JONNY

JONNY

MY AUTOBIOGRAPHY

headline

First published in 2011
by HEADLINE PUBLISHING GROUP

1

Cataloguing in Publication Data is available from the British Library

Hardback ISBN 978 0 7553 1339 6
Trade paperback ISBN 978 0 7553 8605 5

Typeset in Bliss by Ben Cracknell Studios

Printed and bound in Great Britain by
Clays Ltd, St Ives plc

Headline's policy is to use papers that are natural, renewable and
recyclable products and made from wood grown in sustainable forests.
The logging and manufacturing processes are expected to conform to
the environmental regulations of the country of origin.

HEADLINE PUBLISHING GROUP
An Hachette UK Company
338 Euston Road
London NW1 3BH

www.headline.co.uk
www.hachette.co.uk

ACKNOWLEDGEMENTS

It is going to be very difficult to get this part right and do justice to so many who have done so much for me.

In terms of this book, thank you to all the guys at Headline Publishing, especially Jonathan Taylor. Thank you to Owen Slot for your tireless effort in writing it with me, and an even bigger thank you for pretending that you enjoyed doing so.

For the stories I have been able to tell in the book I must first of all thank my parents, Mame and Bilks, and my brother Sparks. You will never truly know, I don't think, what a life you have given me. I couldn't have asked for any more support or for a more special family, and to think of all the things I've put you through over the years!

To my beautiful girlfriend Shelley, thank you for being such a great person, helping me stay balanced and for always being there for me.

To Blackie, your knowledge and ability still astounds me every day. I have always struggled to comprehend just how inspirational and selfless one person can be. It has been an honour to tread this path with you. As you, my brother and I well know, our best days are still to come.

To Dave Alred, thank you for letting me in on your genius. There simply is no one around to match you in your field. Thank you for always helping me to get better despite all the stick you've had to take from me throughout the last 16 seasons.

I would like to mention my sponsors Adidas, Gillette and Jaguar as well as all those who have sponsored me in the past. You have made me feel valued and have supported me through some very difficult times. Thank you.

To Tim Buttimore, my long-time friend and off the field manager, thank you for being a really good guy, being straight up, honest and right there when I needed you.

I would like to thank my grandparents, aunts, uncles, cousins and my lovely little niece Matilda.

I would like to thank all my friends, all the players and coaches I have played with, and all those I have played against too. You have all had a big hand in making my career what it has been. You have also all played a massive part in allowing me to remain myself and in allowing rugby to remain what it is has always been to me, the greatest team game there is.

Finally, and this is very important to me, I would like all the supporters who have written to me, sent their best wishes or shouted for me to know just how much you have mattered and what a difference you have made in my life. Those messages and cheers have helped to create unforgettable memories and have brought the best out of me. In darkest moments they have pushed me to get back up and they have helped motivate me to fight on and keep going. You have been amazing. Thank you.

PROLOGUE

I never thought it would come to this. I never thought I could possibly ask the question do I want to play for England any more?

Eighty times I have played for England — more than twelve long years of chasing my dreams. I can't believe I can even consider quitting the chase. Three World Cups I have played and if I can hang on for another year, I could be playing my fourth. Yet right now I don't know if I want to go that far. I don't know how to end my England story. What I do know is that I don't want it to carry on like this.

Today, 9 October 2010, at the Stade Mayol, Toulon, the club I love dearly, play Ospreys, from Wales, in the Heineken Cup. Martin Johnson, the England manager, will be there to watch and tomorrow, down on the seafront, where bars and restaurants overlook the Mediterranean, we are due to meet.

The last time I saw Johnno was a few months ago in Sydney, and I told him that England and I had maybe gone as far as we can go. Maybe it's time for me to stop. But I get the feeling that, tomorrow, he will be wanting to talk about the forthcoming autumn internationals, about England's opposition, about game plans and calls, about my role in the side and how England are going to play. It's my duty to be honest, though. The conversation topic in my head is not what role I should play; it's whether I'm going to play at all.

With England, my confidence has just disappeared. I feel lower than I have ever felt before. I don't want my journey to end here, not like this. The thought of not playing for England again makes me sick, but I simply do not know if I can carry on.

Toulon is a different matter. When I arrive at the Stade Mayol for the game, I could not feel more different. Here, among this group of players from all around the world, I feel high. There is a different handshake for almost every nationality – the Australian George Smith, possibly the greatest openside flanker I've ever seen; Juan Martin Fernandez Lobbe, the ridiculously skilled and driven Argentinian back-rower; Joe Van Niekerk, the Springbok game-winning captain you'd happily die for; Carl Hayman, the rock-like Kiwi prop capable of playing anywhere on the field. These four alone have nearly 250 caps between them.

They seem to gain strength purely from me being here, as I do from them. But our mutual respect is not built on how many caps anybody has won. It's a respect for ability and desire, for what we've been through together, knowing that each player is always prepared to give everything and that each one of us will support the others unconditionally. I belong here. In this changing room, I treasure that sense of belonging. It's not the same right now with England.

We have found our form, too. We've won our last four games and I have been performing well all season. My confidence, which was so shot last summer in Australia with England, is seeping back. I feel like I am worth something here – the responsibility I am given on the pitch, the respect my teammates give me. Maybe I'm worth what I'm paid.

We are on a roll and we carry on that way. The Stade Mayol is humming today, but the atmosphere is always awesome. Last thing, just before kick-off, the crowd do the traditional PilouPilou. This is a chant with a story, and the story is about the players being primitive warriors who have come down from the mountains to fight by the sea. The crowd love the tradition. They belt out the PilouPilou. But it doesn't seem to intimidate the Ospreys players much – not at all. The Ospreys are here to play.

The game is tight and we exchange penalties until the Ospreys' Shane Williams gets away for a try on the hour. That puts us 14–9 down and we stay that way until, with six minutes to go, we are awarded a penalty. I kick it and we are now two points behind. And then, with four minutes to go, I manage to push a long, floated pass over the top of their rush defence to Paul Sackey, who runs it in to score in the corner. To ensure we're five points ahead and not three, I have the conversion from the touchline. I get that, too. It's been a good day against a very good team.

So that's five wins in a row. We do our ritual lap of the field to thank the supporters. In glorious sunshine, we wave to them and they sing their hearts out back. I like it here.

●　　●　　●

The Toulon seafront is usually quiet on a Sunday morning, but today it's filled with gaggles of Ospreys supporters who are over here for the long weekend and are out nursing their hangovers in the sun.

We meet at a café on the front, Johnno, Brian Smith, the England backs coach, and me. I try to start the conversation, but some of the Ospreys supporters come up and ask for a photo with us and we are kind of obliged to say OK.

With regard to my international career, this is the hardest conversation I've ever had, but Ospreys fans are everywhere. We get another request – can you do a photo for us? OK. So we do another photo and then we move on. We find a new bar, but that gets crowded. Again and again we get asked for pictures and so we move on one more time. We finish up in the furthest café at the water's edge, our final option, and at last find some peace and quiet.

I tell them that, from my point of view, I don't feel I'm fitting in to the England set-up any more. I'm not surprised that the team respond a lot better when Toby Flood is in there at number ten rather than me. They seem more relaxed with him. And me? I don't feel like I'm myself around England, I'm not playing as myself, you're not getting the best out of me and I'm just not happy.

I carry on. I tell them how the Six Nations and the summer Australian tour had been such a low for me and that I don't know where I fit in to their plans any more. In the media, I became the scapegoat for our performances in the Six Nations, and it seemed to me that people were happy enough for it to be that way. I was being hammered in the press during that Six Nations and yet, every Wednesday, I was wheeled out regardless to smile politely and answer the questions of the writers who were pulling me apart in their columns.

The point is, I tell them, it's too overwhelming. It's killing me and I don't know if I can stomach it any longer.

Some four hours later, we are finally done. There are no conclusions. Johnno and Brian say to me you should take your time over this. No, we don't want you to stop. So spend a couple of weeks thinking about this hard.

●　●　●

The next fortnight is about as tough professionally as any I've ever been through. How do you end a story like this? I'd like a different final chapter. I'd like at least to end on a high note.

I live here in France with Shelley, my girlfriend, in the peace and tranquillity of the hills, a couple of miles back from the coast. I love the climate here, I love the lifestyle and I feel relaxed in our home, overlooking a valley of vineyards, but this Sunday I return filled with a sense of doom.

My mum and dad are over to stay with us and we debate the topic at length. What is the answer here? The thought of not playing for England again is simply unacceptable to me, and yet when I think of going back into the England environment, I know there's just no way I can face it. I'm doomed if I do and I'm doomed if I don't.

I start to canvas opinion. I ring Tim Buttimore, my agent, and he explains if you retire, the media response could be a big disaster. It could be construed that, because you're not first-choice number ten any more, you just don't want to bother.

That couldn't be further from the truth. I am desperate to be back in there and enjoying it. I am a competitive animal to the core. I have never settled for second best, but at this point, my confidence around England rugby is so low I can't even think about it.

I phone Mike Catt, one of my greatest friends and allies. He understands my pain. And he is positive. He tells me that in the right situation with England, they'd play to your strengths. You'd be straight back in the team and playing as yourself again.

I meet with Richard Hill, with whom I shared so much in the England days and whose career was finished early by a terrible knee injury. He says consider the long-term side of this. You're a long time retired.

I speak to Felipe Contepomi, my great Toulon teammate, friend and captain of Argentina, and he sees both sides. He says he's gone through a generation change in the Argentina squad and now he sees his role as paving a way for the young guys to take over. But my goal has always been to contribute to the team and I can't stop wanting to be the best. I'm just not sure that I know how to do that right now, and the thought of going back depresses me.

Already, since last summer, I feel I have come so far in rebuilding the confidence that was so completely shattered.

I got back from Sydney and spent four solid weeks in Majorca. Every summer, I holiday in Majorca and every time I'm there I train pretty much every day. This summer I did one boys' week with Matthew Tait, Toby Flood, Pete Murphy, an old mate from Newcastle, and another old mate from way back in mini rugby at Farnham, Andy Holloway. Taity and Floody were a bit more professional about their rest than I was. I pushed myself to the usual limits, working out stupidly hard every day. I worked on skills and fitness. Inside, I worked on weights; outside the villa, on the road, I worked on kicking. I did everything I could to ensure I was well prepared and physically flying for the start of the season.

Our second game was a good away win against Biarritz, but it stood out for me because of Iain Balshaw. It's been thirteen years since Balsh and I started playing together. The first time was at England Under-18 level, and he is still as incredibly talented as he ever was. Now he's playing at Biarritz, uncapped by England for two and a half years.

We met in our team hotel after the game and ended up chatting into the early hours. I asked him what is it like? How does it feel to be playing just club rugby, not to be playing for England? I wanted to know. This is the debate in my mind. He told me he's still massively keen to get involved. It's something he hasn't got and really, really wants.

A month later, I got a different message. Toulon played the current champions, Clermont, at the big Stade Vélodrome in Marseille. It was a huge game with a ludicrous atmosphere and 55–60,000 supporters going nuts. After we'd won, 28–16, we did our lap around the ground to acknowledge the fans. I was walking round the stadium with all my Toulon teammates, whom I adore. Thousands of people were standing and cheering us in the sun and the voice in my head was telling me maybe this is enough. I've done it for England eighty times; maybe this is OK for me now.

● ● ●

The longer I continue in this state of indecision, the more I feel as though my life is on hold.

Two weeks after the Ospreys game, we are due to play Stade Français at the Stade de France. I go down to the club for a kicking session and I cannot concentrate on my kicking for this big game because all I can think of is my England career. Is it over or is it not?

The minute I make up my mind one way, I immediately switch and go the other. I hit one kick and say to myself just forget about it all, be happy in life, leave England alone.

Then I kick another, straight through the middle of the posts, and I think I can't afford not to push myself to that level and waste all my hard work over the years. This whole career has been about pushing myself to the extreme, trying to achieve everything. I can't stop.

I hit another couple of kicks and my mind starts to slide again. I think about how it felt with England recently. I think about the media fall-out and watching helplessly as my reputation took a hammering.

But here, at this kicking session, I decide I can't walk away without making up my mind. I can't let this go on any longer.

I think about the 1998 Tour from Hell, when England got beaten 76–0 by Australia. I remember the tour to South Africa in 2007 when an already depleted team suffered from food poisoning, and yet still we had to front up against the Springboks. God did we suffer. Those were mighty hard times, but the point is this: I've never walked away from a challenge.

I can't back down. I can't live with myself unless I feel that at least I stood up and was counted. It's been my way, my greatest value, and I am proud of that. I can't let it change. That is the ultimate non-negotiable. Never give in.

I leave my kicking practice feeling slightly happier. I phone Johnno and tell him I'm in.

I don't know how this story will end, but at least I know that there will be one last chapter. It's not ideal, it's not how I want to feel, but I've got to stand up and be counted one more time.

CHAPTER 1

I'M not sure if I was born a perfectionist, or if I just decided subconsciously that was the way it was going to have to be.

When my dad pulls up the car at a mini rugby game, I immediately leap out and sprint for the nearest hedge because I need to be sick. Sometimes we have to pull over in a lay-by on the way there; sometimes we have got to the club car park by then. The thought of the game ahead just gives me a kind of panic, a deep fear and a sense of doom about what will happen if it doesn't go well.

I am seven and I play mini rugby for Farnham, where Bilks – which is what we all call Dad – is one of the coaches. I am mad about rugby, particularly during weekdays, when Sparks, my brother, and I mess around with a ball in the garden during daylight hours, and then in the living room when it has got too dark outside.

But Sundays are different. On Sundays, we either have a training session or we play matches. The training days I love. I can't wait to get to the ground for training. When a game is scheduled, though, I sometimes feel I can't bear it.

As long as there is still a night before the game, then I'm OK. For some reason, it still seems a long way away. But on game-day morning, I wake up early, five or six o'clock, and now it is unavoidable and the fear kicks in. I feel my heart beating like mad as if my body's telling me that something really bad's going to happen.

I can't do it, I tell Mum and Dad. I can't do it. Please, you've got to tell them that I can't play.

If it's an away fixture, we meet the rest of the team at Castle Street in the centre of town and then head off in our cars. Bilks leads the way in our Mitsubishi Jeep, with Sparks in the front and me in the back with my friend and teammate Andy Holloway. And when we get close, that's when I start to want to be sick.

It's the same every game. Pre-match panic, then we play. I normally play well and we normally win the game. Then we go home for family lunch, I watch the rugby league on the TV and, with a big smile on my face, I talk about what a great morning I've had.

I don't know what the problem is, but it must be as frustrating as hell for Mum and Bilks because they know full well that they will be going through the exact same thing next week.

I particularly like it after home games because Bilks catches up with the other coaches in the clubhouse and Sparks and I can muck around with the rugby ball. Everyone likes doing drop kicks. We try to get them over from the 22 metre line. Most boys like to have one or two kicks and then run off and do something else, whether the kick's gone over or not, but I can't just pack it in like that. I enjoy so much the basic feel of kicking a ball. I carry on kicking and I won't stop. I can kick drop goals like this for half an hour, an hour. I'm seven and I find I kind of slip into a zone where I can do it repetitively over and over again. I won't quit until Bilks comes out of the clubhouse and tells me that I have to because we're going home.

Our garden is built on three levels. The bottom part has the rhubarb patch and the green bin that Dad bought to use as a dog loo. The small middle lawn is our favourite for cricket. Then there is the top bit with a crumbly brick and slate wall – another training ground. I can spend at least an hour kicking a football or a rugby ball against the wall.

I kick the ball with my left foot, and I'll watch my foot all the time, studying the movement of the swing. Then I'll look at my right foot and say OK, I'm going to do exactly the same thing using this leg. I can do this day after day for hours, which completely ruins the wall. I kick with my left, kick with my right, and I keep on like that, completely losing track of time. It's mesmerising.

But I have to go to school the next morning and the panic sets in again. I go to Weybourne Primary and it's like the rugby game. I wake up with my heart thumping in my chest, thinking I can't do this, and I go crying to Mum. I can't go, please don't make me go.

To settle me in, Mum has to come in to the classroom in the morning and stand at the back. As the lesson goes on, she slowly creeps out of the door. School ends at three o'clock, but I insist that Mum's there at half past two, and when I come out she asks me if I had a good day, and I say yes it was great. But Mum knows that tomorrow morning will be a repeat of today.

What I can't stand is the idea of getting the work wrong. I have to get it all right. So I ask Mum can you ask the teacher not to make it too hard?

I'm not scared of hard work, it's just the thought of getting it wrong. Every week we have a spelling test and every week I get twenty out of twenty. One week I spell the word 'gauge' wrongly; I get the 'u' and the 'a' the wrong way round. I sit there, waiting for my marked paper, expecting to see another '20/20', and when I see '19/20', I don't know what to do with myself and I feel the panicky heartbeat. I feel embarrassed and, as the other kids lean over to look at my sheet and remark on my imperfection in surprise, a desperate need to wind back the clock and do it again.

In the playground afterwards, all my friends are running around laughing. These are people who have probably spelled 'gauge' and other words wrongly, too, and I wonder how can you be laughing? How can you be having such a good time? I just focus, all the time, on trying to get everything right. Mistakes, and the panic, make me so meticulous. If I can be perfect, I can avoid that awful feeling.

The trouble with rugby is you can't be perfect. Yet on the rugby field, more than anywhere else, I need perfection. Especially when it's a Sunday game, when there's a result, something on the line, and it matters to me and my teammates and I feel responsible for it all.

In the Under-8s, I'm played at full-back as a sort of sweeper, a last line of defence. We play in a festival at nearby Alton rugby club and I'm in a team with boys a year older than I am. At half-time during one game, we make a lot of changes. We now have a weaker team and I sense the other boys are looking at me for help, so in the second half I just run around tackling everyone – make a tackle, get up, make another, clatter anyone you can. It feels a bit like I'm spinning plates and I can't stop working for a second. I can't let these plates stop spinning, because if I do, this other team are going to beat us; they'll score and it'll be my fault. And I can't live with that. I make a covering tackle next to the touchline and while getting up off the floor, I say to Bilks I just can't do this any more, it's too much. I want to come off.

I am mad about rugby but I hate the sense of doom that comes with every approaching Sunday fixture. Sometimes I think that if there was an option to be propelled forward by three hours, providing you could tell me it had gone OK, I would seriously consider it, even though that would mean not playing.

But I do like being full-back. I like the challenge of having to be the tackler; it makes me feel valued. When someone in the opposition breaks the line, people can say oh don't worry, Jonny will sort that out. And I love that. I love to be needed like that. But in order to keep on being seen in that way, I realise that I cannot afford to let people down.

On the pitch, it's easy to see what happens. Every team does the same thing. They give the ball to their fastest man, or their key player, who runs across the field, arcing round everyone, and then sprints up the touchline and scores. So when I see that happening, I do the opposite. I run straight to the corner to cut them off. I get into this habit of sprinting down touchlines, desperately trying to smash people into touch. I don't know why. It's like there's a switch inside me. When I see those guys racing round to the corner, I don't just want to tackle them and get them down, I want to knock them sideways on to the next field, and I want to shock those parents watching from the sidelines, too.

One Sunday, we are playing against Alton and there is a girl in the opposition team. She takes off down the wing with the ball the way everyone does, and I'm thinking to myself do I smash her? What should I do? But I don't get to make a decision, because as I run over to cover, she runs off slightly into touch, round the corner flag, back in and then touches down. And the ref awards the try. That's so unjust. How can that be allowed to happen? And how does that make me look? They have scored and it's the girl who's scored. I look for Bilks on the touchline and I'm crying. It's just not right.

Another Sunday, we are playing an Under-8s game against Basingstoke, and I get a bump on the ear. It's not foul play, but it hurts enough to flick that switch inside me, and my response is to raise the level of aggression.

I charge round putting in the heaviest tackles I can manage. They are not fouls, either, just big hits for a small kid. And I hurt the boys I tackle. From the touchline, Bilks indicates that he is bringing me off. I've done nothing wrong, he explains. It's just best for everyone that I have a rest.

What I really like, though, is midweek when Mum picks me up from Weybourne Primary and we drive on to pick up Sparks from the school I will go to next, Pierrepont. Sometimes we get there early and while Mum sits and waits in the car, I get the ball out of the back of the car and take it into the middle of the school rugby pitch. A proper, full-sized rugby pitch. I kick the ball up in the air and catch it, and do the same again, and again, over and over. I can get completely engrossed and lose myself for twenty minutes while Mum and Sparks look on. Holding, catching and kicking a rugby ball in the middle of a big pitch – this, for me, is a real special treat.

●　●　●

Sparks and I have a video that we have become a little bit obsessed about. We like it because of one thing in particular – a kick by Gavin Hastings, in which he is wearing a quartered shirt. He takes the conversion from about 15 metres in from touch on the 22 metre line. The kick is not the hardest but it's a beauty. I'm not sure exactly what it is about it, something to do with the way the ball flies through the air, but it is my idea of perfection. We love that clip, we play it over and over again.

All I want to do is copy it. I know I need to kick with my right foot as well as my left, and I want to be perfect at that, too. So Sparks and I spend a lot of time imitating Gavin Hastings. When we can't kick outside, we kick inside. We construct our own posts from toilet rolls that we stick together with Sellotape, and we create our own balls from other toilet rolls stuffed with toilet paper.

Our house is called Lapa Kaiya, so-named from Mum's native Zambian language, Bemba. It translates as 'Our Shack'. The annex in Lapa Kaiya is our training ground. The room is a perfect length for toilet-roll kicking, and a sofa-bed on one side is good for unleashing a Fosbury-flop-style high jump after a particularly good kick.

Toilet-roll kicking may not be very sophisticated but it's OK for technique. I watch how Gavin Hastings' leg swings. I watch how my left leg swings and I try to copy Gavin Hastings, and then transfer the same movement from my left to my right leg. Again and again. I can spend hours doing this.

We have another video, from *Rugby Special*, from the autumn internationals of 1988–89. There are loads of great highlights on it, from England against Fiji and Wales against New Zealand in particular, but, again, one particular moment is the most fascinating. We rewind and play it, rewind and play. It features Graeme Bachop, playing scrum half for New Zealand. He can pass the ball off his wrists for miles. It's outrageous.

So we want to be able to pass like Graeme Bachop. We use one of those mini rugby balls, the ones that you get players to autograph, and we pass back and forth, back and forth, just working on using our fingers and spin-passing off our wrists.

All our practice is fun, but it does have a deeper purpose. I write everything down in an exercise book. It's full of doodles and drawings, most of them of me kicking a rugby ball over a set of rugby posts. After the first World Cup, in 1987, I write down my goals. I haven't done this before. I want to play for England, I want to be England captain, I want to kick for England, I want to be involved in a World Cup, I want to win a World Cup, I want to play for the British Lions, I want to be England's number ten and I want to be the best player the world has ever seen.

That final one is the big goal. I want to be the best rugby player in the world.

When we watch England games on the TV, I'm not just hoping they win. I'm watching what the players are doing to see if maybe I can learn to do it too. I watch Rob Andrew, England's fly half, in particular. I study his kicking routine, take notes in my exercise book and then try to copy him in the garden.

Writing down my goals like this seems to give everything added purpose. So when I play matches, there is more meaning to them. I am not just playing for Farnham or my school; I am in the process of trying to fulfil my goals.

 •   •   •

At my second school, Pierrepont, there are a lot of strong players, which is lucky. We have a good team, captained by Sparks, and we go through an entire season unbeaten. The dubious prize is BBC Southern Counties Radio asking if two boys can come to the studio in Guildford to be interviewed. Dan Fish and I are chosen.

A female presenter fires questions at us. How did you get into rugby? Dan is a bit more confident than I am and plays the lead role; I have a bit of a blank and a panic but recover enough to mention the international players I like watching on TV and how I try to imitate them. I think I do pretty much OK.

When I get home, I explain this to Mum. I tell her some of the questions, particularly the one about getting into rugby. What did you say, she asks. So I tell her and she says well done, and did you mention your dad?

Suddenly, it dawns on me. I didn't mention my dad, the guy who is responsible for everything, who is the reason I started playing rugby, the guy I watched playing rugby, the guy who put the ball in my hand when I was three, who has coached me since I was four and has been there always.

I cannot believe I have done this. How ungrateful can I be? I cannot believe I have let my father down in such a way. After everything he has done for me, I've not given him the credit. My heart is going into overdrive; I'm in full panic mode. I have a real feeling of desperation. Mum, I need to go back to the radio station because I didn't mention Bilks.

Mum says oh, it doesn't matter. People will have forgotten by now anyway. No, I say, I need to go back. I can feel myself welling up. I have to get back there and put this thing right or else life will never be OK.

Mum says she has the answer. I'll write them a letter, she says, to ask them to put the facts right. That kind of helps but not for long. I cannot get this thing out of my system. The next day after school I am no less desperate. I am in tears again. I can't believe I let Bilks down. I feel devastated. I go to my room and think about what to do. I write my own letter to the radio station. Would it be possible to re-air the interview but allow me to add in a different answer?

I write a lot of these letters over the coming days. I don't send any of them. I spend most of the time in tears, just writing these things, screaming at Mum and Dad, saying that I have to change it, that I have to do this. I have to do something. It's as though something incredibly serious has happened, the end of the world.

Bilks says don't worry. He tells me over and over that he is not bothered. Not at all. But that doesn't really help. It does die a bit over time, but occasionally it comes back, haunting me, like a ghost. I'll be playing basketball outside with Sparks and suddenly I am miles away. I feel the panic and I know I need to go inside because something's not right. I stop the game. I need to go and say sorry to my dad. Sorry about not mentioning you in the interview. And maybe I could ring that radio station.

Mum, I ask, weeks, months later, did you send that letter? Do you think they'll say anything on the radio?

• • •

It is not long before I find my next reason to flip out.

I come home from school and see a blackbird on the ground, struggling, half-dead. It must have flown into the window. Wouldn't it be great to pick it up and take it inside, help it out? So I do. Mum helps me put it into a shoe box, padded out with tissue, its own little living room. Then I go upstairs for a bath, and afterwards mess around in my room, forgetting about the bird, until Mum calls me for supper. When I go downstairs, the bird is dead.

It's dead because I wasn't there to help it. I was too busy having fun to care. This is my fault. I have killed the bird. I am overwhelmed by what I have done. The tears, the screaming, are back. This bird was my responsibility and I have let it down. How can I make amends? Mum, what can I do? I have killed the bird.

Don't worry, she says. You did your best. It would have died anyway. There's nothing more you could have done. But I have to atone. I cannot live with this. I start writing letters again. Most of them are to God. Sorry. I am so sorry I didn't look after the bird better.

I cannot stand this intense, choking feeling. Mum, I let the bird down. I am screaming. What if I have to live with it for the rest of my life? I can't do it, I can't do it. I have to get rid of this feeling somehow. Mum and Dad and Sparks all say the same thing. This isn't achieving anything. Everything will be all right. You need to forget about it and move on.

But I am not just obsessive about kicking rugby balls. I can grapple with this problem pretty single-mindedly, too. I cannot put aside the image of the bird and my responsibility for its death. I have to try to work it out, find a solution to a situation that doesn't have one.

● ● ●

Sparks and I have a strange fascination with my left calf. It has got a massive bruise on it and the feeling in it has kind of gone.

It happened down at Farnham Sports Centre on the bouncy castle. I bounced off and landed on the floor and then this big guy, who must have been six years older than I am, landed on top of me. He was supposed to be in charge, monitoring the kids and general behaviour on the castle, but instead he was bouncing around, and the moment I bounced off, he came off too, both knees flat on my calf with all his bodyweight.

It hurt big time and took ages to get up and walk. But I managed it, and somehow I managed to get through an Under-11s tennis tournament the next day. I wore a big tubey grip bandage on my leg, which made me feel very proud.

Now my calf is swollen, and the sensation in it is a little weird. So, in our bedroom before bedtime, Sparks and I are sitting on my bed playing a game to test it out. It's a simple game – we just hit the calf with our knuckles to see how hard we can do it before it hurts too much. Sparks has a go and then it's my turn. It's hilarious how hard you can hit your leg when the feeling in it has gone.

But in the night, I wake up with serious pain. I get up and hobble through to Mum and Dad's room. They look at it. We'll get on to it first thing in the morning, they say. About an hour later, I'm back. It's really, really hurting, I say.

So off we go to Aldershot Military Hospital. The doctors explain that I have burst a blood vessel, there has been internal bleeding into the calf, and an infection in the blood has caused an abcess. It is poisonous, pussy and generally horrid. And they need to cut it open. I'll have to stay overnight, and for the next two nights as well.

I look at Mum. I'm not staying overnight on my own. I can't stay on my own. Mum understands the problem. OK. We have a deal. Mum stays, too.

Eventually, we get home and I am carried into the house like a wounded soldier, taken to the annex and laid down on the sofa, which has been pulled out as a bed. The doctors' instructions are simple and specific – rest, please, no exercise at all. Perfect for me because Wimbledon is on the TV. Awesome. So I settle in.

But there is only so much Wimbledon you can watch. After a while, I wonder about my toilet-roll balls; could I kick them? That would be pretty harmless, wouldn't it? I'm sure I could do that. I get one out and try. Not too bad.

Mum catches me in action. She's not too impressed. You're not supposed to be doing that, she says. I know, I know.

I know she is right. I settle back down to Wimbledon. But then I get up and kick my toilet roll again. How can I become a better kicker if I don't?

●   ●   ●

Normally, when Sparks and I play games, we find a way of playing on the same team. We like helping each other out. We get a massive buzz out of it. But I am obsessing a bit about a computer game we have for the Commodore Amiga 500 called Speedball II. You have a team dressed in big, metal robotic suits and you have to throw a ball into a hole at the other end of a wall. I spend ages learning all the moves and controls. I work out all the different and elaborate ways of scoring points and when I think I have perfected it, I ask Sparks, who has hardly played it, for a game.

Sparks doesn't take it as seriously as I do. In fact, he spends the whole time laughing and taking the mickey. So I play this tremendous game, build up a massive lead and even start feeling sorry for Sparks. Then, at the last minute, he exposes a monster flaw in the game. He tries punching all the buttons on the joystick and the result is that his character on the screen starts grabbing the ball, throwing it to one of my players and then, just as they catch it, he punches them clean out and takes it back. Sparks scores three times by doing this, while laughing hysterically.

This really annoys me. It shouldn't be allowed. It gets down to the last seconds, the last play of the game and I'm still ahead, but only just. He lays out all my players and then turns to my goalkeeper.

Don't do it, Sparks. I tell him. Don't you dare. But he does. He drops my keeper with a massive left hook and, on the buzzer, hammers the ball home for the winning goal. And I just want to explode.

My frustration level is probably as high as I have ever known. I don't know whether to scream at him, fight him, or what. So I storm out of the back patio doors and down to the bottom of the garden to the rhubarb patch. I sit on the concrete slab by the rhubarb and work out my plan. I'll stay here until he comes and apologises. He has cheated me out of victory. He has to apologise. Has to. I won't let it go, I cling on to it. I can hold on for a long time.

So I stay by the rhubarb for a good two hours. And Sparks doesn't apologise. In fact, he seems to have forgotten I'm even down here. Mum says what on earth are you doing down there? Come in for your dinner.

● ● ●

The rugby coach at Pierrepont is keen on working both my feet. From the left-hand side of the field he has me kicking conversions with my right foot, and from the right-hand side with my left foot. He says it is important for

me to be able to push myself with my skills, and put myself under pressure. I probably put myself under enough pressure anyway.

We are a good team, but our pitch is not of the very best quality. There is farmland all around the school grounds and our first XV pitch is quite uneven.

In one game, we score a try in the corner. On a full-sized field, this is a long kick for a prep-school boy, and that's without taking into account the ball, which Mr Wells likes to inflate really hard so that it is possible to hear my teeth clatter each time I strike it. It doesn't help that, because the kick is from the touchline, some parents are standing right behind me. So while I'm lining up my conversion attempt, I'm thinking it'd be pretty amazing if I get this. The parents next to me will think I'm brilliant. With this positive image in mind, I commence my run-up.

But when I go to kick the ball, disaster strikes. I tense my foot hard, preparing for a massive contact, but my pointed toe catches a clump of turf just before the ball. By the time I make contact I have lost all the power in my leg swing. I uproot a clump of grass and have just enough momentum left to make the ball topple over and roll once.

Although I manage to shut this out of my mind for the rest of the game, when I get home, I start thinking it through, over and over again. The replay of that kick invades my mind, coming back to haunt me, like a horror film.

What did that kick look like? What did those people standing right by me think of it? What do they think of me now? I become obsessed with the questions. I can't change what's happened, and I hate that. I get the fast heartbeat, panic sensation. That kick is part of me, part of my history, something I have to live with for the rest of my life. And what are those touchline parents thinking?

We have a nice family dinner and watch some TV. Then suddenly, the switch is flicked, the tiny kick is on replay again in my head. The next thing

I know, I'm running around the house for a good fifteen or twenty minutes in a massive state of distress, just trying to find some way of appeasing the pain. What must those people think of me? I just can't bear the thought of it.

Down in the annex, I am screaming at my parents. That kick! The embarrassment! Mum has an exasperated look on her face. Bilks says look, those people will not even remember it. They have got more important things to be worrying about, I'm sure.

He says the same a month later when the thought is still haunting me and I am in tears over it again. It's like the bird and the radio interview, an image my mind refuses to let go. I am convinced that Bilks is wrong. Those people on the touchline – they're all going to be thinking about it and they're all going to be talking about it. I'm never going to be able to forget it, I'm never going to be able to change it. It's with me for ever.

If there was ever a reason to go out and spend hours practising kicking, the Clump of Earth Kick is it. It causes such intense pain. This is the reason I want to be perfect, because it just hurts so much when you're not.

● ● ●

I am not a great sleeper, I never have been, and, at Pierrepont, that becomes a greater challenge when we go away on tour. I worry not only about how I will do on the rugby pitch, but about sleeping in a strange place. I'm jumpy, panicky, I don't feel very comfortable or remotely safe. I am always touring with boys a year or two older than I am, and I'm not sure I would be able to get through it if it wasn't for Sparks, who is captain, and Bilks, who helps out with the coaching and comes with us.

Every year, Pierrepont goes on tour to Senlis, near Paris. When we go in 1991, I'm twelve and I'm thinking about these Senlis kids, the ones I'm going to have to tackle, who, we've been told, are going to be a year or two older than our team and thus two or three years older than I am. How big are they going to be? When the opposition team turns up for a game, the first thing I always do is look across to see how big they are.

So I pull hard on Sparks. My brother and his mates are all good guys, but I stick to Sparks; wherever he goes, I go too. On tour, we always go to the adidas warehouse and buy one of the Wallabies' rugby balls, the big, round, fat, yellow ones with the black tips. We love that. But every mealtime, I worry about what sort of food will be served up, and I try to sit next to Sparks. He makes me laugh, tells me what's going on, puts me at ease.

The nights are hard. We are billeted with local French families and I am sharing a room with a French boy, but feeling very much on my own, lying in bed, not going to sleep. One night, I work myself up into an enormous panic and tell the boy's parents I need to get hold of my dad. I keep badgering them. I need my dad.

I have no idea how they get hold of him, because there certainly isn't such a thing as a mobile phone around. But they track him down to an event in town, the big annual social event of the tour when all the coaches of the two sides are together, having their big rugby dinner. He comes on the phone and I tell him I can't stay. I can't stick this out.

At this point, he knows he has no option but to come and get me. He comes to the house where I'm staying and soon we are back at the dinner and I'm having an extra place laid for me at the opposite side of the table from my dad. They get me a Coke and I tell them that I am sorry but I can't eat the gourmet five-course meal that everyone else is so excited about. Can I have chicken and chips, please?

The men do lots of toasting, lots of talking and laughing. It all goes way over my head, but my chicken and chips cheer me up pretty quickly. Across the table, my dad keeps motioning are you OK? Is everything all right? I tell him I'm fine, which I am until the moment I reach out for the salt and knock my Coke clean over.

Now I've done it. I've embarrassed my dad, I've ruined his evening and these guys all hate me. I get massively upset about it and start to beat myself up for being so stupid. So Bilks is required, again, to come and save the day.

● ● ●

Ball games at Lapa Kaiya cause regular breakages but Bilks doesn't mind too much. He understands, he likes ball games. He is quite good at replacing panes of glass, and he has to do a fair amount of work on the basketball net.

On the side of the house, down the driveway, in front of the garage, we have a big bare wall, and the area makes for a perfect basketball arena. We are obsessed with slam-dunking and hanging off the net the way the NBA players do. We are quite into our NBA. The net, though, sometimes comes off the wall, but Bilks just screws it back on using bigger bolts each time.

The joys of basketball are twofold, and nothing to do with winning or losing. We are obsessed by dunking and blocking. We have our friends round, my mate Ed Morgan and Sparks's friend Luke Cromwell-Parmenter. Ed plays with me, and Luke with Sparks. For the match, I have created an NBA-style scoreboard out of a big cardboard box. I like the stats; I like filling in my cardboard box with a big marker pen.

Ed and Luke think this is a proper game, and we are happy for them to remain under this misapprehension. This way, I can set Ed up for a shot, which is actually really a way of setting Sparks up for a block. Likewise, Sparks will create situations so that I can dunk on Luke.

The teams here aren't really Ed and me or Sparks and Luke. The only real team is Sparks and me, fulfilling our desire to dunk and block. Beautifully, Ed and Luke have no idea that they are merely the downtrodden supporting cast in our own game. Afterwards, we don't talk about who won and who lost; it's just Sparks and me reminiscing about the highlights, our best dunks, our top blocks.

When there are no teams and it's just me at home, I go back into kicking mode. Lapa Kaiya is on a quiet cul de sac, which means I can use the road for training and the hedge as my target. I kick endless spiral punts. I kick with my left foot, collect the ball out of the hedge, then walk back down to the bottom of the road and kick another with my right foot. Left spiral, hedge, right spiral, hedge, on and on. I can discipline my mind to keep going, not to get bored or want to watch television, or even to consider anything else. It's as if I'm flicking a 'Tunnel Vision' switch. That way, I can keep destroying the hedge for hours.

● ● ●

One of the things I enjoy most is tackling bigger people, although that's not necessarily how I feel when I first see them.

We are back in Senlis again the following year. I am almost thirteen, and this time we stay in a dormitory, which is fun. The night before the game, we are mucking around, chirpy and happy, but the next morning, as soon as I wake up, the familiar, chronic nervous panic is there. I don't want to go near the rugby field and I'm worried about everything to do with the game.

Later, we walk down to the pitch, which is a football pitch with football goals, and we see the opposition, and it's one of the scariest sights I've ever seen. They are like full-grown men.

Not long after kick-off, Sparks, our captain, is knocked out, which hardly helps. He is helped off the pitch and sits down on his own on a grassy bank in front of a bunch of French schoolkids, who start shouting at him.

But the occasion is memorable more for what happens towards the end. I have been watching Rob Andrew, the England fly half, and have tried to study what he does. I want to copy it, particularly because he drops a lot of goals. So from about 25 metres out, slightly to the left, I strike a drop kick, off my right foot. It flies nice and true over the goal. We win the game. That is the first drop goal I have ever kicked, and it's over a set of soccer posts!

● ● ●

Summertime, and my mate Andy Holloway is cast in the supporting role.

We have been watching a highlights video of the England cricket team's 1994 tour to the West Indies, and we love Curtly Ambrose, Courtney Walsh and Kenny Benjamin. What we love is the high-bouncing stuff the bowlers deliver around the batsman's head. We love to see the batsmen ducking and the fielders responding. We watch and rewind, watch and rewind and then we go out into the garden to reproduce.

We have the perfect setting for it. The middle lawn is the batting wicket, and it has a slight rise just where the bowler pitches the ball. Sparks has got a great arm and is evil even off a very short run-up; Sparks can really hit the bump. To spice it up more, we pour a bucket of soapy water on the grass, so the ball comes through even faster. That's where Andy comes in.

Andy pads up. Helmet and all. He has to face Sparks. And I go up to the top lawn to play wicketkeeper. The perfect delivery is when Sparks hits the bump, Andy gets an edge and I take the diving catch; or I'll settle for Andy ducking the bouncer and me taking the ball up high around my head. Sparks is bowling for himself and for me. I am looking for the dramatic catches. The golden moments of summer are played out for hours as we recreate our version of the West Indies, and Andy tries to stay alive.

Soon, though, Sparks and I are allowed to play with Bilks's Sunday team, the Aldershot Officers Club. We go to the nets on Wednesday nights and I work on my shots; they have to be perfect. I badger Bilks, wafting airshots with my bat.

How's my defence?

Yeah, fine.

How's my attack?

Yeah, fine.

Over and over, I play my airshots and study my style. It has to be spot on.

A few other lads are allowed to play with the dads' side, but no one else gets such pleasure from fielding as Sparks and I do. They always field Sparks at deep, because he has such a long throw, and I'm usually in the covers because I love diving around. But our secret joy comes from throwing the ball in to the wicketkeeper, Mike Smailes. The game is to bounce the ball in front of him, just where wicketkeepers like it least, so he can't quite get to it and the ball bounces up and hits his fingers. That's just Bilks, Sparks and me – always aiming for Mike Smailes's dislocated and increasingly more deformed fingers.

I enjoy the Wednesday nets the most. I love it when they pull out the catching cradle and three or four of us are catching at each end. What a great piece of kit the cradle is. As the light slowly fades, the crowd gradually thins out, and every Wednesday, the three Wilkinsons are the last to leave, still throwing and kicking balls to each other in almost complete darkness.

● ● ●

Sparks and I are back on the basketball court. This is the last time in our lives that we will ever allow ourselves to get into proper one-on-one competition.

It isn't even supposed to be that way, but we have watched an NBA clip of Patrick Ewing and Dennis Rodman in a game between the New York Knicks and the Detroit Pistons. In one epic moment, Ewing is driving towards the net and as he leaps to dunk the ball, Rodman throws himself in the way and manages to make the block just in front of the rim of the basket.

We want to recreate the moment. It's simple. Sparks is Ewing and I am Rodman. He wants to dunk, I want to block. Those are the roles that we decide upon, everyone is happy. So Sparks dribbles the ball once and then jumps off one foot and tries to dunk the ball into my face while I run in and try to block him.

We try it once and then we try it again. And the more we try it, the more competitive it gets. He tries to go harder and harder, and I'm trying more and more desperately to stop him, knowing that every time I do, that's a win for me. We become more and more aggressive. I get so determined, I almost break my wrist over the rim of the ring. We start pushing each other hard.

It all comes to an end when he dunks one with full power, pulls the ring off the side of the house and it collapses over my head. We both know that we should not be competing like that, not against each other, and although we don't say as much, we will never do so again.

But there is a happy ending to this episode. Bilks doesn't put the net up on the side of the house any more. This time we upgrade to a spring-loaded, professional-style ring and a gangster-style chain net, which we put up at the bottom of the garage. We take Sparks's ghetto-blaster down there and play for hours on end, but not competitively, never again.

CHAPTER 2

AT the age of fourteen, I am not prepared yet for failure. I am sitting in Bilks's car, having completed the second round of trials for the Surrey Under-15s, and I've got this excited buzz about what it could mean to be a county rugby player and what those games might be like to play in.

I have been told that, potentially, I am a good player. I have been playing in age groups above myself. So now I am sitting in the Mitsubishi Jeep, waiting for Bilks to come back from the clubhouse, where the selectors are announcing who's made it into the squad.

I don't like trials. You've got no lineout calls, no backs moves, you don't even know the name of the guy you're playing with. It's a lottery whether you are behind a good pack or not, and your teammates are a bunch of guys who just want to show themselves up in a good light. In reality, for the purpose of identifying quality players, they are a pretty terrible idea.

But I am still not prepared for it when Bilks gets in the car, grabs the steering wheel and says sorry, you didn't make it, they didn't read your name out. That hurts. It hurts like hell.

But I get a second chance. Farnham is on the Surrey–Hampshire border, so I can trial for Hampshire, too. Bilks takes Andy Holloway and me. This time we both get in, me at number ten and Andy at scrum half, and we forget our complaints about trials. You don't have the whiney stories when you're on the right end of the roll call.

Andy and I seem to progress well together. The following year, we go from Hampshire Under-16s into the London South East Divisional team. Then we both get picked for the Under-16 England side and travel to games against Wales and Portugal, but they pick a guy called James Lofthouse at number ten. Andy and I sit on the bench throughout both games and leave with two perfectly clean sets of kit.

The selectors tell me I'm not demonstrative enough, too shy, too quiet. James Lofthouse seems like a nice enough guy, and it is pretty obvious that he's stronger in the areas where they think I could improve. I can't say the selectors are wrong with their advice to me, but in my head, I am still convinced that I am capable of playing rugby at that level.

● ● ●

During a Hampshire Under-16s game against Sussex, I make a tackle I'll never forget. I line up the ball-carrier, but he steps slightly and my head gets caught on the wrong side, between my shoulder and the man. It hurts. Down my arm shoots a strange pins-and-needles sensation, heavy, burning, white hot. I don't think I can possibly play on, but then the feeling passes and I'm OK. I carry on.

This is a stinger. My first. It comes, I am informed, from a compression of the nerves between the vertebrae as they branch out from the spinal column. The problem is that once you have had one, you have opened the door to more. And the more the door swings open, the easier they come. So I start seeing a physio at Aldershot Town football club and he does good things with my neck. The point is I want to keep playing and this guy is helping me get out on the pitch.

What I need is a run of three or four games without a stinger, because that helps me reset, shut the door – but get another unfortunate hit and the door is open again. Bang, bang, bang, I get another load in a row. One morning after a game, I wake up and I can't move my head in any direction. This is scary. There's no way I'm going to school today. Instead, I'm straight to the doctors for a neck brace. The nerve in my neck is trapped that badly.

Still, I hardly miss any games. But I have established a pattern; I might get one stinger followed by about three or four others, and then a break for three or four months without any.

It has developed into a bit of a chronic problem. This becomes pretty clear when the cricket season comes round. I am coming in to bowl and there it is again, that hot, burning sensation down my arm.

● ● ●

One of the unspoken rules in rugby is not to blame the kicker. When I miss six out of seven, though, our coach ignores the rule – as if I don't feel the hurt enough already. But I am also being propelled towards one of the most significant moments in my entire career.

The game is London South East Under-18s against Midlands, I am a year younger than the rest of my team and I have one of my worst kicking days ever. I don't miss the uprights by much, but I don't really quite know where any kick is going to go. And, as it turns out, any one of the six missed kicks would have been the difference between victory and defeat.

Naturally, I feel horrible. I know it is my responsibility and, later, when I go into the team meeting, I am pretty sure that everyone else is thinking the same – that I've let them all down, and it's my fault.

As it happens, this is how the coach sees it, too. He says we played well in parts, we'd have won with better kicking, and assures the team that we won't ever have a day like that with a kicker again. I don't know where to look and settle for staring at the floor.

But I also have a solution – be obsessive about making sure this doesn't happen again. In other words, go out and kick some more balls. So the next morning, I'm out there kicking, trying to drive the memories of yesterday from my mind. It's not that I enjoy the business of kicking well; it's that I detest the imperfection of kicking badly. I can't get out there quickly enough to erase yesterday's memories and ensure they are not repeated.

And I can stay out there for two or three hours if required. This is my response. Flick the Tunnel Vision switch and carry on with barely another thought in my mind.

A few weeks later, Bilks and I are driving to Bristol to meet a guy called Dave Alred. This has been arranged by Steve Bates, a chemistry teacher at school who is also the rugby master. Steve plays for Wasps with Rob Andrew and Rob works with Dave. He has arrived at Lord Wandsworth College, the school I now attend, at a good time. I'm at the stage when career advisers try to work out what you might do one day for a living. All I can say is I want to play rugby. They say that's not really a career. Steve has given me hope that it might be.

Sending me up to see Dave Alred might help, he suggests, but I feel slightly ambivalent about it. Alred is a kicking coach, but I reckon I'm about a seven or eight out of ten kicker who has the occasional bad day, and I'm not quite sure what he can tell me about kicking a ball that I don't already know.

I've been to a kicking clinic before, last year with the England Under-16s. All that happened that day was that we were asked who wanted to be kickers, a bunch of us, including props and number tens alike, put up our hands, and then we all did lots of kicking together. The height of the technical advice handed down was after one of my teammates asked should he be looking at the posts or the ball when kicking for goal.

As our car pulls into the Bristol University sports ground, what I don't realise is that the guy I am about to meet is not only a kicking coach, he is by far the best in the world.

He is immaculately turned out in adidas gear – just three stripes from the top of his shoulders down to the underside of his feet. He seems to be about forty years old, but I later discover he is a wee bit more than that. We say hello and chat for a bit but he is quite keen to get down to business and I like that.

I assume we are going to kick some balls around, but he takes me straight to a flip pad and starts drawing. The diagrams are a demonstration of kicking through the ball, not across it, about the line of the kick, your body position and the feedback you feel through your feet.

I didn't expect all this scientific stuff. This is new. Coaches tend to tell you what they want you to do, and here was a guy telling me how to do it.

But the bomb is yet to drop. He doesn't stop at telling me how; he then goes and does it himself. Fifty metres farther down the touchline, there are two cones, five metres apart. He says I want you to be able to pick your spot between those cones. He then hits a perfect spiral kick. As soon as it leaves his foot, it's going straight between the cones, doesn't even deviate from its line.

This is the wow moment – the one that lets someone know for sure that he has your attention. And now Dave has all of mine. My mouth drops open. Did that really happen?

When I try, of course I fail, hitting neither a spiral nor the cones. Dave goes again. Same perfect outcome, followed by a trademark smartarse comment – so the money's mine, then.

So astonishing is Dave's ability that I am slightly distracted. The noise when he kicks his ball is different from when I kick mine. The flightpath is different. The success of his kicks is inevitable. The difference is so gaping he must, I conclude, be kicking a different ball from the one I'm kicking. But I am wrong.

I thought I was a seven out of ten kicker. Suddenly, the scale has gone up to 100. I am stuck on seven and here is a guy in the high nineties.

At the end, Dave gives me a video of our kicking session and goes over the lesson in précis form. Imagine the path you are sending the ball down, visualise the feel of the ball, the contact, the successful outcome. This is the crucial message: you can control the ball and where it is going, and this is how.

This is eureka!

I have a hell of a lot of work to do, but my eyes have been opened. At the end of a long tunnel, there is a light and I am determined to reach it.

● ● ●

When we left Dave, I had an extraordinarily positive feeling. What sweetened the deal even more was that I also had a new pair of adidas Predator boots. As if he needed to do any more to impress me, back at his house afterwards, we saw, stacked up in his toilet, boxes upon boxes of Predators. Oh my God! I like those boots. And Dave just nonchalantly asked me what shoe size I am and handed me a pair. I like Dave, too.

But now it's down to work. Sparks and I have always kicked together. At the bottom of our road is a park where we take the dogs for walks and you are likely either to turn your ankle or step in something one of the dogs has left behind. We call this 'Ankle Turn City' and we can kill an easy ninety minutes here, standing forty to fifty yards apart, kicking an Australian Rules football back and forth, with the dogs looking at us, wondering when they can go home.

That is just part of life. Now I've met Dave, though, my approach has changed. I've seen something I want, something I need to master.

On most days, now, with time running out until the start of the school term, I get up early and around seven o'clock head off to Farnham rugby club. I get myself some breakfast, then I make some more toast, smear it in Marmite and wrap it in foil and put that in my bag together with a drink and an apple to take with me. I go on my mountain bike with a rucksack of four rugby balls on my back.

That is the routine. Normally, I'll do an hour and a half's kicking, but I'll stay there until I'm satisfied. I want to be the best, so this is what I have to do, and now Dave has shown me that it's possible, that's the deal, no excuses. Getting my kicking right gives me satisfaction, but now it has become a necessity. I can't move on with my day, or with my mind at peace, until it is right.

My problem is that I haven't completely and correctly understood what Dave has taught me. Down at Farnham rugby club, though, I don't know this. I kick my four balls and then I go to the other end of the pitch and kick them back. These sessions are almost entirely punting, back and forth, back and forth, and I can't bear it because my kicks aren't flying remotely the way Dave's were.

One day my attempt to emulate Dave is so poor that I am in bits. Exasperated. This is so important. I kick four balls, get angry with myself, run after them, pick them up and kick them back. Then I get angrier and angrier and angrier. This is not how I want it to go. And I don't know why it is going this way. I become more and more frantic and my kicking reflects this. I start shouting out loud, turning the air blue with my frustration.

But my obsessive switch has been flicked and I'm not going to stop. I can overcome problems like these, I know I can. Other people might decide to stop, do something else to take their minds off it, but I can't take my mind off it. I can work hard on this. It's not insurmountable. I can change it.

A black Suzuki soft-top turns into the club car park. It's Mum. She looks a bit ticked off. She says to come home, she's been worried sick. Where the hell have I been all day? Do I know what time it is?

No.

It's 11.50, she tells me. I didn't realise it, but I have been kicking for almost five hours non-stop.

Mum says to come home for lunch. I tell her I can't; I need a few more kicks. But that doesn't go down too well. So we go home for lunch. The kicking is on my mind, weighing me down.

You don't need to go back again, Mum says. That's enough for one day.

I tell her I have to. I have to go back. Then I start getting self-destructive. I tell her I'm finished, you should see the way I'm kicking, it's rubbish, I can't go on like this, I'm not going to succeed.

Mum tries the sensible approach. You've got plenty of time, she says. You've got next week. Tomorrow you can go and do some in the morning.

And I'm saying I have to go now, I have to go now.

So we settle on a compromise. I leave it until early evening, around seven, pack up my four balls and cycle back to the rugby club. I kick for another hour and a half. And it's a little bit better. Just enough for me to sleep that night.

●　●　●

What frustrates me is that I know it's my fault. I'm putting in all these hours of practice and effort – and I don't mind that at all – but it's not working. Must be my fault.

In the evenings, I watch the video Dave made. He filmed me kicking and then he filmed himself kicking. I watch this over and over. I don't get what it is I'm doing wrong.

It just makes sense to me to work harder. I drop into my obsessive zone. I know that with hard work I can prevail. This gives me strength. This is my advantage. But this time, it's just not working.

I kick with Sparks. I kick with Bilks. I kick with them for hours, screaming, genuinely crying. They don't know what to say to me because almost anything they do say touches a nerve. Their patience is huge. I can't get it! I shout at myself. It's not right!

Sparks's role almost becomes time-keeper. Listen, mate, he says, Mum says we should go home for dinner.

I'll just do a little bit more, I interrupt him. Look, you go. I'll be along soon.

I start phoning Dave and he listens but I can't crack it. So eventually, with Sparks and Bilks, I go back up to Bristol to see him. I kick one ball and he sees the problem.

Hold on a sec, he says, you need to be doing this.

Oh, you mean not like this?

No, no. Like this.

Oh my God. I want to tell him what I have just been through, but I'm more interested in soaking up his information and getting it right.

What I have totally misconstrued is the part of the foot I should be kicking with. I've been using the inner part, and following through straight, like Dave. What I should have been using to strike the ball is the top of my foot as a flat surface. Suddenly, it all starts to make sense.

Thus Dave does it again. He doesn't tell me what to do, he tells me how to do it. And then he shows me by doing it himself. And then he gives me the key points, the essential set of focuses to remember so I can go away and get it right.

Sparks and I stand down one end of the field while Dave kicks to us and we find ourselves laughing with admiration at the ridiculous height and perfection with which he strikes almost every ball. As I watch him, I feel this enormous respect and confidence in him. It's already clear to me that this is a truly special guy, and if I'm really serious about wanting to succeed, I need to learn from him everything I possibly can.

● ● ●

Back at school, the volume doesn't go down. Not at all.

Every day, we have forty minutes for lunch and then Activity Hour. You are permitted to use just one Activity Hour a week for sport. But I have a mate, Duncan White, an inside centre with a deceptively slow turn of pace, and we go out kicking every single Activity Hour of every single day. In fact, we keep lunch to the minimum and make it an activity hour and a half.

You are also not supposed to be out kicking rugby balls during your free periods – you are supposed to be inside studying. But my studying tends to take place out on the rugby field behind the trees by Sutton House. You have to be careful not to be seen, so you have to control your kicks so they keep beneath the height of the trees. On Thursday afternoons, when I have a free period, Bilks takes time off work, comes down to Sutton House and shares the studying with me, always keeping balls down low, beneath the top of the trees.

It has become a major privilege to see Dave, and I'm beginning to get my head round who he is. As well as coaching many rugby kickers and being a fan of the Naked Gun films, Monty Python and Tommy Cooper, he has coached in Aussie Rules, and he used to be a kicker in the NFL for the Minnesota Vikings. Besides that, he was a top-flight player in rugby union and league. Quite handy credentials, those – all of them.

The third time up to Bristol, Bilks comes with me again, so that he can understand and help me more, and when we arrive, Dave is kicking with a player I recognise, Mike Catt. Catt has just taken over kicking duties for England, and I am astounded by how approachable he is.

Dave works mainly with Mike, and I am down the other end. But when we get together, we chat and Mike and I both marvel at how amazing Dave is at kicking the ball. I kind of marvel at Catty, too. He has a great way of making you feel at ease, and by the time we leave, it is as if he and I are mates.

I also have another new pair of Predators tucked under my arm, and Bilks has tucked away some of the Dave coaching manual. Now, when we kick behind the trees at Sutton House, a perfect reverse spiral is known as an 'Alred'. Occasionally, Bilks isn't afraid to put in a pretty decent Alred, too.

● ● ●

After a year spent playing for the England Under-18A team, 1997 is my opportunity to force my way into the Under-18 first team. I badly want to be in this team, not least because I know there are some impressive guys around – Mike Tindall, whom I have just faced in an epic Daily Mail Cup semi-final schoolboy match; Iain Balshaw, a really pacy full-back; two imposing locks, Steve Borthwick and Andy Sheridan; some impressive front-row contenders, including Lee Mears and David Flatman; a back who can play anywhere, Simon Amor; Alex Sanderson, who loves contact sessions; and two guys who will one day be my clubmates, centre Tom May and scrum half James Grindal.

What I am not too enthusiastic about, though, is that the Under-18s are still holding trials, which I think are a nightmare; and they hold them over long weekends up at Castlecroft, the national youth rugby centre, near Wolverhampton, which I am not particularly fond of, either.

I'm desperate to do well and also desperate not to oversleep. I share a room with two other guys and, on the morning of the trial, I continually wake up in a panic about being late. When it's light outside, I open our room door and block it so it doesn't lock shut, and then I walk around the hotel, convinced all three of us are late. I do this maybe three or four times, at six o'clock, quarter to seven, half seven, anxious to know the time. We don't have to be up until half eight or nine, but I am constantly nervous, determined to get everything in my preparation right and make a good impression. It would help, I guess, if I had a watch.

I don't get off to a great start in the trials but that's partly because our team are not winning much ball. We are playing into the wind and up the slope. I look forward to the second half, but my heart sinks at half-time when my opposite number, James Lofthouse, who has played pretty well up to this point, goes off with an injury and doesn't have to play the tougher 40 minutes, up the hill and into the wind. So I am not remotely surprised when I hear that James has got the number-ten shirt. Geoff Wappett, our coach, cuts an imposing figure, stern, tall and permanently puffing on a pipe; and he is a very good coach, very assured, and responsible for some fairly brutal contact sessions in which I attempt to take on Alex Sanderson. Wappett is the rugby coach at Sedbergh School, where James is a pupil, so he knows James's game better than he knows mine.

When you don't hear your name being read out, it's an horrendous feeling, but a week later we are back at Castlecroft for an England warm-up match against Midlands and the word around the camp from the coaching staff is that the team selection is not set in stone. This is everyone's opportunity to play for their place. So I am revved up like mad. This is my time, I'm thinking. I'll show you what I've got. It's time to set the record straight and show you that you've made a big mistake.

Before the game, we are in the changing room and Geoff says he has a small announcement to make. They have decided to appoint an Under-18s captain for the season – and it is going to be James Lofthouse.

And that just feels like the final kick in the proverbials. It means that not only have they discounted me from the first team but they have pretty much discounted me from playing any games. I feel stitched up in every way possible.

●　●　●

A few weeks later we are at Twickenham for the first game of the Under-18s version of the Five Nations, and I have my chance. James is injured. We are playing France and I am starting.

This is the biggest game of my life, and the rest of the guys feel the same. You can tell from the way we are all getting pumped up. Then, in the changing room before we go on, our full-back screams out that this, for us, should be the second Battle of Agincourt, and the mood is killed. Some guys are no doubt trying to work out what Agincourt actually was, while others are thinking that the comparison is a touch over the top. But we are still pumped. In the team huddle in the big space between the changing room and the showers, we are bouncing around, so fired up that we keep bumping into the shower buttons, turning on the water, getting sprayed, shuffling along to a dry spot and then knocking into the shower buttons again.

So we take the field slightly damp, I sing my first ever national anthem on the Twickenham turf and a new team takes its first steps towards success.

We beat France and I kick all four of my goals, including an important conversion from the touchline. The following week, at Lansdowne Road, we survive a streaker-on-the-pitch experience, and well beat the Irish, even though their team has a strong back line including Brian O'Driscoll, a player of whom we have all heard.

Scotland are next. We play them up at Preston Grasshoppers. I get a try and kick seven goals. With that 55–18 win behind us, we head to Wales in search of a Grand Slam.

The atmosphere around Narberth, where we play, is noticeably hostile, gritty. The teams on the pitch are pretty hostile, too. Previous results suggest that we should win, but with us going for the Grand Slam and them intent on stopping us, the game is very tense.

In the absence of our captain, Tony Roques, I am captain for the day. I am also given an early taste of the kind of aggression with which this entire game is played. In fact, I will look back on this game as involving probably the worst shoeing I've taken in my entire career.

Only five minutes into the match, on the far side of the field, I'm on the wrong side of the ruck. I try to get out of the way but can't because I'm being rucked to pieces. It feels as though the opposition are just running up and down my back. Later, we take photographic evidence of the scars, but for now, I get to my feet and feel an intense burning sensation. The heavy cotton of our shirts seems to stick to the wound and exaggerate the pain. And I'm thinking great, that has just got me super fired up.

The game is close and edgy. In Gareth Cooper they have an electric scrum half, and we struggle to keep any kind of lead. We get to the dying seconds of the game 17–15 down.

What we need is a drop goal, but drop goals have not really formed a huge part of my decision-making on the field up to this point. I like to attack. I have only ever kicked two drop goals in my life, one six years ago in Senlis. The other was a few weeks ago, right at the end of my last game for Lord Wandsworth, in the Hampshire Cup final, when our hooker Dave Barker ran over to me and said if I win this scrum against the head, you'll have to take a drop goal. That was his deal – bizarre – but I stuck to it.

Here it's clear what we need. We know what we are up to. We drive the ball up the middle a few times and it comes back to me too far out to be a decent bet, about 40 metres. I hit it with my left, the contact is good but it might not have the distance. Only when the referee hears the Welsh full-back swearing is he convinced that the ball did indeed creep over.

We have a Grand Slam. And a last-minute drop goal feels good.

●　　●　　●

The Grand Slammers soon depart on a major trip – a five-week tour of Australia. This is the biggest thing, rugby-wise, that has happened to me, and it is also a major experience in terms of leaving home. We are staying in billets and a part of me is still thinking oh God, I don't want to be billeting on my own. So at the first opportunity, I sneak a word with the coaches.

Look, I say, with all the kicking practice I need to do, it'd make sense if I'm billeted with Simon Amor. Very wisely, they agree.

Simon is one of the other kickers and happens to be a mate. We stay in some amazing places and the high spirits on the tour, as it slowly works its way down the country, are boosted by the fact that we pick up win after win *en route* to Sydney, where we will finish with a schoolboys' Test.

The journey is further improved when Sparks hitches a lift. Sparks is here playing rugby for some local grade teams, but he soon starts following the tour, as does Duncan White, my mate from Lord Wandsworth, who is over to take up a teaching post.

Generally what happens is that we arrive at a new billet, introduce ourselves to our hosts and quite quickly the conversation turns to the fact that my brother is also here with a friend, trying to follow the tour and looking for a place to stay. Invariably, and very kindly, they extend the invitation to Sparks and Duncan.

At one stage, the tour manager tells me that he doesn't want Sparks staying with me any more. But we carry on nevertheless, and Sparks becomes so much part of the tour that he hitches rides on the tour bus. One time, we have him hidden under a pile of bags and coats in the middle of the bus, and I'm wondering what the hell the manager is going to think if he turns round and finds him.

We end up just having a huge holiday. In Queensland, we stay with Kris Burton's parents – I next see him fourteen years later, playing for Italy against England at Twickenham. Farther south, we take part in the most hilarious and physical game of beach 'touch' rugby with Alex Sanderson, who doesn't really do non-contact. An Aussie guy, gamely trying to join in, ends up taking a monster shoulder charge from Sparks and having to be rescued from the waves before he drowns.

The tour, of course, peaks with the Test, in front of 9,000 people at the North Sydney Oval. I play centre – outside James Lofthouse and inside Mike Tindall – against a side captained by Phil Waugh. Their full-back, Ryan Cross, scores two tries, but we are very strong, one of the most successful schoolboy teams England have ever had, and we win 38–20.

Great tour. Huge fun – before my life turns very serious indeed.

CHAPTER 3

FOR my first training session at Newcastle Falcons, I watch from the main bar at the Kingston Park ground, an 18-year-old new arrival sitting at a table with his dad. Outside on the pitch, meanwhile, one of the most élite groups of rugby players in the professional game has gathered.

The list of international players is phenomenal. From England: Tim Stimpson, Tony Underwood, Rob Andrew, Dean Ryan, Garath Archer, John Bentley. From Scotland: Gary Armstrong, Alan Tait, Doddie Weir, Peter Walton, George Graham. From Ireland: Nick Popplewell and Ross Nesdale. And from Samoa, two giants of the game: former All Blacks Inga Tuigamala and Pat Lam.

I had, for a while, been expecting to take up an offer of a place at Durham University, but when Newcastle asked me if I would try going full-time for a year, I needed no second invitation. I got back from Australia, trained hard for a couple of weeks with Sparks and made my way up north, feeling strong, confident, raring to go. And now I sit here, waiting for the ice-breaker with my new international teammates.

The first person I shake hands with is Inga. I don't know if there could be a better way to start. He greets me with an infectious, ear-to-ear smile and sits down opposite us. Hi, how are you doing? What's your name? Where are you from? Great to have you here. What an awesome guy.

Next up is Pat Lam. Same thing. And Tony Underwood and Tim Stimpson are not far behind. What a difference that makes. What a start. The selection policy here has clearly placed great emphasis not only on the quality of player but on the quality of person. Among the players, the so-called superstars are, in fact, the most approachable.

And for me, I am now being paid to be a professional rugby player. I am getting around £12,000 per year, which is fantastic for an 18-year-old, although pretty soon I start spending almost all of my wages on taxis.

My problem is that I don't drive yet. I share a house with three other young guys – Chris Simpson-Daniel, brother of James, Mark Bentley and Charles Yeoman – and they all drive. They give me a lift to the club when they can, but I hate the feeling of putting them out. I definitely don't want them to hang around after training while I do my kicking. So it becomes a bit of a strain. I constantly don't ask, because I don't want to, and I hate the fact that they might feel they have to help, or they should do. It's a bit awkward.

The result is that my earnings go to the local taxi firm. I'm constantly on the move. I need cabs back from training, and I get £15 taxis to the gym in the evening to chill with a swim and a Jacuzzi, and then £15 taxis back. In an average week, I can spend £100 just on going to the gym. It's lucky our membership is free.

But I won't give in to asking for lifts and affecting everyone else's lives just because mine happens to be so obsessive. I start travelling on foot. If I need to go somewhere, I'll often walk or run there, even if it's miles away. My most horrendous problem is the weekly shop. I run to the supermarket, a good mile and a half away, and I do my entire week's shopping, six or seven full carrier bags' worth, which I then carry back. The mile and a half home is torture – a quick burst of strongman walking for a hundred yards or so, then stop, put the bags down to save the tips of my fingers from falling off, get some feeling back in my hands, and then off again.

It is fairly clear – I need to pass my driving test.

●　●　●

My first impression of Steve Black comes from what I hear about him from the other players. Dean Ryan and Inga have such respect for him. But I've never heard of him. I'm surprised that a fitness conditioner is talked about like this. The message seems to be just do what the hell Blackie says and don't piss him off.

My first sessions are on the exercise bikes. I train with the back-rowers and the nines and tens, and Blackie, this former boxer, sprinter, power-lifter and professional footballer with a big beard and a bigger Geordie accent, is in charge. Blackie says up the level on the bike and we do, but we don't know for how long. Most fitness trainers would say for thirty seconds or a minute. He doesn't do that; with Blackie you just get on with it. Mentally, it's tough. People start muttering under their breath. It gets to the point where you're looking for someone else to give up so that you can give up, too. But it's inspirational. Blackie waits for everyone's breaking point. He wants to know how we respond to challenges.

He chats during training, watching how we tick, how we train, how we prepare ourselves. He gets to know our bodies, but he also learns our hopes and dreams. And while we are pedalling, he is constantly in rugby, forever creating visual images and making us play the game out in our heads.

Right, he says, take it up to the maximum level. I want you pedalling at 110 revs-per-minute, you're now sprinting back to help out in defence, you're driving your legs in a tackle, up off the floor, what's happening in front of you? Stay in the game, keep your head in the game. What can you see? What can you hear? What's the next move? How can you contribute? Where do you need to be? It's like match practice on bikes.

But it's not a dictatorship. When you arrive, he asks how you are, how you feel, how you slept and how you're eating. And he adapts accordingly.

The deal is simple and I understand what Dean and Inga were saying. You come here to give 100 per cent. It's not acceptable if you don't, and he makes your life a living hell if that's the case. When Blackie lets fly at someone, it's aggressive. You keep your head down, but really, you just want to get out of the room.

Blackie, it becomes clear, gives everything for the team and I just don't want to let him down. He's available whenever we want, day or night. He'll go as far as we want to go. And I like that. Here is a guy who is as obsessive as I am. And that seems a perfect opportunity.

●　●　●

On the pitch, I feel better about life. On arrival at Newcastle, I'd been told that the thinking was that, all being well, I could develop into the long-term replacement for Rob Andrew at number ten, so I wasn't expecting much first-team rugby for a year at least. However, I am pretty much straight into the first-team squad, playing second-team rugby and keeping the bench warm for the big boys.

I get my debut off the bench against Edinburgh, and it could hardly have gone better. I am on with 15 minutes to go; my housemate Chris has come on, too, at scrum half. I have barely got on the pitch when the ball squirts out of the scrum, Chris picks it up and sets off through a gap, steps the full-back and pops up the ball to me, and I sprint the final 10 metres and dive in to score. That's my first touch of the ball in a Newcastle shirt.

It's not always going to go like that, of course it's not, and when it doesn't, I really feel it. In fact, I make sure I do. My full debut, a huge occasion for me, is at home in the Cup against Exeter, a division below us. Kingston Park can be subject to the most horrendous crosswinds, and as I will learn, those crosswinds can completely destroy a game. This is one of those days.

Rob plays number ten. I am at inside centre, but Rob hands me the kicking duties, and it is a tough, tough day to be kicking. I do my best but end up missing three goalkicks from three, and I miss touch with a penalty when the wind almost blows the ball out of my hands.

In open play, I actually do well. I put Tim Stimpson through a couple of times and I have a hand in a couple of tries, but my mind is on the other stuff. At half-time the message is that, with the wind in play, the game is a bit more edgy than we'd expected. So Inga is going to come on for me and basically sort it out. As a decision, it's an absolute no-brainer. Inga dominates in contact, he intimidates people in defence, he goes forward, he is exactly what we need.

But it is not what I need. The expectations I have of myself are so high that I cannot stop those missed kicks and my substitution from overshadowing everything else I have done. I just wasn't good enough, obviously. On the bench, in the second half, everyone says well done to me, but I am convinced they are saying it more in consolation than encouragement, and are actually trying to hide the fact that it hasn't really gone very well for me at all. I cannot stop myself thinking I've screwed everything up, I've let people down, I've let myself down.

In the changing room afterwards, I manage to hide my feelings, but just at the end, when almost everyone has changed and gone, and just George Graham and I are left, he notices that I'm trying not to cry. He gives me a look as if to say don't you dare. You've done really well, he says. Don't be stupid. This is what sport is like. It's going to get a lot worse than this.

Yes, this is sport, but for me it's part of the bigger goal. I want to be the best rugby player in the world. This is the thought that is lodged permanently in my head, the ultimate challenge. For now, I am standing at the foot of it; every new level is another small mountain. Can I get up and over this one? That is what I keep asking myself.

That is why, when I met Dave Alred, I thought I'm going to give this guy everything I've got. Hold nothing back. If I'm going to get to where I want to go, I need him, and I need to drain every last bit of ability out of my being.

That is also what I feel with Blackie. Blackie can get me over those mountains. In fact, he'll climb them right alongside me.

● ● ●

Blackie knows that, at 12 and a bit stone, I am too light for professional rugby. He says that if Newcastle are going to play me at centre, my body will not stand up to it. He wants me nearer 14 stone and he starts pushing me in that direction quickly.

I feel the extent to which he is taking me under his wing, the way he talks to me and gets to know me. It hasn't taken him long to see my intentions. With Blackie, it is not so much wanting to be the best; he understands that not being the best is just not good enough for me. I have to be the best in the bike sessions, on the weights, in shuttle runs, at kicking, passing, tackling, professionalism. Everything.

Blackie knows us outside the club, as well as in it. From his early days working the doors as a bouncer in the Newcastle nightclubs, he has contacts thoughout the city. He knows where we've been and what we've been up to.

One Tuesday morning, I'm recovering from a night out on the town with Pat Lam. We are on the bikes again when Blackie gives us a random change, sending us outside to do shuttle runs on the grass, and my throat is burning. I'm in all kinds of trouble. In the Jacuzzi afterwards, I have to bolt and make a mad dash to vomit in the changing-room bin. It's one of those bins with a swing-lid and as I vomit, it swings back and what I've unloaded finishes all down my own feet. Pat smiles as if to say you'll learn one day, youngster. Blackie no doubt knows anyway.

But it is a lesson. Have I got the capacity to behave like this? I know, of course, that the answer is no. And if Blackie is going to help me fulfil my goals, it is not the life that is going to get me there with him.

Blackie never was and never will be just a fitness conditioner. He just happens to be the best in the world at understanding sport and the intricacies of the movement, how to get the best out of players, how to improve performance, how to get inside their heads. There is no comparison with anyone else. His knowledge and experience take him off the chart. I have no doubt that if I am to go anywhere, I need him with me.

● ● ●

I have long had an appetite for the big collisions, but one of the worst ever comes at Headingley. I will never know for sure, but I think this is the one that will undo me several years from now. What is certain is that I am already sowing the seeds of future fitness problems.

Before arriving at Newcastle, selection for representative team rugby had been the be-all and end-all. However, when I'm invited for the North Under-21 squad trials, I feel quite relaxed. On a weekly basis, I'm trying to fit in with a team of full internationals, so it's nice to feel the anxiety lift for once – if only a little.

And I'm straight into the team. James Lofthouse is in the squad, too, but this time I get the number-ten shirt.

We play Midlands at Headingley and the game starts brilliantly. The scrum half makes a break, he passes to me and pretty much my first touch is a 50 metre run-in. Almost straightaway, I'm part of a try down the right. And I knock over the conversion.

But then, after 25 minutes, I fly in for a big tackle and get my head caught on the wrong side. My head compresses dead straight back through my neck. I feel the all-too familiar searing heat of a stinger but this time it goes shooting down both my arms and lasts longer than usual.

After being poleaxed like that, there is no way I can carry on. So I watch from the bench, consoled by the fact that I got a reasonable start, yet massively disappointed about having to come off.

It doesn't stop me going out with the boys that night in Leeds, and neither does it stop me sleeping on Ian Leek's floor. Ian is a friend from Lord Wandsworth days, now studying at Leeds University. Sleeping on his floor is probably not the best idea I've ever had. The next morning I cannot move my neck at all. I put it down to experience.

● ● ●

More representative honours follow. From North Under-21, I get the call-up to play for England Under-21. We beat a New Zealand team going by the name of Nike New Zealand and starring a young Byron Kelleher, and the bar afterwards swarms with agents. I've not seen agents like this before. They introduce themselves. They explain what they do – I'd be interested in looking after you. I'd be interested in helping you further your career. One comes and then another, three in all, the same chat every time.

What are you supposed to make of that? Thank goodness I am with Bilks. We say thanks very much. Really we mean thanks, but no thanks. I don't like the atmosphere or this business-like approach to the sport I love.

We play France, which goes well. In a tense, close game, I get a kick in the dying minutes, which turns defeat into victory.

A few days later, in Newcastle, I am round at the house Tim Stimpson shares with Martin Shaw, and something astonishing happens. Stimmo flicks casually to Ceefax and the new senior England squad for the Wales game in the Five Nations has been announced. At the bottom of the screen, last mentioned, almost like an afterthought, is my name. I stare at the screen. What's my name doing there? Is there another J. Wilkinson playing rugby?

CHAPTER 4

THIS is a huge challenge. I am 18, I am joining up with England and I am greeted in the England camp by a bunch of taunts from Austin Healey. Austin asks me if I'm a prize-winner who has won a competition to spend the day with the England team. He asks me if I've got my autograph book with me; he asks if I've finished my homework. He carries on like this for years to come. One day I appreciate the jokes, but right now, he has no idea that he is quite so close to the bone.

When I arrived at Newcastle, it took three months for me to feel comfortable or that I belonged. That's how long it took before I felt I had earned the right to talk, if only briefly, to the senior boys. That's three months of walking into the changing room, sitting wherever I could find space and getting changed in silence before making my way out, first, on to the training field. With the younger guys, and obviously my housemates, it was easier. But Inga, Dean Ryan, Pat Lam, Richard Arnold, Nick Popplewell and the other older guys inhabited the other end of the changing room. I didn't talk to anyone from that end until someone there spoke to me. It's called doing your apprenticeship, earning your place, and I respect that.

The one serious downside to the Ceefax moment was that one of the significant names that had been left off the England squad list was Stimmo's. That was disappointing for him, because I felt he deserved to be there, but also for me. He is such a good friend, and in the corridors of the Petersham Hotel in Richmond, where I join up with the England squad, it would have been nice to have had his company.

At least I have Garath Archer and Tony Underwood as friendly faces. And Rob Andrew knows what I am facing and prepares me well. Just enjoy it, he says. It's clear that he has been in communication with the England coaches. He would not have let me go unless he thought I was ready for it, although it quickly becomes clear to me that maybe I am not.

My first roommate in an England squad is Dorian West, ingeniously nicknamed 'Chief' because he calls everyone chief. Chief is an easy guy to get on with, absolutely no ego, very relaxed — ideal. We share a small, dark room in the far corner of the bottom floor of the hotel, and this is where I hide.

The guys in the squad are people I know because I have seen them on TV — Jerry Guscott, Martin Johnson, Lawrence Dallaglio, Jason Leonard, Phil de Glanville, Kyran Bracken, Tim Rodber. I am very wary of my place. I wouldn't dream of opening my mouth to these guys before being given the green light to do so. I find it very difficult to approach them when I meet them in big groups. I introduce myself very formally. My name is Jonny, nice to meet you. I stop just short of calling them sir.

I guess this is a different environment from Newcastle. It's competitive here, and we all come from different clubs, so people don't know each other as well. There is no welcoming moment as there was at Kingston Park, no Ingas and Pat Lams coming over to say hi.

It's at its worst at mealtimes. You get your food and who do you sit next to? I find myself scanning the dining room quickly and if I can't spy a friendly face, I double back to my room. I'll stay hungry and come back later.

There is a form of escape in Dave Alred, who is England's kicking coach. Training at Twickenham finishes around 5pm and then Dave and I stay and kick for hours. Kicking under floodlights at Twickenham, with the whole place to yourself, is a schoolboy's dream. Often I don't get back until eight, which means I'm late for dinner, which is good because there is no one in the dining room.

I enjoy training, too, because there's loads of contact. In particular, I enjoy a drill called murderball, which is basically fifteen on fifteen, a very small pitch, completely full-on. Physically, I act like I'm almost invincible, and I try to hit whomever I can, the biggest, smallest, just smash them. Quite what the senior guys think of an 18-year-old upstart running around trying to put them into hospital, I have no idea. But this is my release; this is my opportunity to be me.

Kicking with Dave means I get to know Paul Grayson, who is England's kicker and number ten, and I start to spend a lot of time with him. I feel comfortable with Grays. He is a genuinely decent bloke.

I feel comfortable with Catty, too. I don't know why but he is just different. Hey Wilko, he says as his greeting. He jumps on my back, puts his arm round my shoulder. Just for a brief second, I feel I'm back at Newcastle among friends.

But when everyone is back together again, the mood changes and I revert to an awkward silence. I find the backs meetings particularly hard. Everyone gets to the meeting room early and chats while waiting for proceedings to start. I just sit there, fold my arms in my lap and find something to stare at.

It's uneasy, uncomfortable, but I so desperately want to play for England, it doesn't matter. If that's how it has to be, so be it.

On the Thursday of the Wales week, I am released, as expected, from the England camp so that I can play for the England Under-21s. We do well, we score some decent tries, running the ball from all over the field, and I feel the obvious contrast. I am part of this team, I feel valued and I walk around with my head held a bit higher. With England, I am, rightly, at the bottom of the chain.

Three weeks later, I'm called back to the England senior team for the Scotland game. Clive Woodward, the head coach, wants a word. He says he is thinking of putting me on the bench.

At least Clive is not intimidating. He seems welcoming, and he seems to have a great deal of confidence in me. I feel as though he actually believes in me, and my call-up is not some crazy one-off, but he has a genuine plan and I'm a part of it.

I also know that he thinks I'm too quiet, not demonstrative enough, and his way of dealing with that is to ask me questions in team meetings, just to get me to say something out loud. So it's not long before the team meetings down on the bottom floor of the Petersham Hotel are something I begin to dread. The other players seem to wander in, relaxed, yet I sit there totally paranoid, as though I'm waiting nervously for an oral exam, because I know it's going to come, my question, my moment when I'm going to have to say something.

There is one good team meeting, though, and that's the one when Clive lifts the paper on the flip chart to show the team sheet, and there it is on the subs' list: my name. My name on the England team sheet. It's also a bit embarrassing. A lot of the players congratulate me, but I wonder oh God, do these people think I deserve it? Do they really want me here?

Then I look at Dean Ryan, Newcastle captain and coach, who has been called up to join the squad. How does he manage it? He doesn't seem remotely nervous or anxious, or at least if he is, he doesn't let it on. He just seems himself. What an impressive way to be.

We fly up to Scotland and, inside the Murrayfield stadium, I sit on the bench, completely torn in two. I desperately want to get on. I want to be able to say I've played for England; I don't want to be so close but not close enough. At the same time, the game seems to be going in the right direction. Maybe these guys are doing well without me. Maybe I'll just learn from this and be ready for the next one.

A fortnight later, I'm at the next one, still waiting, back on the bench for the Ireland game at Twickenham. England are winning quite well and time is fast running out. Scott Benton, the reserve scrum half, and I go down to the bottom end of the pitch to warm up and while we are there the game stops because Catty, who has been playing on the wing, is down. Hamstring. The thing is we have no reserve winger. Scott and I look at each other, knowing that this means one of us is going on. Dave Redding, our trainer, tells us the answer. It's me.

I shake off my tracksuit trousers. Deep breaths, puff out my chest, there's no hiding now. It's all very well having this image of the England player-in-waiting, but now you've got to prove yourself – which is not so simple on the wing. I have never played wing before. And it is so obvious what's going to happen – Ireland's first lineout, a box-kick to the new boy. I jump and catch it, and I'm not smashed as expected because Neil Back runs an awesome block line on their winger's chase, for which he is then penalised. Thanks for looking out for me, mate.

My five-minute debut is gone in a blur. The pace of the game is so frantic, it's absurd. But it's done and I have played for England. On my list of goals, that is one I can now tick off. I wanted to play for England before I turned 19 and I have. I'm told I'm the youngest England player for seventy-one years. My teammates congratulate me, the atmosphere feels fantastic.

After the game, we have to meet some corporate sponsors in the marquees in the car park and I go along with Catty and Neil Back. I hear people talking about me as we walk past. They want to shake my hand. They want to say well done and can we have an autograph, and as we walk from one area to the next, we are greeted with applause.

It would be so easy to get carried away with all this, but there is something else on my mind, and it's been there since Clive flipped the paper to show the team for Scotland. My singing ordeal. When you make your England debut, you have to sing a first-cap song. I know that as soon as we are back on the bus, it'll be my time.

At the after-match tea, I head to the bar and down a couple of beers to help me. Pretty much as soon as we get on the bus, cheering comes from the back. We've got a new cap on board! They're like animals sniffing fresh prey.

Normally, I have a good memory for lyrics. I've too many stored away for my own good, including half of Bilks's sixties and seventies record collection and the entire Beatles back catalogue. But right now, at the front of the bus, my mind goes blank. It doesn't help that, for the first time ever, wives and girlfriends have been invited to the black-tie post-match dinner, and so they are on the bus, too. I can think of literally nothing to sing, absolutely nothing, and along the aisle in front of me I can see the faces of Guscott, Leonard, Johnson and the rest, looking grossly unimpressed.

Eventually, I break into 'All Things Bright and Beautiful'. It doesn't go down well. They abuse me loudly. I should ignore this and carry on, but I stop. OK, OK, I say, I don't know any other songs. The silence is teeth-grindingly awkward.

Sing anything, they shout from the back. But I can't think of anything. This is horrible. Just sing 'Wonderwall' comes the cry. So I do. Badly.

At the dinner, I am introduced to another mandatory game for the new cap. This is the one where the other twenty-one players in the squad all buy two supposedly identical drinks, one for themselves and one for the new cap. It's the red wine and whisky coming my way that I find most troubling. No surprises that before we've even sat down for dinner, first up is Austin Healey.

The women come to my rescue this time. Don't be so mean, they say. What are you doing to him? Leave him alone.

Thanks to them, I just about survive. I am presented with my cap, a genuine cap. I actually manage to walk up to the stage unaided to receive it. Then I wear it, as tradition dictates, throughout dinner. Next stop is the Café de Paris nightclub in the centre of town. I have never been out in London before so when I offer to get a small round of drinks, I discover I haven't got nearly enough money. Thank God for Dean Ryan, who helps me out. I end up using his money to buy him a drink.

Thank God for Dean again, for getting me home. And I haven't even lost my cap. The next morning, I am awoken by knocking at the door. It's Mum and I'm still fully dressed, lying face down on the bed. I have never felt simultaneously so bad and so good, and proud and very fulfilled.

5

IF you are a young impressionable kid and you want to be the best player in the world, there are probably no two better people to learn from than Inga Tuigamala and Pat Lam.

At Newcastle, I have Rob Andrew as a guiding light, showing me the composure and mentality required to play number ten, to control and manufacture victories. And I have Pat and Inga as my inspiration. It's not just that they are the best two players in the Premiership – that's my view, anyway – it is their spirit and their approach.

They love playing rugby, and every day in training, you see them pushing the boundaries, with big smiles on their faces. It is as if they are opening a door and allowing me a peak through – this is what's out there, if you really want it.

In one training session, we practise a move that starts with Pat coming off the back of the scrum. My job is to hold the tackle bag to stop him when he comes through to set the ball up for the next phase. We run the move twice, and when we run it a third time, Pat runs towards me as planned. I go to hit him with the bag and he just completely steps me; he makes me look stupid. My lesson for the day – be ready for everything, never switch off, not for a second, not even in training.

For a big guy, Pat has a lethal step. I love that. And he has a phenomenal ability for timing a run on to the ball.

Inga's supreme skill is beating three, sometimes four, five, six defenders, and then still, always, off-loading. And although we'll spend all week practising moves for the weekend, in the middle of the game itself, he'll start calling something completely different that he has just dreamt up. The English response is to consider the possible risk, but his enthusiasm takes him away from that. He just says why not? I think because it'll be me who shoulders the blame.

Every week, Pat and Inga show me that anything is possible. Every week, they inspire me to be the best.

In the weeks away from the England camp, being back in Newcastle feels like being back at home. I feel more at home in the team now, too, regularly playing at number twelve. And sometimes, I can even hold a five-minute conversation with a senior player. Playing twelve is a privileged place to be – outside Rob, the great controller, and inside Inga. You can give the ball to Inga in any situation. If Rob feels he really needs experience for a game, he brings Alan Tait off the wing and into the centre instead of me, but towards the latter part of the season, when we are making a charge at the league title, I mostly keep my place.

In April, with six games to go, we have lost just one league game all season. We play successive games in London, against Saracens, who beat us with a last-second drop goal, and against Wasps, who beat us by a single point. Our title hopes are in danger.

The Wasps game is tight and awkward. Towards the end, I'm not quite sure how to help. I don't want to get in Rob's way and it's against my instinct to hide. The tension is killing. By the changing rooms afterwards, I meet Bilks and I can hold it in no longer. He is greeted with the same panic and tears he has seen so many times before. Have I let people down? I want to know. I feel so frustrated. I ask Bilks am I doing my job right? What else could I have done? I don't feel completely clear about what I should be doing, about my role. What more can I do? Maybe the pressure is wearing me down a bit.

And I look at Rob. With a last-minute, long-range penalty, he had an opportunity to win the game, and he hit the post. How can he be so calm and philosophical? Why do I seem to feel it so much more?

We finish with three big games – Leicester and Bath at home and Harlequins away. If we win them all, we win the League.

I love having Blackie in the changing room before games. He gives the team talk, such is the standing in which he is held by the team. We are half shit-scared of him, and 100 per cent respectful, so there is no better person to deliver messages about commitment and honesty, and what makes a difference.

He asks us to focus on what we've trained on during the week, but he also talks about aggression in contact, and the fire in our performance, in our desire. He talks about inspiring each other, and our roles as players and leaders. When he speaks, it's an aggressive, inspirational sound track pumping through the changing room, and we listen.

On a sunny Bank Holiday Monday, the Leicester side we face is full of the big names I have been hiding from in the England camp, plus Joel Stransky, South Africa's World Cup-winning fly half. We play well. We run a perfect double-switch, Rob linking with me and then me with Pat. Pat runs his line so fast and close to my back that I feel his speed like a ghost going through the back of my shirt. He explodes through the hole at full pace, has just one defender to beat and out-gases him to the line. Great try from a great player.

We beat Leicester 27–10. Against Bath, I help us to build a lead and then watch from the bench as we successfully defend it, 20–15. Finally, on a hot mid-May Sunday in London, we complete the job at Harlequins, 44–20. I have been here one season and we are Premiership champions.

Naturally, this kick-starts a week of partying – serious, proper, night after night celebrating – which isn't too smart, because at the end of the week, we are at Twickenham for the Sanyo Cup. The new league champions play a seriously classy Rest of the World team starring Chester Williams, Philippe Bernat-Salles and David Knox.

We start by playing like people who have been drunk for half the week. Inga's first involvement in the game – beating three players, then a blind back-handed offload – makes it obvious that he is teetotal. Very quickly, we find ourselves 31–7 down, but we recover to 31–19 just before the break. And we want to win this. We pull ourselves back into it and the last half hour becomes the Pat and Inga show. We win 47–41.

But the point is this. I am on the receiving end of a lot of success at a ludicrously early stage in my career. And physically, I feel kind of invincible. This path is one I am finding a little too easy to tread. Harsh reality, however, is but a game away.

● ● ●

Off the pitch, life is moving fast, too. It's clear I need an agent and Bilks and I are put in touch with Tim Buttimore, an ex-Leicester player who looks after Martin Johnson, Neil Back and Clive Woodward. That seemed a pretty decent recommendation.

I like Tim. He's not like a lot of other agents – no fast talking, no promising this, promising that, just very supportive, genuine, honest. I feel comfortable that this is someone I can get on with.

The relationship starts well when Tim tells me he can bring in a boot sponsor. Adidas? I'd almost sell my soul to be with adidas. Ever since Dave Alred gave me that first pair of Predators, I've worn nothing else.

So I get a little bit of money, all the kit I could possibly need, and boots. My excitement when that first pair of boots arrives from adidas is like a child's at Christmas.

● ● ●

The day after the Sanyo Cup, I join the England squad for the Tour from Hell. At this stage, we are just a young group, excited to be going on a long England tour of the Tri-Nations countries. We don't know yet that this is the Tour from Hell. That name is applied five weeks later and sticks for ever more.

What is clear at the start is that we do not have anything approaching a full-strength England team. Many of the senior players have been advised to use the summer to rest, but at least we have Neil Back and Stimmo. Stimmo is one of the best physical specimens I've ever seen on a rugby pitch. But on the morning we meet up, Backy has a quick chat with Clive and suddenly goes from the squad list to the injury list. When you see a guy of that quality walking back to his car with his bag, that is a big blow.

We train on the Twickenham pitch, a particularly hard, physical session with John Mitchell, the forwards coach, screaming at the shirtless forwards, telling them individually how fat they are. Off the pitch, Clive stresses the point by asking Josh Lewsey to take his shirt off.

What? Josh was not exactly expecting this.

Take your shirt off, Clive tells him.

Josh does what he is told and Clive points at him and tells us that, if we are serious about playing for England, this is what we all need to look like.

Somewhere hidden in this act, genetics aside, Clive may have the semblance of a point. I am getting more used to his interesting ideas. To improve communication, he once had the Under-21s back line training with pillow cases over their heads. Also in the Under-21s, he has tried playing Paul Sampson, a phenomenally fast winger, at number ten because he wanted to see what it was like to have the quickest number ten in the world.

His other idea for this tour is to start me at number ten. The result is that pretty much the minute we get to Brisbane, I am being sat on a park bench having my photo taken and being interviewed by Australian journalists. Naturally, I try to play it straight and I go on about the enormous respect we have for the country we are visiting. Nevertheless, 'The Boy Wonder' is what they call me in the papers the next day; they big me up as England's young hope and I feel massively uncomfortable with it. Look, I say, I'm 19, just walked off the plane, never played number ten for England before, only played five minutes of international rugby at all and that was on the wing, and when I was here this time a year ago, it was on a schoolboys' tour. But the Boy Wonder tag sticks. This was what the Australian media were going to write whatever I said.

●　●　●

In a park in Brisbane, Dave Alred does something incredible. For my kicking, he is trying to focus my approach on hitting the target. Rather than trying to kick the ball through two posts, the idea is to start aiming for the middle of the middle. It's like darts – rather than aiming for the board itself, you aim for the bullseye. And the more you practise, the better you get at hitting it; the more precise you get, the more the margin for error is reduced, and the easier it becomes.

The park in Brisbane is littered with palm trees, so we do a lot of kicking over the trees. Then we start goalkicking and he turns to an electrical pylon with six hexagonal panels round it, 20 metres away, which we're going to use as our bullseye. He's got a ball set on his kicking tee and, from the back of his run-up, he is talking body position and bodyweight. He is halfway through his sentence when he sets off and kicks the ball in front of him. The ball flies smack into the central panel and rebounds along the same trajectory, straight back at us; he traps the ball with his right boot, a foot from the kicking tee, and continues his sentence without pausing for breath. Genius. As if I needed any further affirmation that this is a guy I need to listen to!

* * *

When the flood gates open in rugby, sometimes the water rushes through so fast you get swept away. This is what happens against Australia. This is what happens when an understrength team, such as ours, plays against probably the best in the world in their own backyard.

On the touchline are four local players who have made a charity commitment to do press-ups to match the total points on the scoreboard every time Australia score. They don't know what they have let themselves in for.

We start OK. We don't get much ball to attack with and we hold our own for quarter of an hour, but we fly round like maniacs just to keep our heads above water. God, is it hard work. I throw myself into every tackle and get a huge hand-off in the face from Matt Burke as my reward. He just palms me to the ground. The Wallabies are clinical. Their organisation, their precision, is just bang on. Their plans and their roles are executed so well.

The strength of a team shows in its collective resilience when things don't go well, in how you manage to stop the rot, how you change your plans, how you adapt. But we don't have the ability to do this. After 30 minutes the score is 6–0; by half-time we are 33 points down.

We come out in the second half trying so hard, but we leave ourselves more open and we have nothing left with which to defend the odd ball we turn over. The game gets crazy very quickly. Ben Tune and Stephen Larkham score a hatful of tries. I have two kicks at goal. They are close, but I miss them both. The final score, 76–0, is the biggest defeat ever in the history of the England rugby team. The Australian fans jeer in a manner I will never forget. Even the press-up brigade have to call it quits and revert to sit-ups instead.

In the changing room afterwards, I catch Stimmo's eye and we allow ourselves a wry smile, as if to say what the hell was that? Did that really happen?

That is the last smile for a long while. At the post-match function, the embarrassment starts to kick in. I can't look the opposition in the eye, not at all, not after that. I feel shame rising in me, the shame of not being able to hold my head up, of being totally second class in every single way. It's done and I can't change it, and the thought sets my heartbeat soaring. I need to get out of here.

I am suddenly desperate to get into my own space to let it all out. I thought I was on this perfect path – I've scored a try with my first touch in the Premiership; I've been in the England team aged 18; I've won the League with Newcastle; I've won the Sanyo Cup. What happened to that invincibility, to my perfect path? All ruined, all gone. It's almost too much, now, to carry on. What will people think of me now? How can I ever recover?

This devastation has a faintly familiar feel about it. It's the same as that fateful kick of the turf at school, except that was in front of a handful of parents; this one was in front of 26,000 people, and it was live on TV.

I am rooming with Austin and when I return, it is a good thing he is not back. I start walking round the room, crying, shouting my frustration, panicking. Planning on being the best in the world! Who am I kidding? Those dreams were all a pile of shit. I'm a joke, I'm pathetic.

I want to hide. I want the ground to swallow me up. I don't want to have to face anyone. I just don't want this to have happened.

• • •

I am still in tears when I get through on the phone to Bilks. From the other side of the world, he can recognise the tone of voice and the state of mind, and he is straight with me. He would have known this call was coming. His response has a big effect.

Look, he says, what's in the past you can't change. The only thing you can decide now is how you move on. You've got to decide very quickly. What are you going to do about it? Because if you don't like it, you can stop. Do you want to stop now? And go out like this?

What he shows me is a massive fork in the road. He pulls me from my torture, my self-denigration, and appeals to that other person in me, the person who plays with pride, the one who is competitive to the finish. What am I going to do about this? One thing I know for sure is that I'm going to struggle to live with 76–0, but I'll struggle to live with myself a lot more if I bow out just because it got a bit tough a bit early and I couldn't take the strain.

Then I get it. That 76–0 is a bit like kicking with Dave Alred. Dave shows you what being the best is; he makes you realise how much work you have to do and how far you have got to go. The Australians have just done the same. They have shown me what being the best looks like. They've shown me what I want to look like too, and how much work I have to do in order to be that way.

And now that I know, I make a promise to myself – I am never going to feel this way again. I'm never going to feel so helpless, never going to feel so second rate, never going to allow myself to feel as unvalued as that. Never. The day we were defeated 76–0 is one of the worst and most important days of my life.

* * *

The pain does not just evaporate. Usually, the day after a match, we do our recovery session in a hotel pool, or in the sea, a stretching room or a gym. But Clive tells us that today we are going to do it in the park outside the hotel, right out there where everyone can see us.

The deal is that Phil Pask will take us for a run. Pasky is one of the team physios, a truly great one, but more to the point, he is a former Northampton player turned Iron Man fitness freak, and he appears to have no concept of how fit he is.

We go out in our England-branded training kit and we are soon being heckled, taking abuse from all sides. It doesn't help that we can't keep up with our physio and are slowly strung out in a long line behind him. We get abuse for that, too.

Life doesn't get any easier when we arrive in New Zealand. In Dunedin, the All Blacks await us and their team is full of my schoolboy heroes, including Walter Little, who would have a good shout at making my all-time dream team, Michael Jones, who was a big hero of Sparks's too, Andrew Mehrtens, Jeff Wilson, Josh Kronfeld and, yes, Jonah Lomu.

I don't have long to think about how I am going to deal with Lomu because, surprise surprise, we are hardly into the game when he takes a pass from the base of the scrum, running straight at me. This first time, I hit him full on with all I've got, fairly high on the ball, just enough to halt him for a second for everyone else to dive in. On the second occasion, I have no time to prepare myself and am not so successful. We're five metres from our line and I know that if I go high, he'll carry me over and score anyway, and then probably toss me into the crowd, so I sink down low to try to get round his legs and I just get smashed. He knocks me on to my back and runs over my chest.

But I don't play well. I'm short on confidence – would you believe it? Halfway through, my leg gets trapped and I'm lucky to escape a serious break. I get away with strained ankle ligaments, but that's me injured and out of the game. We lose 64–22. My tour is over – well, kind of over.

We move on to another defeat in Auckland and then another in Cape Town. Hanging around on crutches, just watching and soaking it up, is a horrible experience. You hear what people are saying about you, what they think of you, and they don't seem to respect you. Maybe this is exactly what I need. There was I a few weeks back feeling kind of invincible, and it couldn't be clearer now how mistaken I was.

CHAPTER **6**

NOW I have seen where I want to go and where I need to be, I want to get stuck in as soon as I can.

Back at Newcastle, I have a wish list, both on paper and firmly ingrained in my mind. The obsessive switch is flicked on, and all my energy is focused in one direction. I want to take the whole thing by storm; I want to follow Pat and Inga's example and tear up the field with ball in hand; I want to lead games by my decision making; I want to be the completely reliable, machine-like kicker; and I want to smash people in defence. That's really what I want to do. I want to smash people.

At the end of the Tour from Hell, I was taken aside by Roger Uttley, the team manager, who told me we appreciate this has been a really difficult tour, we don't want you to feel you've let anyone down or failed or anything, and with regard to future selection, we'll take that fully into account. I appreciated the chat, but I'm not kidding myself, either. I sense that I'm now bracketed as too young, not quite ready.

● ● ●

When the next England squad is announced for the autumn series, my name is not on it. Actually, it gives me a certain freedom about the task in hand. I'm so fired up, working so hard. Blackie, sadly, has moved jobs to work with Wales, but we remain in very close contact. I so need to continue working with him.

Out on the pitch, I am so determined and so passionate that I start getting carried away and mouthy with the opposition. It's not a conscious decision and I hate myself for it afterwards, but I can't seem to help it. My pre-game anxieties and nerves are as bad as ever, and when I'm caught up in the game, they manifest themselves in impulsive comments and aggressive taunts.

I love putting in the big hits, but I start following up with some back-chat on the ground: How do you like that? Or one of my most cringeworthy: Take that, served first-class delivery for you! It's weak, disrespectful and not very clever, but I can't seem to control it.

We play London Scottish away and I am angry, frustrated. The game isn't going well, the Scottish boys seem a little cocky and I start having an ongoing exchange with their back-rower, Simon Fenn. We run our double-switch move and I block the player defending me so he can't get to the next tackle. I am right in Fenn's ear, letting him know all about it, shouting: It's a missed tackle, your missed tackle, that's your man and it's your fault.

It doesn't end there. We are constantly on at each other in open play, in rucks and even during breaks in play. After the game, we go through their tunnel and everyone says well played, as you always do. But I seem to be the exception. Their players just carry on abusing me, calling me an idiot and far worse. It is quite an achievement to have made an impact like that in eighty minutes. I deserve it, but it shocks me.

A few weeks later, we have London Scottish again, back at Kingston Park, and I still haven't learned. We are in the process of scoring a try and, away from the action, one of their second-rowers is in a wrestling, slanging tussle with Rob Andrew. Arrogant, confused, but trying to be clever, I charge in to break it up.

Listen, I say to their big number four, and point to the uprights. You go over there now, my friend, and stand under those posts while I kick this ball over.

Then I see that we've scored in the left corner, and so I line up the conversion thinking I've just made this kick even harder now. I've really set myself up for a big fall. If I don't get this, I'm opening myself up to a whole load of abuse.

I don't strike it brilliantly but the sight of the ball going through the posts triggers intense relief. Yet I am making life needlessly tough for myself. I don't need it. If only I could control it.

● ● ●

The good news is that I have passed my driving test at the first attempt, which will help me get around, and means my entire wage does not go to the local taxi firm. The bad news is that I am not the best behind the wheel.

Now I need a car, particularly since I have become a proud house owner, so no lifts to training, and what I save on taxis has to go on my mortgage.

The area in which I live does not have a brilliant reputation. I guess I should have twigged when some enthusiastic kids knocked on my door asking to borrow some golf 'bats'. Slightly bemused, I lent them a couple of my clubs, although this is a built-up area, and there aren't exactly many golf courses around. I can't really be sure what the clubs were used for. Suffice it to say, I never saw them again.

And just up the road, there was an armed siege on a house. The neighbours were told to stay away from their connecting wall because there was a chance that bullets might be flying through from the other side.

But I feel good round here, a sense that is massively enhanced when Sparks moves in with me after getting a job as a conditioning coach with the club. There are good people around, too. Jim and Sue, a truly lovely couple over the road, become like surrogate parents to me. But the real reason I have no worries is because of Blackie. With his reputation and all his local connections, he basically puts the word out that no one is to touch my house, no one is to go near it, because his mate is living inside. That is a seal of approval that gives you confidence.

As for my suspect driving, it began when I was a learner in Farnham and managed to take out a concrete gatepost in our driveway. Up here, I have randomly crashed into the car of my teammate Ian Peel in my own driveway when it was parked next to me. That cost me some £350.

My first car is a red Peugeot 206, and I have managed to drive it up on to the grass island in the middle of a roundabout. I'm not entirely sure how, but I stopped at a shop off the roundabout to get a drink, and then somehow managed to rejoin the roundabout by going the wrong way up the exit sliproad. Other cars were heading straight for me and I could see terror in the eyes of the drivers. So I swerved and finished up parked in the middle of the central island.

The sight of my red Peugeot on the island was ridiculous – obviously – and as other drivers slowed down to see what the hell was going on, I decided to pretend there was something wrong with the car and started banging the steering wheel, to show that I was really angry and totally blameless. I then just ducked down and hid in the footwell for three or four minutes, occasionally peering up to see if there were any cars around, and when I finally saw that there weren't, I slipped quietly back on to the road with a perfect execution of the trusty mirror, signal, manoeuvre technique.

But now I'm wondering what to say to my teammate Jim Naylor, or whether to say anything at all. After a recent game at Kingston Park, driving away from the snowy car park, a notebook fell from my door compartment. It landed under my feet and I didn't want it to go under the brake pedal. So I reached down to grab it, simultaneously veered a little and managed to ride my 206 up against another car.

In the dark, I checked the other car up and down properly, and I couldn't see any damage at all. I didn't think mine was damaged either, although the cold light of the next day showed that I was clearly wrong.

A week later, I'm back at the club, relaxing in the physio room. Someone comes in and asks have you had a bit of a prang in your car? The front wing is pretty dented.

Er, yeah, I reply. It was after that game with the snow last week in the car park. I think someone drove into me and then just drove off. I can't believe someone would do that.

It just so happens that Jim is right next to me.

I don't believe it, he says. That's exactly what happened to my blue Escort, on the same night.

I don't tell Jim. But I do sprint outside and vigorously scratch off the blue paint from my Peugeot's front end.

●　●　●

The season hasn't been going long before Rob wants a word. It's my defence, he says. You need to back off a bit, leave it more to your teammates, mainly the back-rowers.

OK I reply. I'm not sure I'll find that easy, but I realise it's a good idea.

It's not just Rob who delivers this message. I've heard it before, anyway. It comes from the other coaches, too, and to be honest, I can see it kind of makes sense. If I'm able to back off a bit, I'll be slightly fresher for other parts of my game. Almost everyone is of the same opinion. I speak to Blackie. He understands me. He knows that I am all or nothing and that tackling fuels the rest of my game.

It's not as if I wake up in the morning and think I'm going to go out and really try to smash people today. Not at all. I want to change the course of the game for my team. If I am able to damage the other team's game plan, dent their confidence by getting in a good hit and make them think twice about coming back next time, I won't hold back.

But it's not just that. It's also something I feel on the field of play. That ultra competitive switch in me gets flicked when a ball-carrier looks at me as if to say I'm going to run straight over you. I feel kind of belittled by that. I find myself thinking there's simply no way I can cope with just tackling you to the ground now, that would almost be your victory, that almost means you win. No, I'm going to have to show you you've made a mistake.

It's just pure competitive instinct and desire to show what I'm capable of. It's why I train the way I do; it's what I live for.

But trying to explain that to coaches when they're talking from a purely tactical mindset doesn't work. I can't explain my natural desire. I can't explain why I have only one way and no alternative.

So what I say to Rob becomes a stock answer given each time we have this same conversation in all the years to come. OK, yeah, it's a good idea I know. I'll do my best.

● ● ●

At home in Lemington, in the West of Newcastle, just before Christmas, I'm preparing dinner when there is a knock on the door, a pleasant gentleman in his sixties.

How can I help?

You've been notified for a drugs test, he tells me.

This is like being subpoenaed; once you have been notified, that's it. Refuse and it counts as a negative sample. This is my first home visit.

The problem is I have only just been to the toilet. So I invite him in. I have almost finished making dinner and apologise that I didn't make enough for him.

We sit on the sofa together in my small lounge and watch *The Simpsons* in silence while I eat. Poor guy. It's a little awkward, but I can't deliver what he wants yet. The drug-tester seems easygoing, and patient. He is not allowed to let me out of his sight, which means that when I go to the kitchen to make us a drink, he comes too.

After two and a bit hours, I can finally deliver what he has come for. I go to the toilet and he joins me in my tiny bathroom. That's part of his job. He has to watch; I am not allowed to shut the door. It feels more awkward than it did before.

But he is just the first. This is the life.

● ● ●

In the new year, I am recalled to the England squad for the Five Nations.

It's great to be called back, and this time I really feel I've earned it. But it means going back to the Petersham Hotel and that intimidating atmosphere, where I am so uninvolved in the day-to-day chat that I really don't know what the squad think about me. Am I taking the place of someone else they feel should be there? A friend of theirs? Someone else who fits in more?

Playing for England is, of course, a dream come true. It's meeting up with the squad that I start to dread, like the back-to-school-blues. You spend Sunday at home relaxed and then Monday morning rolls around and you feel uncomfortable and are constantly in a state of panic.

I don't know how much of this is just me and my insecurity, but Clive isn't having it. He can see I'm still not demonstrative, not saying enough in the meetings, not giving my opinion. I'm picked to play inside centre, and he makes it clear to me that if I'm ever going to play at ten, I need to be able to boss people such as Martin Johnson and Tim Rodber, tell them where I want them to go and what I want them to do and what they're doing wrong, regardless of their status or position.

In meetings, Clive starts pushing me towards the front even more than before. More questions come to me. He asks me to talk through some of our moves. I understand what he is doing and why, but at this point I don't have it in me. In no way do I have the ability to give what he wants from me. I still feel there are guys in the room who don't necessarily want me here.

However, being first choice and starting for the team does give me an increased sense of belonging. I feel less like the guy who just won the competition. The night before our first game, against Scotland, I find a note that's been slid under the door. It's from Lawrence Dallaglio, our captain. He tells me about his early experiences of playing with England and what it meant to him, and that he is now proud to see me here doing the same thing.

Thanks, Lawrence. What a difference that suddenly makes.

● ● ●

We beat Scotland 24–21, a decent start to the Five Nations, even if we let them back in at the end, and I feel that I have done OK despite a couple of fairly simple defensive errors. I still have a lot to learn, obviously, but I think I show I am capable of getting around at that level.

Next up is Ireland, my best day so far in a white shirt. For the first time in international rugby, I feel as though I've found my feet. I get the opportunity to show some skills, to engage in the decision-making, to push everything forward. I make a late break and come within inches of scoring. I feel I have actually imposed myself here. It feels great. It's awesome playing alongside Paul Grayson. I learn a lot from him. And I am starting to enjoy playing with some of my other teammates.

The old nervous anxiety is still throbbing away, though. That doesn't change. There are times when it feels like hell, when I can't sleep the night before the game, when I am thinking about it all the time, the game and nothing else. But I have to cope, I have to get through it. I still feel I'm at the bottom of the mountain, looking up and wondering what I can achieve.

In the week before the France game, I split my ear so badly in training it rips slightly from the side of my head. This is a recurrence of an old injury and it means that I have to play with tape around my head. I hate that. I feel so self-conscious out there. But the game goes well, I kick seven penalties and we win 21–10. We are a good team and now we are going into a Grand Slam decider against Wales.

And I am slowly finding people I relate to in the squad, younger guys such as Dan Luger, David Rees and Matt Perry. For the Wales game, Barrie-Jon Mather is in the team at centre. What an awesome bloke. And Steve Hanley is on the wing. He's a great bloke, too. There's a bit of a younger feel to the squad and I like it. At mealtimes I can normally find somewhere to sit. Occasionally, I can even manage a smile.

We play the Wales game at Wembley and it's one of the greatest surfaces I've ever played on. Absolutely beautiful.

We play good, attacking rugby, but we cannot get much of a lead because we keep on coughing up the odd penalty and Neil Jenkins, the Welsh number ten, kicks everything from everywhere. What we will remember, though, is that towards the end, we have a penalty to stretch the lead, but Lawrence elects to kick for the corner and go for the try. We all agree with his decision.

It would have been a perfect call if it had come off, but it doesn't. We then concede a tough penalty from a massive Tim Rodber hit on Colin Charvis. This is deemed to be a shoulder charge and from the ensuing lineout, Scott Gibbs breaks our line, scores under the posts and leaves Jenkins with a simple conversion to finish us off. Wales take it by a single point.

That's that. Grand Slam lost. If there is any consolation to be had, it's the sight of Blackie so happy with his team. But the pain is incredible. This is not a feeling I ever want to repeat.

● ● ●

I might be an England player, but I still feel very much a junior among the big names at Newcastle. Nick Popplewell, a nice, funny, hard guy, who is coming to the end of a long, impressive career, and struggling badly with a heel injury, is exactly the sort of player I respect hugely and would like to think well of me.

We are in the back bar at Kingston Park and the coaches are showing video clips from a game against Bedford. In one move, Rob had taken a pass coming from one side of the ruck to the other, and I spot that their defenders are all looking at him. I then run a line off Rob catching one of the defenders ball-watching and end up clean into space, step around the full-back and score.

I am slightly embarrassed that this is being shown in front of everyone, but Popplewell saves my embarrassment with liberal use of the F-word.

Fucking brilliant, he says, repeatedly. Screw tactics, screw all that. That is just fucking brilliant.

And that makes me feel immensely proud.

● ● ●

In the changing rooms at Kingston Park, the lights have been set up for me to do a photo-shoot for *GQ Active* magazine. I haven't really done this kind of thing before. I thought it was going to be a simple interview and a photo, but they are saying they want me to take my shirt off for the picture.

Opposite the changing rooms are the club offices. I feel embarrassed enough without all this going on in front of the office staff. But I don't want to take my shirt off anyway.

It's for the cover shot, they say. They always do it this way.

Yeah, but it's just not me, I reply. It's not what I do. Not what I want to do.

They tell me that it's what they always do and that the last cover shot was of Lennox Lewis. If the world heavyweight boxing champion can do it ... The picture's not going to have any impact if it's just you standing there in a T-shirt. You'll be fine.

But I don't feel fine about it at all. I feel embarrassed. I don't want to take my shirt off. It's not who I am or the image I want to portray. On the flip side, I hate the idea that I'm letting these people down. But I'm a private person. Surely they can understand that.

I get on the phone to Tim Buttimore. What do I do? I don't want to let them down, but I don't want to do the picture, either. Tim speaks to the photographer. The photographer then tries to convince me not to worry. It'll be fine, he says. It'll look great. I later find out that Tim actually said no to the photographer. But that's all too late.

We end up with a compromise – shirt off, yes, but doing a press-up. The picture is taken from the front, so all you can see is my arms and a slight angled view of my chest.

I feel bullied into doing this. I don't like the way this world works. I feel I've betrayed my values and been played for a fool. If I can possibly help it, this will not happen again.

● ● ●

Our domestic season ends back at Twickenham at the Tetley Bitter Cup final, which Newcastle lose to Wasps. The defeat is hard enough to take in itself, but when I meet up again with England for our summer tour to Australia, Clive wants to talk about it. I ran the ball too much, he says. I need to kick it more.

This is on Clive's mind because, he says, he is considering taking me to Australia not as a number twelve but as first choice number ten, which entails another level of pressure. I was just enjoying finding my feet at twelve, and now I am a ten. And Clive wants even more from me in meetings. He now wants me to start presenting meetings to the whole of the team.

We fly out to Brisbane where we have a long training camp on Couran Cove. Couran Cove is a resort island, ideal as an athlete's training facility and popular among sports teams. For me, though, being trapped here becomes sheer hell.

All of a sudden, I'm right back to where I started with England. I don't fit in, I find it impossible to relax, I hide in my room and I'm back to my old ways at mealtimes, dipping in and out of the dining room when I can't see anywhere to sit, or sitting there at breakfast with nothing to talk about. I don't feel wanted or that I have anyone to hang around with. Thank God for Tim Stimpson and Barrie-Jon Mather, who I almost cling to for company. We play endlessly on the table-tennis table or the baseball machine that pitches balls at you.

But around most of the guys, I still don't feel welcome. I do feel under constant pressure, constant scrutiny. I dread going to the meetings, where I am the number ten and I am supposed to take control.

I hit a low point at training. We are doing a simple three-on-two drill to warm-up and Brian Ashton, the backs coach, says to the defenders: Don't try to do too much. For the purpose of the drill, just go up and get drawn by the pass.

I go up at second defender. Guscott is going to be running against me. As he passes the ball, I realise I've run up a bit too quickly, so in order to avoid colliding with him, I move to his side, which is also the side where he's passed. This may look as though I'm trying half-heartedly for an intercept, but I'm not. It may also make Guscott look as though he's not doing his job, although that's not the case, either.

I'm going back to the queue when Guscott silences the whole group. What the fucking hell do you think you're doing? He says it to me, loud and clear. You should fucking listen, maybe you'll learn something.

Ever since I joined up with England, Jerry Guscott has had an aura of the untouchable about him, and as the young lad coming in, I'm certainly not the one to challenge it. Nor, on this occasion, is anyone else. Everyone hears what he has said, players and coaches alike. In the awkward quietness, I feel myself shrinking. I feel a foot tall. And then everyone just gets on with the drill again as if nothing has happened. No one stands by me, no one says: Whoa there, that's a bit much. Or: Don't worry about it, Jonny, just forget it, that sort of thing. No one says anything.

I don't blame the other guys. It would've been pretty damn hard to react differently. But I feel totally alone and hugely taken aback. Was what I did so bad that I had to be put in my place like that?

But because no one says anything, this just confirms it for me. I don't fit in here, it's impossible to blend in. All my goals and aims in life demand that I am here in Couran Cove, but I just don't want to be. I hate it.

To poor old Barrie-Jon I therefore become some kind of a stalker, forever knocking on his door and asking what he's up to. I have a good day out to the mainland with Stimmo, but as soon as we are back on the island, I feel the enjoyment draining from me and the dread rising.

To top it all, I pick up a terrible bug, gastroenteritis. I become a prisoner, locked in my own room with my vomit for company. Harsh to say, but that is how the England dream feels right now.

●　●　●

Once we go into game-playing mode, life regains some simplicity. We play a warm-up game against Queensland and it goes well. Almost exactly a year since the 76–0 trauma, I call long-distance to Bilks again but this time, at last, the message is more positive.

We finish with a single Test against Australia, the best team in the world, and I'm back starting at number ten but with a vastly more recognisable team around me. And down in Sydney – or, more to the point, away from Couran Cove – I can direct my thoughts and concerns into the challenge ahead. Eighty more minutes of rugby and then I'm on holiday.

Since this is the Centenary Test, we are given a one-off strip, which is my favourite England shirt to date – dark blue with thin stripes and, as always, embroidered on to the bottom right-hand corner is the date of the game, the name of the opposition and, for me today, the number eight, signifying that this is my eighth cap. In the changing room before the game, Clive talks to me, studying my shirt, looking at the number on it.

Eighth cap already? He says it in a kind of complimentary tone, as if to suggest that's not bad for a 20 year old. But he is pushing me all the way. In handing me the number-ten shirt, he is giving me extra responsibility, an extra onus to do something, to coordinate, organise and run the side. It feels like massive pressure.

The game goes well, but not well enough. Matt Perry scores two tries for us, the second with his head bandaged up. He is an absolute stalwart, a word-class player, one of the most courageous I've ever played with or against.

I think I do OK. With Mike Catt outside me at twelve, I find I can almost enjoy it. Catty is just so good at taking pressure off those around him.

Although 22–15 to Australia is not the result we want, we head back home with our rugby in reasonable shape. Almost exactly a year ago, we lost 76–0. When it comes to the game itself, maybe that England dream doesn't feel too bad.

Top left: Playing for Farnham and looking a little bit too clean for my liking.

Top right: Showing some real gas at an early age, which soon disappeared.

Middle: This must be a break in play. I look as though I'm stuck.

Bottom: The team. Farnham U13s.

Opposite:

Top: Lord Wandsworth U15s.

Middle: A very shy schoolboy meeting his rugby idol, Rob Andrew.

Bottom: Lord Wandsworth First XV. As they say, definitely up there with the best years of my life.

Top: Fully padded up with a freshly cut flat top, and perfect technique.

Bottom: The Officers Club XI, with Bilks as captain, Sparks bowling fast and my good friend Andy Holloway in there as well.

Right: This photo is a family favourite. Sparks looking after me in Bath.

Bottom left: Matching clothes, haircuts and Velcro shoes. The world was our oyster.

Bottom right: Sparks and I at Christmas. Sparks eyeing up my presents.

Right: Proudly
receiving the PRA
Player of the Year
award, with Mum and
Dad there to share
the special moment.

Above: The Lions First Test. A great win, and a
great feeling to be able to share the moment
with Bilks.

Right: Mum, Dad and I ... and an MBE. A real
honour for me in every way.

Below: Mum and I and the great man, Inga
Tuigamala, in New Zealand in 2005.

Top left: Warming up before coming on in another of my many comebacks.

Top right: Training and playing with my bro is always a pleasure. He has a great rugby brain and takes on much more than his share of the responsibility.

Middle left: A proud moment for me as Sparks shines on the field at 12 and me at 10.

Middle right: Talking shop during a break in play. Sparks still looking after me.

Left: I wish there could have been more days like these. Sparks and I together on the field again.

Me, Sparks, Peely, no idea, Machin and Murph. Great days.

Dinner out in Majorca for my friends and I. Sparks taking the photo this time.

A 'bad shirt' night out in my home town of Farnham.

Left: In my younger days, fresh-faced and ready for anything.

Middle: The England U18 Grand Slam-winning team with some familiar names in the line-up.

Bottom: The only team ever to beat the Rest of the World team. My first start at 10. Inga and Pat Lam were on a different level for this one.

Schools International

Wales / Cymru			England / Lloegr
15 Cerith Rees (Llandovery College)	Full Back	Cefnwr	(Stonyhurst college) Iain Balshaw 15
14 Daniel Rogers (Strade)	Right Wing	Asgell Dde	(Durham School) Lee Best 14
13 Rhys Williams (Cowbridge C.S.)	Right Centre	Canolwr De	(Q.E.G.S Wakefield) Michael Tindall 13
12 Jamie Evans (Gowerton C.S.)	Left Centre	Canolwr Chwyth	(Tonbridge School) Tom May 12
11 Chris Landrie (Pontypool College)	Left Wing	Asgell Chwyth	(Bedford School) Simon Brading 11
10 Gareth Bowen (Neath College)	Outside Half	Maswr	(Lord Wandsworth College) Jonathan Wilkinson 10
9 Gareth Cooper (Pencoed C.S.)	Scrum Half	Mewnwr	(King Henry VIII) James Grindal 9
Edward Rees (Cowbridge C.S.)	Loose Head Prop	Prop	(Dulwich College) David Flatman
2 Gareth Williams (CAPT Bryncy C.S.)	Hooker	Bachwr	(Colston's Collegiate) Lee Mears 2
4 Gary Powell (Llandovery College)	Tight Head Prop	Prop	(Dulwich College) Johnathan Dawson 3
4 Adam Jones (Olchfa C.S.)	Lock	Clo	(Dulwich College) Andrew Sheridan 4
5 Scott Morgan (Neath College)	Lock	Clo	(Hutton Grammar School) Stephen Borthwick 5
6 Adrian Chiffy (Greenhill C.S.)	Left Flanker	Blaen Asgell	(Sevenoaks School) Anthony Roques 6
7 Nick Howard (Cowbridge C.S.)	Right Flanker	Blaen Asgell	(Sevenoaks School) Michael McCarrick 7
8 Chris Hughes (Amanford C.S.)	No. 8	Rhif 8	(Hampton School) Andrew Beattie 8

16 Andrew Jenkins (Neath College)		
17 Ian Higgins (Whitchurch H.S.)	Referee:	(Colston's Collegiate) Phillip Greenaway 16
18 Phillip Wheeler	Eddie Walsh	(Hampton School) Simon Amor 17
19 Craig Hawkins (Gorseinon C.S.)		Daniel Smaje 18
20 Duncan Jones (Neath College)	Touch Judges:	(Colston's Collegiate) Richard Siveter 19
21 Mark Troake (Barry C.S.)	Donald McCourtney	(King Edward VI) Alan Hubbleday 20
22 Gavin Evans (Gorseinon College)	Martin Williams	(Kirkham Grammar School) David Giles 21

The Welsh Schools' Rugby Union (Senior Group) are very grateful to Narberth R.F.C for staging the Schools International and Welsh Water & Pembrokeshire County Council for their financial support

Teams Accurate as of Thursday 21st May 1998

NEWCASTLE FALCONS		WORLD XV
15 Stuart Legg	Full Back	Paolo Vaccari 15 (Italy)
14 Jim Naylor	Right Wing	Chester Williams 14 (South Africa)
13 Va'aiga Tuigamala	Centre	(Captain) Philippe Sella 13 (France)
12 Martin Shaw	Centre	Philippe Bernat-Salles 12 (France)
11 Alan Tait	Left Wing	Stéphane Glas 11 (France)
10 Jonny Wilkinson	Stand-Off	David Knox 10 (Australia)
9 Gary Armstrong	Scrum-Half	Agustin Pichot 9 (Argentina)
1 Nick Popplewell	Prop	Marius Hurter 1 (South Africa)
2 Ross Nesdale	Hooker	Raphael Ibañez 2 (France)
3 Paul Van-Zandvliet	Lock	Cameron Blades 3 (Australia)
4 Garath Archer	Lock	Hannes Strydom 4 (South Africa)
5 Doddie Weir	Lock	Warwick Waugh 5 (Australia)
6 Pat Lam (Captain)	Flanker	Massimo Giovanelli 6 (Italy)
7 Richard Arnold	Flanker	François Pienaar 7 (South Africa)
8 Peter Walton	No 8	Tiaan Strauss 8 (South Africa)

REPLACEMENTS FROM	REPLACEMENTS
Chris Simpson-Daniels	Eric Rush 16 (New Zealand)
Rob Andrew	George Leaupepe 17 (Western Samoa)
Graham Childs	Arwel Thomas 18 (Wales)
Tony Underwood	Richard Cockerill 19 (England)
Ross Beattie	Darren Garforth 20 (England)
Steve O'Neill	Troy Coker 21 (Australia)
David Barnes	Sinali Latu 22 (Japan)
George Graham	
Richard Horton	

Referee:
Stewart Piercy

Touch Judges:
Grant Ashton-Jones
Ashley Reay

SANYO

CHAPTER 7

AS the 1999 World Cup approaches, one of the big messages from Clive is about performing and thinking under pressure. With that in mind, he takes us to the training headquarters of the Royal Marines in Lympstone. What these guys have to deal with in their daily line of work is incredible. And there was me thinking my job had a lot of pressure.

What the marines have in store for us is also seriously good fun. The star prize of the entire trip goes to Victor Ubogu for his magnificent commando-style Arnold Schwarzenegger impression, machine-gun in hand and trying to take down an enemy fort all by himself.

We are subjected to a simulated helicopter crash – the helicopter goes down into water with everyone strapped in. It spins and twists 180 degrees, and you are in total darkness. What happens is unbelievable. Guys try to get out without even undoing their seat belts. Instead of players managing to escape, the only thing that goes out the window is the training we've been given. The highlight is Dan Luger who, totally disorientated, swims back under his own seat and repeatedly bangs his head on the inside of the fuselage as if that is going to get him out.

We are divided into groups and sent into a smoke-filled building, which is on fire. With gas masks on and almost zero visibility, we have to find our way to the bottom floor to put out the fire. My group fumble around in the pitch black, walk into a dead-end corner and eventually get split up. Everything we touch is boiling hot. Some of us find our way to the basement, where the fire is, and while we wait for the lost members of our group, we get very hot. We don't know what's going on, or even if anyone knows we're there. We try to ignore the heat on our faces and suppress the instinct to panic.

Suddenly, Phil de Glanville cracks and starts screaming out loud for one of the marines. Sir! Help me! Sir, my face is burning, my face is burning!

The evacuation takes about twenty seconds. It takes even less time to ensure that neither Phil's face nor anyone else's is on fire. Phil then has the piss ripped out of him mercilessly. But he was only giving voice to what we were all thinking.

As always seems to be the case, Clive throws in something extra for me. We have another task. We are in a simulated submarine, which springs a few leaks. Water starts pouring in and as the level rises worryingly high, we have to hammer in plugs to cork the holes. We are instructed how to do it beforehand, and it looks a lot of fun.

The trouble is we need someone to coordinate the group and that's where Clive steps in. He has a word with the supervising marine.

Right, that's decided. Jonny, he says, you're in charge.

It's all part of his issue with me – be a number ten, communicate better, be more assertive. Take the decisions and tell everyone else what to do.

So I end up ordering people around, telling them where to go and what to do, and I feel I am being evaluated as a leader. What looked fun becomes an exam. And as I'm issuing my commands, I'm wondering how did Paul Grayson, the other number ten, do on this? If he did better, does that mean I'm not going to get picked?

At the end of the trip, the marines give their feedback to a meeting of the team leaders, which, as a number ten, I somehow qualify for. They tell us the squad works well in terms of roles and relationships. But they stress if you really want to be a team, if you really want to win this World Cup, you need a firmer one-in-all-in ethic.

That is a crucial lesson. It tells us we need to be strong as a group, we need a set of rules and we need to stick by them together. We start to set down a Code of Conduct. Personally, even more than before, I analyse how I contribute to the squad.

● ● ●

Just as I'm leaving Newcastle to head south for the England camp and my first World Cup, Dean Ryan stops me for a quick word. I think it's going to go really well for you guys, he says. And I've got you down as my player of the tournament.

That's a nice message to hear, and it reinforces in my own mind how important this part of my career is about to become. My first World Cup. A bit of a step into the unknown.

It kind of swallows my bigger ambition. I still want to be the best player in the world, but it is also clear how far away I am. I've yet to show that I'm truly capable of surviving at the top level. But I am becoming more and more aware that individual performances have very little to do with it at times. It's those around you who count. My team.

Down at the Petersham, the new thing is nutrition. Two specialists,

Adam Carey and Roz Cadir, have been brought in and it seems we are taking their subject very seriously. They want hair samples from us so they can study what's in our bodies and what our bodies need. They want stool samples from some of the boys – not me. I make any excuse I can to get out of that one. And they want to weigh us and our food before and after every meal.

Huge emphasis is placed on knowing what substances might be banned. On the other hand, we are put on so many supplements. Some people are on up to thirty different pills and tablets every day. It gets to the stage when some of the boys are waking up in the middle of the night so they can take their protein drinks at regularly spaced times.

This is a massive change for us; it's very full on. I've not really heard of soya milk and tofu until now. And suddenly I am supposed to be eating steak and broccoli for breakfast.

In a room in the Petersham we call the War Room, Clive discusses strategy with us. You need to take the initiative more, is one of his messages. Play what you see in front of you. Don't play by numbers.

One example: when we get penalties that are out of range of goal, don't kick for the corners all the time. Keep your head up and look down the middle of the field where there might be no cover. Put in the kick, chase and see if you can isolate a full-back and turn him over under his own posts.

This is not exactly what our forwards want to hear, and it's the kind of thing a young number ten feels a bit hesitant about. But I try it in our first game, against Italy, and it turns out OK.

The Italy game is a good start, and I score my first England try – three of us chasing a bobbling ball and me getting the lucky bounce – and then indulging in an appalling impromptu celebration.

I have hardly touched down when I'm up on my feet, running towards the crowd in the south stand with my arms wide apart. It doesn't take me long to realise what I'm doing and how much I wish I wasn't doing it. It couldn't be further from my usual style. I never go in for try celebrations. I think it's just shock that I've actually scored a try for my country.

●　●　●

The Italy game is generally viewed as merely the opener. Everyone knows that the next one, against New Zealand, is very probably the one that will define our route through the knockout stages, and so influence our chance of winning. If my career has been a series of 'biggest games so far', this is now it, especially playing at ten. I am asking a hell of a lot of myself. Some big names are playing against us, Jonah Lomu for starters.

At dinner later, the nutrition police relax a bit. Bread and butter pudding gives us a chance to go a bit heavier on the carbs. I know all too well that after this last treat, the minute I put down my spoon, it's all business.

As I walk into the dining room for the Last Supper, I catch Austin's eye. He purses his lips and makes a familiar bathroom noise, which tells me that he can see I'm already clearly suffering from pre-match nerves, and that he is shitting himself too. It's good to know that I'm not the only one feeling it.

●　●　●

To try to relax and take my mind off what's to come, Leon Loyd and I go to the cinema. It's not far into the centre of Richmond but we drive, which is our first mistake. We can't find anywhere to park. We drive round and round until we eventually decide to cut our losses and park round the back of the cinema in the hope that no traffic wardens are doing the rounds, because they wouldn't be too impressed.

That is our second mistake. After the film, we return to a clamped car. It's now around 11 o'clock, there is a massive World Cup game the next day and we are standing around in the dark, making phone calls and trying to get someone to unclamp the car.

This takes God knows how long. And it's not good for me. Before a game, I like to know where every hour is going, so that every part of my preparation is right. I can't handle unforeseen events. I start getting edgy. I should be in bed.

And that's it. Never again do I go to the cinema the night before a game.

● ● ●

The game starts at an incredible pace. It feels more urgent, intense than ever. I feel I am working massively on instinct.

I take a pass from Daws, dummy-switch with Phil de Glanville, hold the ball, step, spin, find more space, offload. It's going just about OK, practice and hard work are paying off, but it feels like it's taking all I've got merely to stay afloat. We are matching the All Blacks on the scoreboard. The intensity, however, is unreasonable.

I have the ball again. I'm looking around at where to play next and make a miss-pass out to Jerry down one side, shouting to him use Lawrence, use Lawrence, who is outside him. As a strong ball-carrier, it's an opportunity for Lawrence to truck it hard and find his way forward through some weaker arm tackles.

Jerry kicks the ball instead, a good kick under pressure, which bounces into touch by their 22. He then turns to me and shouts: Don't ever fucking throw that shit at me again! That's your responsibility, you deal with it!

Just what I need. Physically and mentally, I have taken on all the responsibility I can anyway, and the message here is that all the decision-making is to come back to me, the whole lot. I have now got my outside centre and star player, who is, like me, clearly a little stressed, telling me that he only wants the ball when it's bang on for him. I wish I could make the same demands for myself but against New Zealand, the perfect situation doesn't often come around.

I'm almost thinking that the wide part of our back attack is largely out of use, out of order. It reduces my options and I'm now not only having to play against New Zealand and make my own decisions, I'm having to be careful about my own team.

I'm not sure it was that bad an option, anyway. But while I understand his frustration, why not tell me he didn't want the ball? When I don't want to be thrown a pass – which happens often – I make sure I don't get it by saying so very loudly. That's what communication is for. He could have told me there's space, kick long, right. I would have appreciated the help.

And accompanying all this in my head is the nagging thought that if we lose this game, it's going to be my fault. Our future path in the World Cup, any disappointment, is going to be traced back to me.

It doesn't help that I miss a couple of early penalties. We are in touch, but having to chase. Into the second half, we have the scores level again when Lomu finally gets away. I sprint across the pitch, too far away to make any impression, watching him on the outside, looking unstoppable, going through one, two, three and then a fourth tackler. It is almost like I am 16 years old again, sitting in front of the TV watching the semi-final of the 1995 World Cup.

After that, we don't score another point.

● ● ●

I can't get my head around defeats like that. Final score 30–16 to New Zealand. I want to deal with it. I want to break it down in my mind, understand just why it happened and what it means. I want to know: How did I really do? No one has the answers. Instead, I'm left with a feeling of helplessness and intense disappointment.

I could sit around the hotel wallowing in it, or I could accept an invitation from Phil Greening to go out and escape. So, for once, I make a half-decent decision. I say why not? We go out purely in order to change our surroundings, because it's too painful sitting there, and we end up in Home, a Leicester Square nightclub, a huge place with a number of floors and a VIP area where we encounter footballers Paul Gascoigne and Neil Ruddock.

This is kind of weird. There are women floating around and every time any of them get close to one of the footballers, a TV camera appears and tries to film them. I don't quite get it. Is a documentary being made here, or is this just what life is like when you are a celebrity?

Also, it clearly costs a bit to live in this environment. I'm drinking half pints of Diet Coke. When it's my turn to buy a round, it costs me £250. Thank God for my England match fee.

● ● ●

The Tonga game is next. I'm rested and watch from the stands as we move past them with thirteen tries, two from Jerry, and not too much trouble. But the problem with losing to New Zealand is we now have an extra round in the knockout stage, which means we have Fiji five days after Tonga, and then, all being well, a quarter-final against South Africa four days after that.

I actually enjoy the Fiji game. I like playing against a team with that sort of attacking mindset because they never stop trying to come at you and you are pushed to the limits of your fitness, really blowing. I like to be challenged like that. It makes all the lung-busting anaerobic sessions really worthwhile.

What I don't enjoy, though, is the two-on-one at the end of the second half, when I pass to Phil Greening, he scores a simple try and I run straight into a stiff-arm across the face from their hooker. He gets a red, I get carted off and don't really come round properly until I'm on the physio bed in the changing room. That is one of the worst bangs on the head I have ever taken.

So we go to Paris to play South Africa, a game for which our preparation time is minimal. In my hotel room, where I spend a lot of my time, I get a call from Clive. Can I come and speak to you? The moment he says that, I know what's coming, and by the time he's at my door, I am resigned to it.

I have done really well, he says, I am definitely moving along the right lines, doing a great job for England. But for this massive quarter-final game, they want to go with someone who has more experience, is more used to high-pressure games like these and is a bit more familiar with a structured kicking game.

Clive explains all this at length. He does it well, and although I feel massively disappointed, I have so much respect for Paul Grayson that I don't feel horribly hard done by. I get the message. Move on, these things happen.

I still don't feel too emotional the next day in the team meeting. First Clive has an announcement. Jerry Guscott is injured and his retirement from international rugby is immediate. Next thing Clive does is flip over the flip chart to reveal our team to play South Africa and there it is – my name listed among the subs. Now I feel hot under the collar, embarrassed. I've been dropped and I feel people are looking at me.

Afterwards, Neil Back comes straight over and puts his arm round me.

Don't worry about it, he says, there's still three games to go. It's not over. You'll be back in there, so don't let it worry you.

He didn't have to say that. It catches me offguard a bit and as we walk out to the coach to go to training, I keep aside from the others because I don't particularly want them to see how emotional I feel. It's not that I mind about not being in the team. It's the thought that maybe, actually, some of these guys really care about me. For two years, I hadn't felt as though I was fitting in. I felt that people didn't really trust in me or want me there. And now Backy, a guy with all that experience, whom I respect so much, has just said that.

On arrival, as we run out on the field for training, Mike Catt jumps all over my back. He's on the bench, too. He's great at putting the smile back on my face, and he knows when I need a little boost.

That's two guys now, guys I admire enormously and with whom I'll play for crucial years to come, looking after me well. What a huge difference.

● ● ●

I'm not very good at being on the bench. I don't like it. Surely no one does. Sitting on the bench, watching two big, big sides going at it, and not knowing if you're going on or not, is nerve-racking. All the time you're thinking when am I going to come into it? When am I going to be a part of it? And, as a number ten, am I going to have to play a decisive role at the end?

It's a tight game, going one way, then the other. The problem is that every time South Africa get within range, they send Pieter Muller up the middle, a centre who is about as big and hard to tackle as they come. Their ball then comes straight back to fly half Jannie de Beer, sitting deep, and we can't get close to him. He starts firing over drop goals and we can't stop it.

Joost van der Westhuizen scores a try for them just before half-time and we go in just behind. I come on with 25 minutes to go, and I can feel it. So frantic. But I feel I make an impact. My running game, I feel, creates opportunities, although we never quite manage to put them away. And de Beer keeps stretching their lead. He finishes with five drop goals. That is awesome. It's also the end of our World Cup.

● ● ●

A World Cup campaign is extremely intense and long, even if you don't last into the final fortnight. From mid-June to October, it's been day after day, non-stop, with constant pressure. Before the tournament started, we'd trained long and hard, intense physical work with lots of contact. Sometimes it feels too much. Clive likes to communicate with us by email and we have all been given laptops. At one stage, Garath Archer just handed his laptop in. That was his way of saying goodbye. Thanks but no thanks. He came back again, but it was a statement of what we had all been going through.

So we go out, and this time I decide to go for it. I commit to getting stuck in. I need to blow away the cobwebs and lose my mind for just a little bit before the inevitable 'what if' and 'if only' mindset returns.

I'm disappointed, we all are, but I feel a sense of achievement at having come through this massive challenge, aged 20. I was told to hold the reins, and handled the pressure of being the driver of an international team against some of the best in the world. And I've learned a bit about World Cups. They are so long, and clearly another step up.

Yet as much as I may have taken a step up on the rugby field, it is off it where I have really moved on. All that convincing myself that nobody believes I should be there in the team, I'm letting people down all the time, and being beaten by New Zealand was my fault – I think that is maybe behind me. I can go home knowing that, actually, there are guys who trust me and perhaps even want to play alongside me.

But my attempts to celebrate or commiserate, whichever it is, are not particularly impressive. This is a very rare encounter with alcohol. I find myself drinking with Dave Reddin, our fitness king, and I cannot match him. We also find ourselves, briefly, in the company of one or two of the England women's rugby team, and drink for drink, I cannot match them, either.

So Dave puts me to bed and when I wake up, I see he has put a couple of Lucozades to hand. I have that 'Oh dear, this isn't good' sensation, and it only gets worse as I swing my feet out on to the carpet, and some digested food – chicken and rice, by the way – pushes up between my toes. Definitely no excuses from my end, I have overdone it this time.

That's how my World Cup ends – heading to the airport, feeling a little better about myself, sitting in the team coach, vomiting into a paper cup and being laughed at by my team-mates.

CHAPTER 8

MOST people probably go to the pub or to a party on New Year's Eve. On New Year's Eve 1999, to see in the new millennium, Sparks and I go kicking.

The thing is, because I do so much kicking at the club on my own, I have been given a key to turn on the floodlights on the back pitch. The other thing is that we know the club will be open, because the bar will open for punters. So we also know that, if we can get into the changing rooms, we can get into the main tunnel out on to the first-team pitch and that is where the lock is to turn the lights on. Perfect.

The floodlights are half working, the back pitch appears to have been ploughed, so it's not in the best shape for kicking, and hail is falling lightly. Conditions I am used to. We stay out a fair while, nearly two hours, before we look at the time – 11.30. We get back home in time to see in the millennium with an Indian take-away and *Eurotrash* on the TV.

The freedom of Kingston Park is a luxury, and I make the most of it. Any time of the evening, I go there – eight, nine, ten o'clock – flick on the lights and kick. Not another soul around.

It's another luxury having Sparks here. He is well versed in my ways. The following year, I will have him down here on Christmas Eve and Christmas Day. And the year after that, I will have him down here on Christmas Day in the snow, standing under the posts, freezing his backside off and knowing full well that when I say we're going to kick a few balls around and have a bit of a laugh, it's inevitably going to turn into a fully fledged, very serious kicking session.

And he knows exactly how my mind works. He knows that I always like to finish on a set of six perfect kicks, and that if I mess up the sixth, I'll start again. He knows that if I'm hitting a set of twenty drop goals and the last two aren't absolutely perfect, I'm going to say sod this I'm doing twenty more. I can see that Sparks is thinking oh my God, that's another thirty minutes on the session, and I had plans for tonight. I'm quite likely to say to him right, mate, you go. You take the car. I'll find my own way home. And he knows I mean it. But he never leaves. He stays and helps and kicks the ball back. Actually, it pisses me off a bit that there am I practising and practising, and he won't practise as much even though he has a natural ability to strike the ball as well as pretty much anyone I know.

When the obsessiveness does kick in and I won't stop, I am kind of split in two. I feel guilty, a terrible brother, for having him stay, but the other side of me is saying there's absolutely no way I can leave here until I get this right. This actually makes my head worse as I start to panic, rushing to get my kicking right.

And he understands. He can see when I'm struggling with myself. If I start getting mad and I hit a ball that goes somewhere I don't want it to go, we both know that he'll run quicker to get it and kick it back because he knows that I have to erase that with a good one.

What all those hours together have done is create the lifestyle for me to succeed. Yes, it's a selfish adventure, because I'm focusing on myself and my own performance so much. And yes, I wish I had more to give back to him.

● ● ●

This is the way my mind works. I like to imagine myself, my life, as being under permanent surveillance from a video camera. The camera is switched on, following me 24/7. It never stops.

That's not because I like being in front of the cameras; quite the opposite. It's because I want to think that I could play back the tape after any day or week, or at the end of my life, and be able to sign off on it, 100 per cent happy with what I see, totally content that it shows a good representation of who I am as a person and as a rugby player.

It is about being strong in professional terms and having values that never slip. That's why, when it's raining and windy, or things aren't going too well with my kicking, I can never say screw this, I'm going in. I believe everything I do has to make a difference. So I want to do things better than everyone else, not just on the field on a Saturday afternoon, but every day of the week, and off the field, too.

Like many of my ideas, the camera comes from Blackie. He says it's part of *kaizen*, a Japanese philosophy that he follows, about daily improvement. The camera means you cannot switch off. It's not as though getting better is something you do at work and then stop when you get home. Getting better is something you live all the time.

It makes so much sense to me.

● ● ●

Back at home, meanwhile, the toilet keeps blocking and it seems to take the repair man a while to come out for the lovely job of fixing it. Sparks and I find ourselves having to make quick, regular shuttle runs by car to Kingston Park to use the facilities there instead.

That may be mildly amusing, but when you're a nervous 20-year-old who gets particularly tense before games and needs his pre-match preparation to go absolutely perfectly, it doesn't really work. This is just one of many reasons why I feel I need to move house. So I sell up and, having paid solicitor's fees and the rest of it, I blow all the profit in one go – a home-delivery curry for two.

Next stop is a stunning house in Corbridge, a quiet country hamlet. This really excites me. The house is a converted set of stables, full of character, with big arch windows.

We fix it up into a bit of a bachelor pad with a big air-jet corner bath in the bathroom and a few more boys' toys. My favourites are the big, black-leather recliner chairs we buy for watching TV. These are not just any old leather chairs, but chairs with a telephone installed under the arm-rest cushion, a heat facility and a vibrational facility for an in-chair massage.

We have a daily pattern. Train to the point of exhaustion, drive back, stop at the Corbridge Larder, the country farm shop, then home and feet up, Playstation, TV. This really suits me. Spending quality time with your best friend isn't bad, either. I know I am fortunate; it's a taste of the good life. But, foremost, I feel the pressure of rugby life so strongly, it just feels great to be able to come back home and shut the door on it all.

● ● ●

Besides having Sparks at Newcastle, the team around me is ideal for a young man trying to perfect his trade.

I am now seen as the first-choice ten, and I have Inga outside me, loving his rugby, and forever calling moves that he has just dreamed up.

Inside me at scrum half, I have one of the toughest players in the world. We call Gary Armstrong the Junkyard Dog. He is so hard, he doesn't understand the concept of a pain barrier. He will play on with cracked ribs, a fractured eye socket at one point, a jaw problem. He takes huge hits and never lets you see that he is hurt.

For me, he's great because he looks after so much. I'll be looking around from midfield, searching in vain for options, wondering what to do next, and when he sees that, he just breaks off and takes the responsibility himself. Gary doesn't care about making mistakes. If it doesn't go right for him, he just gets on with it, and looks for another way to win the game.

In a way, he plays number nine like Mike Catt at twelve. He doesn't force you to create something out of nothing; he shares the responsibility, allows you to make the right decisions.

I am forever grateful to Catty, for the way he welcomed me in those early England days and made me feel good about myself, and spoke so positively about me in meetings. On England duty, we are now roommates and he has become both friend and kind of a mentor. He loves board games – plays endless rounds of backgammon with Matt Perry – but when I get back from my kicking practice, those hours in our room are often spent just chatting idly about rugby and life.

Through Catty, I learn more about how it's done. He's like my learning aid. I rate him so highly, he is such a damn good player, so great to play alongside, so ready to share the load and help drive a team forwards. I envy him for his relaxed, laid-back demeanour, and I admire his strength, which he needed to come through some harsh media criticism. But what I really like is his rugby philosophy and his attitude to the game. He knows how he wants to play, that's how he'll do it and he's not going to change.

On the night before our first game of the Six Nations, I share with him some of my thoughts, my anxieties, and mention how bad I feel the night before a game. I tell him about my three-hour kicking sessions, and how my struggles with sleep are so bad I sometimes get close to four hours a night. Please, I say, please tell me that dealing with it all gets a bit easier.

To be honest, he tells me, laughing in a comforting, knowing way, it probably gets worse.

And that was from the guy I thought was laid-back and took it all in his stride. He is just very good at making it seem that way.

● ● ●

England seems a little different now. New players have come in – Mike Tindall and Iain Balshaw, my old teammates from Under-18 days, and Ben Cohen, a hard-running wing with the power of a forward and footwork that makes him lethal. It's no bad thing having players such as these running off your shoulders.

And we have moved. With the World Cup behind us, Clive sees everything as a fresh start and part of that means shifting us out of the Petersham Hotel, where England have been based for so many years. Our new home is a hotel in Surrey, the Pennyhill Park. Comparatively, it is luxury, but the real point is it will soon have its own rugby pitch just three minutes' walk down the drive. Ideal.

It already has a good room for football-tennis, even if that's not exactly its purpose. Since I come from Newcastle, farther away than most, I tend to arrive on Sunday night rather than Monday morning, when the other players get in. So I check in, meet Dave Reddin in reception and we clear all the furniture from the big room upstairs. The football-tennis in there lasts hours.

But the surroundings, the personnel and the football-tennis are not the only differences here. Our attitude to decision-making and risk-taking is different, too. We have confidence to take it to the next level.

We just explode on to the Six Nations championship. We play Ireland first, my first senior international with Brian O'Driscoll on the opposition, and we notch up 50 points. But it's not all fancy stuff. In Paris, where England haven't won since 1994, we find ourselves in a very different, monumentally physical game.

I am standing outside Lawrence in defence when Pieter de Villiers, their prop, takes the ball off nine and runs straight at him, one on one. The sound of the collision is chilling and I fear immediately for Lawrence's left shoulder, but both players just shake it off and carry on as though nothing has happened. It's that kind of game. I put in a few decent tackles of my own, including a belter against Emile Ntamack, their wing. I catch him just right, accelerating into a tackle, beating him to the hit, so he's not quite prepared.

We all have an explosive energy and aggression. For the last 15 minutes, we defend our slim lead with resilience and tenacity. This is pure survival. We dog it out and it feels great against a team such as France, in their backyard. It feels great for our sense of togetherness, our identity as a team.

And, for me, it feels great when we come off the pitch and Neil Back puts his arm round my shoulder. He talks about my defence and my lack of consideration for my own safety. You're a man after my own heart, he says. I like that.

We beat Wales at home and then Italy in Rome. The culmination is again a Grand Slam match, this one in Edinburgh, where we find ourselves fighting the weather as well as the Scots. We get off to a decent start but our lineout really struggles. We know that, in this rain, we need to play a territorial game, so we kick long. But Scotland are happy just to smash it back downfield and off the park, and with them then stealing pretty much all our lineout ball, they reduce our options, making our lives hell.

Meanwhile, their driving lineouts are working. They get one well-earned try and with it the lead, and they throw over the security blanket. We need territory, but, because of the weather, our attacks are unthreatening. They don't need their wingers up in defence, which means our kicking game isn't working because there always seem to be three Scottish players in the back field covering.

We try to open up a bit, and at least into goalkicking range, but in such horrendous conditions, every tackle has the potential to knock the ball out of our hands. Scotland don't move the ball at all. They just sit tight in the driving seat, and as the weather deteriorates, that is a great place to be.

Thus, in freezing conditions, another Grand Slam slips by. We shake hands with the Scottish guys and congratulate them. They did deserve to win. But then we leg it to the showers because we are simply so miserably cold. We miss the Calcutta Cup presentation, which is understandably seen as a snub by bad losers, but it isn't at all. It's just a case of not knowing protocol, and an intense desire to get warm and forget about a terrible, terrible day.

We are also judged by the media to have played the wrong tactics in the rain, running the ball too much. That is plain rubbish, just a case of lazy, oversimplified criticism from people who have either never played the game or forgotten what is was like when they did.

We actually played reasonably good tactics. What we could have done was tried a few different kicking options. I could have put the ball up higher, or pushed it just behind their defensive line, instead of kicking long all the time. We really went wide only when the more obvious options weren't working. It wasn't our first resort, it was more our last.

● ● ●

People are beginning to recognise me in public now. I'm not comfortable about that and take appropriate measures.

When Sparks is not on the touchline with Newcastle Falcons, he plays for a local club, Northern RFC, and when I go to watch him, it's generally in the dubious disguise of a big coat with a hood pulled over. I park as far away as is reasonable, so I'm not arriving with any other cars, and I tend to stand by the corner flag, where no one else is likely to be since the view is terrible.

In fact, I'm probably more conspicuous because I look so ridiculous. But if people start walking over from one side, I'll walk round the other way. It's like being chased. If they get too close, I just walk away. If the cameras come out, I leave. It's not a great use of energy, and I tend to miss half the game this way, but sometimes I take my avoidance measures even further.

If I go with Chris Machin, Pete Murphy or Ian Peel, I make sure one of them is behind the wheel and when we drive in, I lie down in the footwell in the back seats. These guys are getting very adept at spotting potentially uncomfortable public situations and, like me, they are working on skills that will be useful for years to come.

But I'm not completely governed by self-consciousness. At Newcastle, we have a hard-working, fun-loving, hilarious Kiwi scrum half, Harley Crane, who has been housed on his own and with no car. So he pretty much ends up lodging with Sparks and me. He introduces us to the sound of rapper Eazy E, and I discover how to make a home-made barbecue that will blow up in your face midway through cooking the peppers. He also introduces me to the hacky sack – a small, round footbag. We go to pick up Sparks from the airport one day and play keepie-uppie with the hacky sack around the busy arrivals hall while we are waiting for him. That is as extreme a display of public behaviour as you will ever see from me.

Spending time with Harley, a free spirit, I come out of myself a little. I see that I *can* relax a bit, and get some evidence that it is not so damaging to what people think of me when I do. This is a lesson I should take on board.

* * *

Dean Ryan, one of the toughest guys in rugby, is now in the opposition. I've learned a hell of a lot from him, especially about putting your hand up when the time comes to be counted. He served in the army while the sport was still amateur, and from the way he trained and spoke about the game, I always got the impression he valued more than most the privileged opportunity we have to play rugby for a living.

Now he is against us, which is not so good. He moved to Bristol as player-coach, and on the eve of our Bristol fixture, Rob Andrew tells us to get into Dean whenever we can, let him know how old he is, wind him up, tell him he's past it.

I'm currently trying to curb my lip on the pitch, so I'm not too keen to get involved in this anyway. But to do this with Dean Ryan? You'd need a death wish.

Some of my teammates don't seem so convinced. Tom May and Michael Stephenson put in a double tackle on him early in the game and then pile in with the verbal follow-up – you should've retired by now, Dean, you're embarrassing yourself! Give up old man!

Dean looks straight at Stevo with a smile on his face. Old man, hey? Oh dear schoolboy, you have just made my day.

I catch Stevo's eye. I've never seen the look on anyone's face change so fast.

But I don't manage to stay so completely out of it myself. Bristol have the ball and I read their move perfectly, Dean peeling round the corner on a ball off nine. I just charge in and hit him with all I've got, right back into the ruck. It feels like a pretty good shot, and I cannot resist the follow-up – oh mate, I've been waiting all day for that one.

But he gets straight back up with the same smile. Not quite, he says, nice try, but not quite.

●　●　●

I don't really drink, but I can still play drinking games.

We've got a pool table at the house and, with Harley and Sparks, we have a new way to play pool. Every time you miss a ball, you have to take a drink. According to the number on the ball, that's the number of fingers' worth you have to drink. And we are talking water.

Then we introduce another rule. When you have downed your water, you have to do the equivalent number of sit-ups, too. This is not a clever game.

Occasionally, very occasionally, I go out and drink alcohol, and because these outings are so few and far between, and because I enjoy being out with the boys so much, I don't want the nights to end. So when the nightclubs shut, Sparks and I tend to find a way to keep the evening going.

Normally, this involves suggesting to Tom May, Pete Murphy or another teammate, why don't we go back to your house afterwards? And then, regardless of their response, we go round telling everyone in the club that there is a big house-party at the following address.

This time, it's Mike Stephenson's lucky night. We go back in a cab with Stevo and when we get to his house, he is slightly surprised to find thirty people outside his front door. He gives us a look that says what the hell is this? But we have a good time and everyone is buzzing – until the police rock up and tell us it's time to move on.

So we leave Stevo's, but on the pavement outside, realise that Ian Peel lives just over the road. So the shout goes up – party at Peely's.

That's fun, too, even if it does result in Peely getting his final eviction notice.

●　●　●

You can really feel the change around the England team on our summer tour to South Africa.

Everything feels so professional – where we are training, how we are training. Clive wants to lead change in international rugby, rather than waiting and following. We are not copying anyone. The desire now is to set the pace.

Although we are on tour, for the first time, we don't move around. We are booked into the Westcliff Hotel in Johannesburg and that is where we stay. We fly in and out for games, but base ourselves in the Westcliff. The hotel is ideal, but the point is that this is no longer about touring. It's about winning.

I feel we are getting our professionalism right. We know we are improving, the hard work from as far back as Couran Cove is paying off, and the consistency in player selection is helping. Players are getting the recognition they deserve. Lawrence is not just one of the best back-rowers, he's arguably *the* best. Some of our other players are being talked about in similar tones.

Me? I'm young, still making my way. I'm still a fan of the other number tens around, with Stephen Larkham, Andrew Mehrtens and Carlos Spencer leading the way. The way Larkham dominates the attacking game, knowing when to turn on the pace, when to run on to the ball, picking his options, is awesome.

Mehrtens is an outstanding linkman and tactician. It must be nice playing with athletes such as Lomu, Wilson and Cullen, but they're only capable of great things when he creates the opportunity and brings the best out of them.

I want to be great at playing rugby. I want to have the most impact in tackling, the most accurate goal-kicking, the best passing, running, workrate, everything. Apart from scrummaging and lineout, irrespective of my size or speed, I want to master every skill better than anybody else. So when I look at videos of games, I don't really review how I helped the team, my decisions or how I ran the game. I look at my individual moments, my passes, my tackles and my breaks.

Clive has got a different message, and he is going on about it so much that I can't avoid it. He pushes it in team meetings, and even more in one-on-ones. He talks about momentum, building a score, and drop goals. He wants drop goals.

But it's not in my nature to give him what he wants. If we are trying to attack, I won't concede defeat. I have eyes only for the try. I won't admit it if the opposition defence is holding us and we are achieving nothing, and I convince myself that the next phase of attack will be the one that works.

Yet Clive wants our score to keep ticking. He wants us to show that we can always make our dominance pay; he wants us to build a lead that is more than one score ahead.

He uses video analysis to show me all this, and explains the psychological battle. If we've given them our best shot and they turn the ball over and we come away with nothing, they are winning. But if we come away with points every time we're down their end, it has the opposite effect.

When you've got a good shot, just sit back in the pocket, he tells me as we prepare for South Africa. Think about that drop goal.

• • •

I'm uncomfortable the night before games anyway, but the night before the first Test, in Pretoria, I feel genuinely sick. It's the beef I had for dinner. At midnight I start vomiting and at two o'clock I start hammering on the door of Terry Crystal, the team doctor. When he eventually stirs, he gives me some tablets, but I'm still up vomiting until about half past five.

After two hours' sleep, I'm still feeling pretty rotten and thinking I've got a game coming, I've got a game coming. I tell Clive and the coaches. They say if you're not 100 per cent, don't play.

But, for me, turning down playing for England is not really an option. On the other hand, I haven't prepared. Usually, I do some kicking practice with Dave Alred on the morning of the game; not this time. I'll usually be checking my game notes, fully focusing on what is to come. But now I don't just feel sick; I feel unprepared. I phone Bilks and asks what he thinks.

Everyone agrees that we should come to a decision as late as possible. Only after walking into the changing room is it plain to me that I'm not up to it, and thus Austin Healey discovers that he is playing fly half against the Springboks instead of me.

Thanks very much for all the warning, Austin says. Now just watch me set this game alight.

And he does a pretty good job. I watch from the stands. The team play well, we match the Springboks, the video ref denies a try surely scored by

Tim Stimpson and we lose by five points. Most importantly, though, we feel we now could be, should be, ahead.

● ● ●

Our second chance comes a week later, at Bloemfontein. The atmosphere is hostile, threatening, and I can deal with that. What I find harder is the fact that they stage a practice game before the Test, which, for a kicker who likes to practice before a match, is a nightmare.

Before an international, wherever possible, I have a very specific warm-up routine. It includes 40 punts of varying style and trajectory, 20 off each foot. Then 15 to 20 goalkicks from almost along the try line, each side of the posts; the acute angle helps focus, accuracy and precision. Then four or five more from in front of the posts, just to check that everything is in place. Then I do restarts, six little scoops from virtually under the crossbar. Then a few grubber kicks and chips. This is a process carefully worked out with Dave over the years and it takes around 40 minutes.

On this occasion, though, we can hardly get on to the pitch. Dave and I go into the deadball area, while the game is in full swing, and start kicking backwards and forwards, stopping every time play comes in our direction. The Springbok supporters near me shake the perimeter fence, shouting and screaming my name aggressively, and yelling that I'm rubbish. Half of it is in Afrikaans, so I can't understand, but it doesn't sound much like good luck.

The intensity increases when the whole team take the field to a bombardment of oranges, Coke bottles and beer cans. At one point during the game, Johnno gathers the team round, just on our five-metre line, and a 1.5 litre bottle of Coke flies on to the ground and bounces right into the middle of the huddle. In our deadball area, I find myself picking up crushed Coke cans and chucking them to the back of the field. We are trying to win a Test match and doing ground maintenance at the same time.

The crowd's intensity is reflected in the game, and I find I am playing it in a slightly different frame of mind from usual. Being the best player doesn't matter so much today; it's more about winning, keeping the score moving, making the right decisions.

And then it happens. We are attacking, stretching their defence, and their players are struggling to cover the holes. So they're not looking up at me, or thinking about charging down a kick. In other words, it's a perfect time for a drop goal. But that's not in my mind. I take the ball one way to attack, and then, as if a lightbulb's suddenly flicked on in my head, I stop. I'm right in front of the posts, not far from the 22. This may be the best opportunity I get.

I take the drop goal. It flies through the posts. There, I've done it now. I've finally kicked a drop goal for England. But I still can't help feeling that maybe I've just wasted an opportunity for us to score a try.

We have a good lead, more than one score, until they score a late try, but despite a panicky last three or four minutes, we manage to keep control. The referee tells us time up. The score is 27–22 and we've got a penalty next to the touchline.

The guys are all saying next time the ball goes out, that's the game. And I'm standing there with the ball in my hands. What a great day it's been. What an end to the season. I've got a 10 yard kick to finish it. I love this moment. Breathe it in and enjoy it.

Afterwards, a kind of pandemonium ensues. The 27 points all came from my boot, so I get the full treatment from the Sky cameras. They don't just want a post-match interview, they want to follow me round the dressing room. They want to know how do you feel? Is there anything you want to say to your family?

What I want to know is can we now stop talking about drop goals?

● ● ●

That game in Bloemfontein is described as a watershed for England, but for me, the real turning point is yet to come.

Five months later, I am facing my first autumn international series, but only after realising that the RFU have messed up on my flight from Newcastle to Heathrow, thus forcing me to take the only other option, which is a taxi. Funnily enough, my Geordie cab-driver doesn't do many trips to Surrey, and we get lost, and it doesn't help much that he doesn't have a map. We stop and ask at a petrol station. Anyone know where Pennyhill Park is? No. Seven and a bit hours and a £400 cab fare later, I rejoin the England squad.

First up is Australia, and this, for me, is the one. This is the team I want to beat, one I've never beaten, the world champions.

It's a tight game, sealed by a late Dan Luger try in the corner from an Iain Balshaw kick-through. It needs the video referee to confirm the try, and when it's given, I ask the referee how much longer? He says just the conversion and that's the end of the game. We are a point ahead, so we've won whatever happens. The conversion doesn't affect the result.

You know what, I say to myself, for once I'm just going to enjoy this conversion because a good, hard day's work has been done. This one will be just for me.

It's rare to stand over a conversion like this and feel so relaxed. And the successful kick caps a great feeling; it feels great to beat Australia. It says so much. It says they're no different from us, just fifteen guys playing with the same ball, and we are capable of beating them. It kind of opens a door to a different future. We start expecting to win. And when you get to expecting, and you're not hoping any more, that's when you've turned the corner.

*   *   *

An Austin Healey joke starts off the week. Martin Corry – Cozza – has a dog called Minton. Minton is not a good dog. Minton eats two shuttlecocks. BadMinton.

Not the greatest of gags. Far funnier is Kyran Bracken, who hasn't got the joke – if that's what you can call it – and asks Cozza about Minton. What breed of dog is he?

That is the last laugh for a while. England are near the end of good year, a near-Grand Slam, a win in South Africa, and now, finally, Australia are on our defeated list, too. Consequently, the RFU is selling lots of new sponsorship packages; everyone is reaping the fruits of our success except the players.

This has been a source of frustration for a while. We have looked at the commercial structures in other professional sports and we know we fare dreadfully by comparison. We have put our case to the RFU and had it dismissed with disinterest. And it is an awkward contradiction. We all started out wanting to play rugby for our country for the sheer honour of it. We didn't set out on any sort of path with the aim of getting rich. We still feel the enormous honour of playing for England, but we are still worth more than a small share of the success others are making from our efforts. And we want to ensure fairer treatment for future generations.

The issue is partly the ownership of our image rights, although right now the RFU want to cut our match fees and give us a bigger win-bonus.

Initially, they wanted to cut the match fee altogether. The feedback from our negotiators, Johnno, Lawrence and Matt Dawson, is that actually the RFU is not interested in compromise and that we are being treated like kids.

Last week, in the build-up to the Australia game, this was a growing distraction. Clandestine meetings in different rooms and talk of possible different courses of action were eventually postponed. Leave it for now, we said, and let's talk again next week before the Argentina game.

While Austin is doing his Minton jokes, Johnno, Lawrence and Matt Dawson are on their way to the last round of talks. At nine o'clock that night, I get the call – squad meeting in Johnno's room.

I have a cold feeling about this. The first news is that the RFU hasn't budged an inch. The question then is do we go on strike? The answer isn't helped by the suggestion, lobbed in, that Clive has said if anyone does walk out on England, he may never play for his country again.

Johnno insists we take that into consideration, and that the younger players should not be swayed in their opinion by the older leaders of the team, who have decent careers already behind them.

I look at Steve Borthwick, my old teammate from the England Under-18s, who has just broken into the squad. He hasn't even made it on to the field. He says: I've literally only just had a taste of it, I don't want this to be the end of it.

That is my point. I'm still only 21. Everything I have done has been about this. But I also feel so strongly what I have been taught about rugby, the values I've acquired ever since childhood – the team has to stick together for what we believe in.

I look around the room, at Johnno and the others for whom I have so much respect – Catty, Lawrence, Neil Back. Johnno would not be wasting his time or meddling in issues that didn't concern the team getting better.

The guys are not about money, ego, power or anything like that. This is literally about bettering the situation – for us and, more importantly, for future generations. Whatever these guys are doing, I'm doing, too. I believe in them enough.

The discussion lasts for two intense hours and then it comes to the vote. Pieces of paper are gathered in an ashtray. Do we strike? Yes or no. Mine says yes. Matt Dawson does the counting. He announces the result. We are on strike.

We inform Clive and he is livid. He questions some of the senior players individually in front of the rest of us; he really puts them under the spotlight. But they respond with honesty. This is not about Clive. There is no shortage of respect for Clive and his coaches.

Next morning, Clive tells us all to clear out of the hotel. Conveniently, Farnham is not far away, so I go home and Ben Cohen comes with me. We may be on strike, but we don't stop work. We are soon back at my old haunt, Farnham RFC, training hard and wondering what the hell is going to happen next.

What does happen is that Ben receives a call from Clive telling him that if he sticks with this, he may never play for England again. Ben is probably not the first to hear this because my phone rings soon afterwards and I see it is Clive. I don't feel I can deal with the conversation and I let him go through on to answerphone.

That night we are all at a charity dinner in London. It becomes part-dinner, part-negotiating room, and the negotiating continues the next morning. Ben and I are in the car *en route* to meet the others when we get the call from Matt – go back to Pennyhill, we have reached an agreement.

So we do go back. We all do. And we go on to beat Argentina, and then South Africa. And, for our troubles, we get the grand sum of £250 more per game.

● ● ●

In our grey suits and blue shirts we celebrate with a squad night out and somehow I end up with Lawrence.

We are in a nightclub in the centre of London – not exactly home territory for me. Lawrence orders at the bar and I go for a wander round the club, feeling very much that I don't belong. My face is hardly known, thank goodness, but for Lawrence it is exactly the opposite. The place is really crowded. I get in people's way, and get bumped around. One lap takes me about twenty minutes. I knock into one guy and he immediately gets angry and aggressive. I really don't like this scene. I tell Lawrence maybe we should head off, and he agrees. So we leave the club and set off to where we think the others might be.

Lawrence walks with big, fast, determined strides. I'm almost jogging to keep up, lagging slightly behind. London seems to rise to him, so I hold back to watch. As we walk down the street, taxi drivers beep their horns, shouting hey Lawrence, nice win today. And he waves back to them all. Other people on the street stop and stare, or stop for a quick chat, and Lawrence indulges them all.

It's amazing to see this commanding figure so at ease with his celebrity, so able to front up to it. This is a guy who just rolls with it and I don't understand how he does it. Hardly anyone recognises me, yet I am barely able to roll at all.

CHAPTER 9

JUST when you think you might be learning the game, when you think you know what the best looks like, how to get there and how the game works, along comes someone who breaks all the rules. Rugby league superstar, and a total hero of mine, code-crosser Jason Robinson is the new face in the England camp. Here is a guy who forces me to reassess what I thought was possible in the game.

Phil Larder, the defence coach, has a defensive drill where one player in a padded tackle suit has the ball two metres from the line, and another player, on the line, has to stop him scoring by tackling and knocking him back, or holding him up over the line. Particularly enjoyable is seeing Jason in defence against Austin in the tackle suit. Austin is very strong, and holding him up is extremely tough, even for the big forwards.

Austin starts with a side step and then lunges, but he almost holds back a bit, as if he is aware of the difficulty of the drill for the defender. Jason tackles him, tussling, grappling and actually holds him up. Austin shifts his bodyweight frantically, realising that he is now in a serious battle. He tries to reach over Jason, tries to spin, tries everything. It's a great wrestle. Jason is so intense, managing to shift his weight around each time to match Austin's moves, and still holding Austin up.

Suddenly, Austin spins himself out and has room enough to lunge over Jason to put the ball down one-handed. It's a bit disappointing but nevertheless astounding that Jason held out for so long. However, just as Austin goes to slam the ball down on the turf, Jason in one movement whips his own legs around 180 degrees and Austin can do nothing as his final lunge grounds the ball on top of both of Jason's legs. It's not a try. Jason holds him there, his face disguising any concern, a picture of pure composure. Amazing.

He is by no means finished. We are doing an offload drill in the five-metre channel. One player has to run, step and then, while taking the tackle, pop up the pass to his support runner. On this occasion, I am the next tackler in line and Jason is in front of me. As I move forward, he has no room to move, so I feel I should go easy on him, which is a bad idea. I also don't want to hit him too hard so he can make sure he gets the pass right. But in making the tackle, I wrap my arms around nothing but myself. I clutch the air. In the space of a five-metre corridor, he has stepped me completely. Cue considerable chuckling all round. If I wasn't just the latest of very many to have missed him, I might have been more embarrassed.

Jason's footwork is no secret, but to see it close up like this is a big learning moment for me. It's like losing 76–0 and learning what professional international rugby is all about, or playing with Pat and Inga and learning about the possibilities in this game. His ability to beat players both ways and make 90 degree direction changes without losing speed totally obliterates what I believed were the limits for footwork and speed.

I watch him, I let him inspire me, I imitate him. And then I go back to Blackie and tell him this is where I need to go next. If I am going to be the best, this is what I am going to have to be doing.

No problem, Blackie says.

In the gym, Blackie invents new drills and exercises for me, which we attack day after day. He has me in front of a heavy swinging punchbag, dodging around it, using my footwork to bounce, step and react. We work on it so much that it becomes instinctive movement, completely second nature. We want to change my game because we've seen what the greatest looks like and we want a bit of that, too.

● ● ●

My new roommate at Pennyhill is Dan Luger. He is not a golfer but he gets quite passionate about our new game of hotel-room golf. The room comes with a practice-putting hole, which we move around, designing ever more complex courses. The tee-off from behind the TV is a good one, and Dan's jumper makes for an obscure hazard. But it is when we get a suite on two floors that the game really comes into its own.

At last, I feel a definite sense of comfort in the England camp, which I lacked for so long. It doesn't make the games any easier, nor does it magic away the pressure and anxiety, but I do at least feel that I belong. The programme Clive has in place now feels so familiar – light day on Monday; training on Tuesday with the emphasis on attack; defence the priority on Wednesday with some full contact, live training thrown in; day off on Thursday; Friday team run; match on Saturday. You always know where you are.

My Thursdays have a comforting familiarity, too. I kick in the morning at Twickenham – there's never a complete day off – get back to Pennyhill, shower and then ring Richard Hill. In Hilly, I find a brotherly soul. On the tense coach journey to games on Saturdays, I always make sure I'm sitting opposite Hilly.

But on Thursday afternoons, the routine is a town visit. It might be Guildford for its shopping mall, or Windsor for its castle, Camberley, Farnham, anywhere to have a wander, a coffee and a chat about anything that isn't rugby. Hilly is definitely up for not talking rugby. So is Catty, who sometimes comes along.

We play a game. Whoever gets recognised the most buys the coffees. This is a game no one wants to win – but mostly it's me. Strangely, in Farnham, my home town, it's Hilly's round.

● ● ●

The 2001 Six Nations starts for us in Cardiff, and that morning I am out with Dave in a children's playground.

Before every game, we disappear off to kick. This is the pattern – just 25 minutes kicking for reassurance, to get some feeling in my legs and feet, and to get my head straight. For home games, this is simple – we kick at Pennyhill. For away games, it involves finding the nearest stretch of grass, or just a decent space, some parkland, a car park, anything. Often this ends up with groups of kids standing round asking for autographs. Occasionally, it involves unusual locations – a golf fairway comes to mind, as does a farmer's field surrounded by cow pats.

But from the St David's Hotel in Cardiff Bay, where we are staying, there is no obvious location. Nothing – until we come across the local school. We have to jump the fence and there we do my preparation for our Six Nations opener – me kicking over a set of swings, Dave on the other side of the swings, standing over those funny animal seats on the big metal springs.

The game goes really well. We score six tries, including a hat-trick from Will Greenwood, and take the chance to illustrate all the elements to our game. Iain Balshaw makes more of his devastating arcing runs from full-back, invariably fed by Catty, the supreme link man.

It is some start. It comes part from us and, in large part, from Brian Ashton, our backs coach. Actually, he's more than a backs coach; he's an Attack Guru, an inspiration in his understanding of running lines, space and width. It is Brian who gives us the freedom to express ourselves and the confidence to do so. And boy are we enjoying it.

● ● ●

When I return to Newcastle from England, I feel a particular pressure to deliver, entirely brought on by myself. It's exacerbated by a guilty conscience because I have been away while my teammates have been here, working hard for the club.

We are not a team that has ever found it easy, we have never cruised, we have never had the dominance of, say, Leicester. We have to work for everything, but I like that feeling of building. I'd rather be in a team that is fighting daily to make its mark than one that is just continuing a long line of success.

We have a notable new recruit this year in Liam Botham. Liam is massively switched on to health and diet, and is one of the hardest athletes I have ever trained with. He doesn't take a step backwards in dressing-room banter, either. Every day, Liam leaves recovery protein drinks in the changing room for after training, and on the one occasion he leaves them in Ross Beattie's space, Ross throws them in the bin. When Liam asks who did it, we immediately tell him. He then takes Ross's underpants and rubs Deep Heat into them.

Not bad, we tell him, but not quite revenge. So Liam cuts the toes off Ross's socks and scoops a handful of Vaseline into each of Ross's shoes. That just about does it.

The good news, meanwhile, is that we have Blackie back with the club. Increasingly, I spend more time with him. We train during the club sessions and outside of them too, and when we are not training together, we go out for the occasional bite to eat. He has become my best friend at the club and the guy I can offload on, depend on, rely on, my mentor, my surrogate rugby parent.

If there is something I want to achieve, Blackie is the one who can make it happen. If it's a new skill, fitness, concentration, Jason Robinson footwork, whatever it is, I say what I want and he just tells me what time to turn up and where. His genius is such that he can improvise with new training techniques and guide me there. I've never lacked for motivation or inspiration, but what I did require was someone to supply me with the techniques and advice I needed to achieve all these dreams and ambitions, to channel my energy and obsessions. I've got that now.

He also makes the club a great place to be. We embark on a Cup run, past Dean Ryan's Bristol, then London Irish, a semi against Sale and into a midwinter Twickenham final against Harlequins, where one of our secret weapons will be Inga's haircut. Normally, Inga is closely shaven, but for some reason, which I cannot fathom, he has a bet with Rob over the accuracy of his place-kicking. Inga loses the bet and the forfeit is to grow his hair. By the time we reach Twickenham, he has a tasteful microphone dome on display.

I so want the final to go well but we struggle as a team, and I struggle a bit from the kicking tee. With five minutes of normal time to go, we are two scores behind, but we know what to do – keep our heads, keep playing our rugby, and just maybe this is still within reach.

We score in the corner with four minutes to go. If I hit the conversion, we can win with a penalty, but I miss. Four points down, we need a try.

Gary Armstrong wins us a scrum and Ian Peel charges for the line. He is bundled into touch. We win the lineout and I see their defence is being sucked in. I miss Tom May and throw a 25 yard left-hander to Jamie Noon, who can make any pass look good. Noonie has been running hard all day, no surprise there, but this time he sees the gap outside and puts Dave Walder through it for the try. Sparks brings on my kicking tee and I put over the conversion. And that's it. An incredible final is made all the sweeter because I get to celebrate it right there on the field with my brother.

Afterwards, though, the press don't want to ask me about the game; they want to know about missed kicks. I should be learning by now, yet I am still taken aback. I think I went pretty well out there, and we have won an amazing game. But I am the kicker and the kicks are the most noticeable part of my performance. When you kick well, they say you've played well, and when you kick poorly, they tear you to pieces for it. When I set out my goals to be the best number ten in the world, this was a part of the deal I hadn't considered.

● ● ●

I need Dave big time, although there are occasions when I am not very good at showing it.

England sometimes train at Sandhurst, and my kicking training is often the last item on the day's schedule. In midwinter, when the days are short, this can be slightly rushed as the light fades, which is hardly ideal. I cannot rest easy without knowing that my preparation has gone well. It's my fix. I can't go home and chill without it. My worst scenario is kicking badly and then having the rest of the night to mull over it.

Before the Scotland game, all these circumstances just get too much for me. We have been doing some contact sessions and I find I hurt my neck in pretty much every contact session I do now. I can't really help that. I'm all-or-nothing in training. I try to defend the way I do in a game, and I always seem to catch my neck. More so even than in games.

So I'm a bit frustrated by this, and the light is going. I know I haven't got long and tell myself this kicking session has to go awesomely well. But I'm worried about the Scotland game anyway, and I'm clearly in the wrong mindset because the session starts badly and everything Dave tells me seems to wind me up. I start shouting at him. I get so massively frustrated that I feel myself tearing up.

As the light goes, I tell myself I'm just going to stay out here and get it right, which isn't too smart because I can hardly see the ball. And the more I can't see it, the worse it gets and the more upset I become.

Dave has seen this before. Plenty of times, unfortunately. He knows that what I'm doing to myself now is counter-productive.

Let's give it a rest, he says. We'll do a couple from dead in front of the posts and then pick it up tomorrow.

That winds me up more. The idea of having to resign myself to the most simple kick on the field is just patronising. I start swearing at him. I tell him the game's going to be a complete write-off, this is bullshit, it's not right, it's not working, it doesn't work, it doesn't make any sense.

Take it easy, he says. That angers me even more.

Dave keeps his calm enormously well. He has a proper explanation. He tells me that I'm not getting a good grounding with my non-kicking foot because the ground is very soft and wet. Jonny, he says, let's return to basics.

In these conditions, we need to go to something simple and more productive that we can control.

But that's like giving in to the challenge. It's a big failure, I'm a big failure, it's almost like saying I can't handle it and I'm not good enough.

When it's all finally over, the poor guy has to give me a lift back to the hotel and he tries to convince me that it was actually OK. I don't think so, Dave, I say, desperate to make this as painful as possible for both of us.

When I get out of the car at the other end, I have finally got sufficient grip of myself to apologise. I'm sorry I put you through that, I say.

But now I know I have a long night ahead.

● ● ●

The week before the France game, Newcastle play London Irish at Kingston Park. We start well and are 25 points up at half-time, but the Irish chase us hard and we finish the match hanging on, frantically defending our lead.

With five minutes to go, I line up one of their centres with my right shoulder, but he cuts back slightly at the last second, which means the impact forces my head to smash against my left shoulder and immediately it's back, that searing heat burning into my neck, across my back and down my left arm. The pain of a stinger usually eases after thirty seconds, but as I lie on the ground, no matter how I shift myself around, this time it doesn't.

By the end of the day, I have caught a flight to London and Pennyhill, where I am supposed to be preparing to play France. I'm put to bed wearing a neck collar. In the morning, I can hardly move my head. I have stiffened up completely. When I do try to turn it, it's agony. Every little twitch is as sore as hell. I can't kick, I certainly can't train, and as I watch training with Hilly and Kyran, who are also nursing injuries, our teammates point at us and drag on imaginary cigars. As if we want to be putting our feet up.

In the Six Nations we are flying. We have already put 80 points on Italy and 40 on Scotland, but it's a big question now whether five days will be enough to get me ready for France. The best person for an answer is Pasky. He describes it as a whiplash injury, the kind of thing you see in car accidents. He and Richard Wegrzyk, the masseur, want to treat it with constant physio.

On the Wednesday, I have a go at training, but as my head movement is still so restricted, a few balls go to ground and more than a couple of passes miss the mark. But Pasky and Wegrzyk – who is known as 'Krajicek', as in tennis player Richard Krajicek, because no one can pronounce his name properly – are winning this battle. In an ideal world, we would have longer, and deep down I know I shouldn't really play on Saturday, but I do. If it wasn't France in the Six Nations, I'd probably be resting, but Pasky and Krajicek are very good at what they do. In an amazingly short space of time, they get me just about ready for international rugby. Physically ready, anyway. We score six tries in a 48–19 victory, but I spend the entire match protecting my neck, constantly in fear that I am going to take another hit on it.

England are on the verge of another Grand Slam. The problem is that there is an epidemic of foot-and-mouth disease sweeping the country and so our Ireland match is postponed. We will have to wait until October to see if we can celebrate.

● ● ●

In European competition, our Tetleys Bitter Cup win means we qualify for the Heineken Cup next season, which is very prestigious. This year, we are in the European Shield, which is great but not quite the same.

We have a fixture at Cross Keys, the Welsh team, and because their pitch is unplayable, we get shifted to the local park. There are no changing rooms at the new venue, so the players have to change on the bus. The Cross Keys chairman tells Rob not to worry because he has sent his second XV to clear off the sheep and his third XV to clear off the droppings. No one is too impressed, particularly Marius Hurter, our South African prop, when one of their forwards goes down on one knee and urinates in the middle of a lineout.

But we take the competition seriously and finish up in a semi-final against Harlequins – again – at Headingley. It's a fortnight since the France game and I am hoping that my neck is OK, but it isn't. Five minutes into the first half, a heavy, accidental knee to head by their full-back, Ryan O'Neill, starts it off. I should probably come off but the game's hardly started, and I haven't even begun my work for the day. I stay on.

I make a few more tackles and each impact seems to set it off again, the pins-and-needles heat firing down my arm. In the second half, Will Greenwood tackles me round the legs and again the electric shock shoots down from my upper spine to my finger tips. My neck is now so ultra-responsive that just the slight judder of hitting the floor sets me into spasm.

By the last minute, I have had more than six stingers and the searing pain has started to spread down both arms, my back and my chest. The medics finally insist I come off and, given that I am starting to worry what the hell is going on, I can now no longer argue.

This time, recovery is not quick. I am sent for nerve conduction studies, where they jab two needles into different parts of the arm and send electrical impulses between them. The results are not too concerning, at least not enough to make any impact on my approach to the game.

It is, though, almost two months before I am ready to play again.

10

HIGH on my list of goals is the desire to be a Lion. I am halfway there, on a long flight to Perth, where this new mission begins.

I chat to Neil Jenkins. He is leaving behind a young daughter. I am leaving behind all that security and belonging that I have finally found within the England team. But that is the challenge for all of us. We have no common understanding, none of the momentum to pull you through that we have spent years building with England. It is time to start from scratch.

What we do have, though, is a fantastic group. Off the pitch, the chemistry seems to work immediately – no cliques, nothing. Having played against Brian O'Driscoll over a number of years, it is nice to be on the same side for once. It is a pleasure, too, to get to know Ronan O'Gara and Neil Jenkins. Neil seems to be pursued wherever he goes by chants of 'Neil-o, Neil-o', even if he has been known to start them himself.

The frustration is being stuck on the sidelines. In Perth, I am also stuck in a roomshare for the walking wounded. That's Lawrence and me. He has a knee injury, I have a groin problem, and both of us are racing to get back in time to compete for places in the Test team. For me, at least, there is the comforting presence of Blackie, who is part if the coaching team, as is Dave Alred. It's no surprise to me that the two people I believe to be the best in the world at what they do have been selected for this tour.

From my watching position, three factors quickly become very clear. The first: we have two training sessions a day, so Graham Henry, our coach, has set out to work the boys hard. The second: to speed up communication and understanding, the coaches present us with an exceedingly structured game plan. We are having to digest tactics that sometimes work several phases ahead. The third: we are plagued with bad fortune. The injury attrition rate is phenomenal. Just as I am reaching fitness, others are already going home early. We lose Dan Luger, Mike Catt, Robin McBryde, Simon Taylor and Phil Greening. And that's even before the Tests.

Meanwhile, O'Driscoll is proving quite handy on the table-tennis table. We have a group game called Red Ass whereby the loser has to pull down his shorts and give the others a free shot with their bat. Predictably, when Austin loses, he does a runner before punishment can be meted out.

●　●　●

After missing the first two games, I am finally given the chance to be a Lion against a good Queensland Reds side. I want it to go perfectly, of course I do. But when we get to the Ballymore stadium, there is a curtain-raiser game taking place, just like at Bloemfontein last year. So where am I going to kick?

Dave and I find a training pitch behind the stadium, which would have been fine were it not for hundreds of supporters arriving from that direction.

They all like to have their say. Yeah, Jonny, don't miss it, don't miss it. That kind of thing. It's hard to maintain your standards and concentration when you have hundreds of people standing around, watching, especially when you have to ask some of them to move even though they are trying to talk to you. Still they come, streaming between Dave and me, sometimes even catching our kicks.

The game goes well. Playing with people you're not used to is our challenge, and I'm learning fast about Brian O'Driscoll and Rob Henderson. I enjoy playing with Keith Wood and Rob Howley. And I manage seven goals from eight; somehow the kicking doesn't suffer.

And of course, it feels great to have worn the Lions shirt. The race for fitness, though, is not one that Lawrence wins and he is soon on a plane home.

● ● ●

We play the New South Wales Waratahs in Sydney and just about survive a physical, sometimes bloody, battle. But it claims Will Greenwood, another injury casualty. We are losing big-name players at a worrying rate, and are simultaneously being criticised in the Aussie press for being a violent team.

We move to Brisbane for the first Test and, as the intensity builds, I find myself looking at Johnno, our captain, and wondering how he does it. He takes on so much and never looks as though he needs any assistance.

Whenever I see Johnno, he stops me and asks Wilko, are you all right? And it's not just a passing form of hello; he really wants to know the answer. I like that.

In Brisbane, I go to the gym to do some training with Blackie, and Johnno comes along. It's interesting seeing him introduced to training the Blackie way.

This is rare but good time together. We both appreciate we are different characters, slightly different generations, and we tend to stick to different groups. But we seem to have a relationship of mutual respect, talking about the game, tactics, preparation. It's just that he takes care of me way more than I do of him.

●　●　●

I have some specific hotel-room rules:

1 No rugby magazines. No rugby reading material of any kind if I can help it. This is definitely the biggest rule of all.

2 At least one item of contraband confectionery in the room. Chocolate preferably. I often travel with a bottle of Heinz Salad Cream, although that's not quite so illegal.

3 Live out of your bag. Only if you are staying somewhere for weeks do you unpack, putting away clothes in cupboards.

On this tour, as well as Lawrence and Will Greenwod, I have roomed with Dafydd James. He's a great bloke, a worrier like me and always concerned about being late. He was slightly perplexed about the number of times I lost our room key.

I have also shared with Neil Back, who is the tidiest man I know and cannot understand why anyone would live messily out of a bag. Whenever I threw some paper at the bin and missed, he'd be straight up to put it in for me the second it hit the floor.

Now I'm with Rob Howley, who is also a great bloke, but a rugby junkie and an arch contravener of Rule 1. Like me, he keeps notes of moves and strategies, but while I jot mine down in a notepad for an occasional peek, he draws all his up and sticks them on our bedroom wall. There is no escape.

Another of my rules is to make the night before a game as restful as possible. But the eve of the first Test does not go to plan. I am lying in bed in the early hours when I suddenly realise I've left my dad's match tickets up in the team room.

In a panic, I shoot out of the room and head for the lift. We are on the fourteenth floor. The team room is on the thirtieth. The lift won't budge, so I take the stairs at a run. The team room is locked. I run down all the way to reception, literally counting the number of steps, trying to work out how much energy it's taking out my legs, how much damage I'm doing and whether I'm losing the game for us there and then.

For a pre-game panicker, this is not good. But at reception, they help me. We even get a lift to work. I get my tickets and eventually I get some sleep. Not clever.

We wake to find a note from Blackie slipped under the door. It reads: 'When you've worked so hard that you feel you may pass out and your body and mind seem to have been stretched to breaking point, and momentarily you think you've no more left to give, hear a voice remind you that there's something far more important than anyone's susceptibility to pain. It is the great tradition, belief and respect of what it takes to be a true Lion. It is then you will become a legendary Lion.'

● ● ●

When you get the chemistry right, everyone on the same wavelength, the right connection between players who have been pulled from international teams because they're good at what they do, the result is exponential and you get a kind of boom effect.

That is what we get in the first Test. There are three minutes on the clock when we pick off a four-on-three down the left touchline, Rob Howley, me and Matt Perry with Jason on the end. What Jason does, one-on-one with Chris Latham and just a tiny amount of space – I love it. It brings me back to that training session at Pennyhill. I sympathise with Latham, who is left clutching the air exactly like I did.

And I love Jason's try celebration. Just pure emotion, no egotism. He celebrates for everyone. It fires me up, inspires me. Such an awesome try. His energy is infectious. And the crowd is very red and very noisy.

We don't drop for a minute. From a midfield scrum, we pull a move – 'Pace' – crafted on the training field to bring in our strike runners, Brian and Jason, and it works to perfection. Dafydd James finishes it and we are still in the first half.

The second half has hardly started when Brian surges through the defence. He isn't even looking in the right direction when he steps Matt Burke. A touch of exceptional individual talent and another try.

I feel the buzz. It feels special, a privilege to be a part of it. There is no formula for it, you cannot just repeat it or reinvent it. It is what it is and then it's gone. But for now it reads thus: Australia 13 Lions 29.

● ● ●

We move to Melbourne for the second Test and the confidence remains with us. Again, we start well, even if this is not reflected in the score. We go in 11–6 ahead and it should be more.

We charge straight back into the second half and the game turns. I throw a pass over the top, but Joe Roff manages to stick a hand out and bat it up in the air. He intercepts it and he is away.

The scores may be tied 11–11 but that is nearly it for us. Australia score two more tries, we get a single penalty. I leave the field fearing a broken leg. Rob Howley is out of the tour with a broken rib, and so is Hilly with a nasty concussion. The momentum has swung and the initiative has switched hands.

● ● ●

My leg is not broken, just severely bruised. The medics put it in a cast, tell me to keep it at 45 degrees and not to move for two days. So I do and I rack up a £250 room bill on films and room service.

By the Thursday, I am able, at last, to join training and stand side by side with the other survivors of this seven-week journey. We aim to play more of a kicking game, to keep the ball in their half. We know it's come down to this, the third Test, one last push.

We wake up to another note from Blackie. He quotes from Rudyard Kipling, Albert Einstein and the world of sport – not a bad range. The message ends: 'A great gridiron coach summed up the effect of determination like this: "Most players are about as effective as they make their minds up to be." How right he was. Make your mind up and be the change you want to see.'

When we arrive at Sydney's new Olympic stadium, there is little doubt that our minds are made up. We go behind early this time, but punch back with a try from Jason. We go behind again, but we pull together with a penalty from my boot. At half-time, we are three points down.

The second half starts well when I deliver my own try – a testament to the punchbag-dodging with Blackie, my own tribute to Jason Robinson. It has nothing of the same quality, but there is an element of the instinctive foot movement. I manage to step around Toutai Kefu and I am over.

But then it slides. We are 29–23 down. Ten minutes to score seven points. We can still win this.

Two minutes to go, the chance appears. We get a penalty, kick to the corner. This is it.

We lose the lineout. But that's still not it. The buzzer goes, we have possession, field position and good numbers, still a chance. Until an Australian hand disrupts a pass and that is it. So close to glory. And so damn painful.

● ● ●

It takes me a while to change and put on my suit. I'm never quick to move on, but especially not tonight. I'd rather sit in rebellious protest. The result should have been different this time. I don't feel like going anywhere.

This is my question: why couldn't I affect it? Why couldn't I make it happen? Why, when my life's work is preparing for this? What have I done wrong? What have I not done? And ultimately, what the hell is it all about? I am miles away from solving that one.

Sometimes there are no real answers to any of this. You've just got to put it down as a lesson learned. As a response, though, that's never been good enough for me.

I do go out eventually. I go out with the boys – properly – and at eight in the morning I am delighted to discover that Brian O'Driscoll's table-tennis game has finally imploded.

You could call all this a drowning of sorrows, but overall I feel it was a great tour. I enjoyed it, which is a strange conclusion, given that we lost. On the day of the first Test, Matt Dawson had a diary column in the *Daily Telegraph* in which he was very critical of the management and the amount of training we'd been doing. He even said that some of the midweek players had been thinking of leaving the tour.

I don't know about that, and I guess I was fortunate to be in the Test team, but I think of guys who didn't play in the Tests but really held their own, such as Ronan and Neil Jenkins. The chanting of 'Neil-o, Neil-o' as they came back, sometimes from a night out, tended to suggest that they were still enjoying themselves.

As for the heavy training, I didn't really get it. I was asking Blackie for extra training, not less.

When you're part of a team, everything you do has an effect on that team, no matter how big or small. That's just the way it works.

● ● ●

At Sydney airport, we are weary, waiting for the flight home. Colin Charvis has his head in a laptop and starts talking about a rugby website with a chatroom, which is getting loads of feedback. Foolishly, I allow my intrigue to get the better of me and take a look at it.

I flick down through the comments. Some of them say I lost the series. A lot of them. My intercepted pass was the turning-point. That, apparently, is the view.

Is this really the view out there? I tend not to listen but I never figured *that* was the tone of the conversation.

It confirms a deepest fear, that when you've given your best, when you've given everything that you can and it doesn't quite work out, there will be people who say don't worry about it, and there will be others who think it's just your fault.

But I can't regret what I did on this tour. I have beaten myself up enough times for my errors on the pitch, but not this time. If I had my 24 hour video camera and could review this tour, I think I could sign off my Lions life with pride.

CHAPTER 11

DAVE and I are at Middlesbrough football club's indoor facility. Our topic, again, is what does being the best really mean and how do I achieve it?

Dave says you need to get the same results with your goalkicking but from farther out. Other kickers have a greater range. I'm convinced that you can kick from farther away, too.

I like the sound of this. It's positive, concentrating on improvement, a great project for the post-Lions summer. Middlesbrough's indoor facility is perfect – no wind, dependable secure footing, a sterile environment, ideal for learning.

We have the whole place to ourselves. Two, sometimes three evenings a week, we drive the hour down to Middlesbrough, we kick between eight and half nine and then we drive the hour back for a late dinner, bed and then up for Newcastle training the next morning.

Dave introduces a new concept: centring. He says to me picture your inner energy like a fire burning in your core area. Channel that fire as you're breathing in and out, and channel the power so you actually feel it going down your leg, like a build-up of explosive energy into your foot as you strike the ball.

It's part visualisation, part a kind of control of energy and part focus of concentration. I follow his words and take a kick. I get an extra six metres. I am astonished. This is the power of the mind and here, for the first time, is the clear evidence. Immediately I realise that this is where I will get my next big gains.

We also work on stripping down and rebuilding my technique. We want to bring in my main quadricep muscle instead of the inside quad muscle, which is not as strong. In other words we want to use less of my instep and a little more of the top of my foot.

When you connect this way, Dave says, you get more power, more precision and it will ping off your foot, fizzing like a golf ball off a low iron.

This is not easy. Numerous times I kick the hell out of the floor before the ball. But then, suddenly, I get it right and the penny drops.

He's not finished there. I have always approached the ball in a slow walk. This gives me a reliable routine but means all my power has to come from my last long step into the kick, which can be difficult to control, especially when I'm tired. We work on flowing into each goalkick, accelerating into the strike, which allows me to use the momentum of my body to achieve the necessary power. In classic Dave Alred style, I get results – greater distance, more accuracy and more comfort, all with less effort.

Who else is doing this? How good will this be if we can perfect it? This is suddenly all I can think about.

When I'm centring, Dave says to adopt a strong position. He doesn't tell me what to do, but I find that the more I focus, the more my hands naturally move to each other. With my hands together like this, I find I can shut out the pressure and crowd noise. This position assures me, very slightly it relaxes me.

To get comfortable with new distances, we spend hours kicking 45 metres, 50 metres, and aiming to land the ball on the crossbar of the goal. We kick footballs to encourage the rolling of the foot – anything to help relearn and perfect my new technique. It's a massive step forward and it's purely thanks to Dave's genius.

● ● ●

The big thing at Newcastle for the new season is the Heineken Cup. We are in a group with Leinster, Newport and Toulouse, so we're not exactly easing our way into it.

I find it hard enough preparing for a game without a TV camera watching your every move. It's worse when you're kicking before the game and going through your warm-up routine, and two guys are moving around you with a camera two or three metres away. For these Heineken Cup games, the TV production side seems to go up a level.

It's the same with all televised games. You get off the bus, get your bag and walk to the changing room accompanied by a camera two feet from your face. The face they choose is invariably mine.

Sparks knows how uncomfortable this makes me feel. Before the game I like my space to concentrate, but the cameras make that so hard. So this is the routine. He gets off the coach first and does a quick scan for cameras. When he sees one making a beeline for me, he walks close in front of me all the way to the changing room, effectively blocking the camera.

I like that minor victory. It works because it gives me the space, but also because I just don't like the way the cameras operate. This is a team, we live in a team environment, so the whole team should have screen time, but they want to focus on one person.

But I would rather the victory was on the pitch. I feel like I kick well against Newport and again against Leinster at their place, but in a well-contested game, they also beat us. Europe, it seems, is for now a bit far ahead of us.

●　●　●

When I started with England, my first fitness tests were straightforward three-kilometre runs round a track. How fast can you do it? Mike Catt was phenomenal. On my debut, aged 18, I got an early stitch and then chugged around, just about managing to stay ahead of the front-row boys. Catty and Neil Back were probably the fittest in the squad. I clearly wasn't.

These tests were tough for the forwards. All that weight pounding down on the hard surface was hell for their knees and backs. At some stage, someone twigged and asked what on earth has running 3km, at the same steady pace, got to do with playing rugby?

So now we have a Team Fitness Test, and it has got into my head.

Starting from a lying position, you get to your feet, run five metres to a cone, backpedal to the start, get down to your chest, up, run five metres out, backpedal again, down to your chest again, then a series of 10 metre zigzag runs before rounding it off with a 30 metre sprint back to the start. That is one repetition. Then you have a 25 second rest and do another rep, then a 30 second rest followed by three sets of two reps with about 45 seconds to sort yourself out in-between, depending on how fast you complete your reps. One final single rep and you have completed the nightmare experience. One rep takes about 20 seconds. One of the coaches monitors you with clipboard and stopwatch. Your combined time for all the shuttles is your score.

It kind of simulates game play, the stop-start, making a tackle, and features recovery – running hard out until a break in play, quick rest, recovery and then ready to go again.

This ability to measure us, to compare us with each other, makes me competitive. When I get back up to Newcastle, I say to Blackie I have to be the best at this test. I want to train for this test. You tell me where I need to be, when to turn up, and what to bring with me. We both know that I'd do better to train for the actual game, but I don't care.

Blackie's response, as ever, is spot on. He sets up similar exercises and he has me doing them wearing a vest weighed down by 10 or 20 kilos' worth of lead. He even manages to make it fun. But I have a new goal here and so I train ridiculously hard for it.

Back down at Pennyhill, the test starts to make me nervous. I find I can't sleep the night before test day. After all this effort, what if I don't win?

But I do win. Just behind me, as always, is Neil Back, but I am consistently at the front. That way I don't feel I have let myself down.

● ● ●

For England, the autumn starts badly. We go to Dublin for our postponed Grand Slam game and we lose fair and square, 20–14. We are short on preparation time and we are slower than Ireland to get the Lions experience out of our systems. In simple terms, we are beaten by a better team on the day. Another Grand Slam is gone.

For me, though, the greater challenge is what comes next in the autumn season – Australia. The media muse over the question who is the best in the world? In press conferences and interviews, this is how they put it: A lot of people are saying now that you're the best number ten in the world, you and Stephen Larkham. What do you think?

I answer honestly. In many facets of the game, I wish I was as good as he is.

Deep down, though, that question strikes a chord. It's a reminder of the goal I wrote down – I want to be the best ten in the world. But I have another goal. Never to be anything less than humble and modest. I make sure I pay due respect to all other players and I'd never dream of talking about myself as the best. But actually, this subject comes like music to my ears. It's like a drug and I can't quite resist it. I want to be the best. It really does matter to me that people think I might be.

By the time the Australia game comes round, this is just one of the thoughts that has worked its way deep into my head. Sitting in the changing room, preparing for the match, the pressure I feel is almost unbearable. If you offered me an opt-out now, the chance to run away, I'd seriously consider it.

I make myself a promise. If I get through this game all right, I'm going to ask for two weeks off after it.

We beat Australia 21–15, I kick all 21 points, five penalties and two drop goals, and I feel good. Not good as in elated, but good as in pleased to have come through the challenge and survived the pressure. And I don't ask for two weeks' holiday.

A fortnight later, we have the Springboks and I am exactly the same, feeling the anxiety and strain rising as the game approaches.

On Friday night, I try to relax by watching TV, but I don't really watch. I spend the entire programme asking myself how much time is left? And am I enjoying this? Am I relaxing? I count the minutes down until it's time to go to bed.

When I go to bed, I read through the notes I've made during the week and then I listen to the CD that Dave has made for me. It's a mental rehearsal

CD with Dave narrating over the noise of a real game. He talks me through tackles and passes, kicks and decisions, using the language I need to hear to visualise my performance. They've moved the ball, your man has the ball, you focus on his thighs and you go forward and hit, driving your shoulder into his legs, wrapping your arms tightly, you make the tackle, it's a strong tackle ... And so on. I listen but I'm still not relaxing.

In the morning, I have my usual breakfast of muesli and an egg-white omelette filled with ham and peppers, and afterwards it's kicking practice with Dave. Then, after a brief team meeting, I have an hour or so in my room to get changed, sit there and mull over it all.

If someone offered me the chance to fast forward five hours now, I'd snap it up. If you could tell me I get through the game OK, I'd take it. I'd miss the whole playing experience just to be sitting back here, knowing it had gone well enough to appease my fears and I'd survived the ordeal.

By the time we get to the game, I've expended so much mental energy, I tell myself again I really need a break. This time after the game, I'll definitely ask for a fortnight off.

But the moment I'm on the pitch, my anxiety lifts and the instinctive, competitive spirit kicks in, and all the training and hard work starts to pay off. We beat South Africa 29–9. I kick seven penalties.

This is how international rugby is for me now. And I never ask for that fortnight off.

●　●　●

If there is an answer to Newcastle's Heineken Cup campaign, it probably comes in the form of Epi Taone – Tongan, massive, brought over by Inga. He is lethal. He is our Lomu. We play him on the wing or in the back row. He is as fast as any of our wingers and bigger than any of our forwards, yet he can step, he can pass, anything. All we need to do is keep him under control and he is an absolute dream.

We play Toulouse at home and Epi just blows them away. On receiving one kick-off, we work the ball back from the ruck, I throw a miss-pass to Epi as he appears late into the line, running from out to in, and Toulouse don't see him coming. He shrugs one tackler, steps another and is clear. He then hands off Xavier Garbajosa, and Garbajosa's quick so he gets back for another go and Epi hands him off again. He goes 85 metres and we score straight from the move. We beat Toulouse 42–9.

But that is a rare glimmer of joy. We play Leinster back at home, or rather at Headingley, because Kingston Park is frozen, and it's a tight, physical game. Clive Woodward is watching from the stands.

At 10–10 their scrum half breaks blind, close to the try line. I'm one of two defenders against three attackers. I try to read the move, take a gamble and commit myself, but the scrum half darts through the gap inside me.

I have to leave the pitch because of a four-inch gash to the back of my head. In the physio's room, Sparks has to hold the sides of the cut together so that the doctor can put in ten stitches to hold it.

After 20 minutes, I get back on to the pitch for the close of the game. We are still seven points behind, but we are dominant and pressing, and finally, with a minute or two to go, Tom May works an opening on the right, which puts Inga over for the try. The conversion ties the game but I miss it. We get one more shot but Brian O'Driscoll smashes me into touch as I go for the corner.

Afterwards the disappointment is intense. I feel responsible. I've let down my teammates, who have worked so hard and deserved more. I feel totally responsible for the try we conceded. I stay on the field with Sparks. I feel so angry I cannot leave.

Clive comes over, I think to say hard luck, but I am totally absorbed in myself and somewhat rude. I don't even look up and Sparks has to cover for me. He explains that I've got a bad head. But Clive won't be surprised. He's seen me like this before.

To work it out of my system, I'm out kicking the next morning. I take 10 balls and hit 50 kicks from the spot where I missed. It's not great training but it does a holding job on my demons for a few hours.

That night I struggle to sleep. It's always that way after a disappointing game. On the second night, when I'm not so tired, I'm not buzzing from the game and my mind is clearer, I lie awake, picturing the action and thinking about what I could have done better. It can take hours to process everything. Images endlessly float round my mind. At 5am, I finally drop off and escape the torture.

● ● ●

I sit down to reassess and, on A3 paper, under the title 'From Here On In', I write out in long hand where I stand:

Goals

• To be the best rugby player ever to have played the game.

• Never to tolerate or deal with underperformance but to persist in following my goals and working harder and more professionally than anyone else.

• To score more tries and never stop working on the pitch.

• To be England captain and win.

• To captain the British Lions and win.

About Newcastle Falcons, I write:

We are in the particularly fragile position of possessing the strength, spirit and ability to win things and become legends in the game – but not realising it. The time we have left as a team to recognise this fact and succeed this year is short and running out fast … We must recognise the advantaged position we are in and make a commitment … There must be a general consensus that to underperform due to lack of drive and preparation is not acceptable … Every time I think of kicking the ball out on the full from a kick-off, or missing touch from a penalty, I feel sick in my stomach from knowing my hard work throughout last week, last year and my life has not been repaid or worth it … To walk into the club after a game and to be approached by fans wanting autographs is a real character test, for if my mistakes and ill performances were to be from lack of hard work or preparation, I would not be able to accept the pen to sign … To feel like I am not progressing in my dream to learn and develop and be the best hurts me as much as it hurts to wonder if the confidence that the players like Inga and Gary have in me ever wavers when I underperform … To know that, come May, we will be saying goodbye to Inga and Pat scares me because I know we have a choice on how we say goodbye to them and I want so badly to be able to say it with medals in their hands.

● ● ●

Sometimes, though, all the hard hours do pay off. The start of the 2002 Six Nations is one of those times.

We play Scotland and win 29–3. A fortnight later against Ireland it feels even better. For 60 minutes, we are flying. We are able to run with the ball, play what is in front of us and everything seems to make sense. I get the chance to run and take people on and vary my game.

And I say thank you, Blackie. Days like this show that everything we do is worth it.

We score six tries against Ireland, and Austin displays his skills. He works best as an opportunist, a floating decision-maker, and I feel his presence. He tells me put it over the top. So, without needing to look, I chip the ball in behind them. He collects it and comes up just short of scoring. He is an outstanding reader of the game.

But then we play France, and they have a plan that works. They send a flyer out on me, just to try to stop the ball from ever going outside. They try to shut me down and take me out of the game. Even if I pass the ball, they hit me to the deck and hold me down while the game moves on.

Serge Betsen, their number seven, sticks to me the whole game. Usually, if a guy flies out of the line like this, it's brilliant because it means that they are defending individually and you've got opportunities elsewhere. But when Betsen goes, the reaction of everyone else in their team is so urgent. They come out so fast it's like their lives depend on it.

For me, that is a challenge, one that fires every competitive instinct. But I can't lose my head. I can't go and smash someone or just sort this out myself. Instead, I have Clive in my head – build the score, direct the game.

But we can't build anything because, at home in front of their passionate fans, they are too good at preventing us from doing so. They play very, very well, and it's actually in attack where they really win the contest. They exploit a couple of minor lapses of concentration in our defence and score two good tries. Five points behind, we cannot claw our way back.

It hurts. It always does when you want something that badly, but there is no fast-acting cure for the pain. It goes down as another lesson – you can go in with the greatest game plan but if it's not effective, you've got a very small window to adapt. So we work on our on-field communication, how to stop the rot. We focus on how to evaluate and change tack, and we set about understanding how to do this under the most severe pressure, when the noise and panic around you are at their height.

If there are any immediate smiles to be found on this day, they come from Henry Paul, another of my heroes from rugby league, who has made his debut and has a first-cap song to sing. We ask him to sing the 'Paul Brothers Rap', which he wrote with his equally famous rugby-playing brother, Robbie. He responds by giving it to us there and then outside the function room where we are due to have our post-match meal. Brilliant.

Then we get a song from Jason, who is over a year into his England career but has still never sung. When you respect a guy that much, it doesn't feel right to abuse him in such a way. Jason is alone in having the freedom to choose when he would like to perform for the boys. The way he delivers 'Saturday Night at the Movies', I don't know why he kept us waiting.

●　●　●

Just once in my career have I consciously moved out of the way of a tackle – and that was to help Inga. The only problem is I'm not strong enough.

We are playing Leeds and Inga annihilates Japie Mulder, the Springbok centre, with a massive hit. But in knocking him flying, Inga gets his head caught slightly on the wrong side, takes a blow to the face and thumps down hard on to the wet, sandy ground.

Leeds recycle the ball and come round the corner straight into my channel, but I've still got an eye on Inga and, instead of making the tackle, I move over to where he is because he hasn't moved. He's been knocked unconscious, he's face down in a puddle and I think he's drowning.

I hook my fingers underneath him and try to roll him, but the guy is just so heavy, it's impossible. I can't shift him. I can see he's looking at me out of the side of his eye, he can't move. It takes Pat Lam to come over and together the two of us just about manage to roll him.

But Inga, being Inga, recovers quite fast. The call from the medics is you need to go off. The response from Inga is no, I'm fine.

I think it's a pride thing. He now wants to set the record straight.

Boy am I going to miss this man when he's gone. I will always remember his spirit, his phenomenal presence on the rugby field and the hand of friendship he extended to me. And I will also remember the day when he was introduced at a rugby dinner as 'the greatest name in rugby history' and 'a household name we will never, ever forget' by an MC who then asked the audience to give 'a round of applause to Egoo Toogamooloo'.

It was the only time I ever saw Inga embarrassed.

● ● ●

The time has come to draw a line. I will no longer read about myself or about rugby in the newspapers. Finished, over, done. They are too powerful, one opinion for hundreds of thousands of readers.

The reason is partly because I have disagreed with too much, but it's also about control. I've always felt the need to be in control. I work to be the best. I insist on a level of training and dedication that allows me to control my performance as much as possible. But I cannot control what is written about me. I am powerless in that area, and I know it has the potential to destroy me.

When I read something critical, I ask myself how can I put it right? How am I going to change that opinion? That is my natural response. But according to the papers, against France I went 'from ovation to aberration'. I guess that means they thought I was poor. Apparently, I was also tactically one-dimensional and so I am now supposed to 'be hurting mentally and physically'.

If you care what people think, like I do, it hurts to read that. But what can you do about it?

It was only a fortnight ago, that I was 'acclaimed as the world number one' and 'simply the best fly half in the world'.

The good stuff is bad for me, too. After Ireland, I couldn't stop myself buying into what was being said. It tapped into life goals. I can read the good stuff and get hooked on it and I don't like that, because if I'm going to buy into one side, I have to buy into the other.

So I've got two options – read it all and deal with it, or don't read anything at all. I'm nowhere near strong or mature enough even to consider option one. I'll take option two.

● ● ●

The France game doesn't send us far off course. We come back with a 50 point win over Wales and then a 45 pointer over Italy. That's the game in which I deliver the last of my appalling comments.

I thought I was through with backchat. I thought I had moved on, but one of their players charges straight for me, eyeing me up as the weak link. I put all my effort into the hit and, with the help of the guys around me, we drive him back and turn the ball over. Before I can stop myself, I say out loud, don't bring that shit down my channel!

No doubt it is in the wrong language to make any impact, but my own teammates certainly hear this despicable example of trash-talking, and they have absolutely no issues with ribbing me about it remorselessly. And that is the last time I say anything like that ever again.

● ● ●

The England summer tour is to Argentina, but Clive and I agree that this is one that maybe I should miss. I've toured for the last five summers. I'd be better off with a proper rest.

But all too briefly does this sound like a good idea. Suddenly, I find myself in virgin territory. The England team are out there working hard and facing challenges head on, and with all the attention on them, I am at home not doing anything. And without rugby, without pushing myself as far as I can go, without working on my path towards being the best, who am I? This is all I have ever known. I didn't realise just how attached to it all I had become, and now it's not there, I am no longer sure.

My entire values system has been created around being the best rugby player in the world and doing whatever is required to get there, but away from rugby, where does that leave me? Under the scrutiny of my own harsh judgement, I don't fare too well.

This starts as a thought, a single negative notion of myself and my life. Yet the more I try to figure it out, the further away I am from an answer, and because this is time off, down time, I have far too much opportunity to think, and so I can't leave the subject alone. Then my obsessive side hooks in and I simply can't let it go. The knock-on effects follow. I start sleeping terribly, three or four hours a night.

This becomes everyday life. On the face of it, this is a great summer – barbecues at home, kicking a ball around with Sparks, relaxing and watching DVDs. These are the things I normally wait all year to be able to do, but it doesn't feel the same. A DVD may be playing but I'm not really watching it. I'm just looking at the TV screen, with no idea of what's actually happening, because my mind is turning over a hundred thoughts a minute about something else.

A sense of helplessness dominates my summer days. Everything feels pointless, and my natural reaction is to treat the problem as I do my kicking – right, work it out and stay here working it out until you have done so. But by focusing so intensely, I just make it worse.

My obsessive side has truly kicked in. I simply won't let it go until I find an answer, but I can't find an answer that's satisfactory to me because the real answer is to move on, and to do that I need an off switch and I don't have one. I want to go with the flow, chill, relax, let it go, whatever it is that people say I should do, but I just can't live like that.

I get back from training one day with this darkness inhabiting my brain. I go up to the Slaley Hall Hotel, which is close by and where they are really nice to me, allowing me to use their spa facilities. Usually, I use their pool to relax physically. This time, I make sure that no one else is around, lower myself into the water until I'm completely submerged, and then I let out a scream of total frustration. I come up for air and then submerge myself again and scream again. No words, just pure desperation. I carry on screaming as long and as loud as I can and I don't stop until I am hoarse. I cannot find any other way of dealing with this non-stop barrage of thoughts and negativity.

I am the problem and I have to come to terms with the fact that I need to change. Right now, though, I am not prepared for it, ready for it or even close to it.

12

WHEN rugby starts again, I start to function again. Pre-season means I can be a rugby player again, which delivers me a way out of my identity crisis. Not a solution, just a way out. Not peace of mind, just some direction into which I can channel my obsessive energy a little more positively.

It's Liam Botham I feel sorry for.

Blackie has prepared an awesome period of pre-season training. Amid all the skillwork, he has us running up and down Tynemouth beach as fast as we can. I know what he's doing. He's testing us, and not just our fitness but our minds. It's less about physical, more about mental, strength. Well, actually it's an horrendous test of both combined. It's classic Blackie. Let's see what you're made of and how serious you are. Anything near to a nine-minute run is a very good time.

When he calls us to go, the group sets off and, as I only have two gears – stop and go – I flick on the tunnel vision switch and start running.

Liam, meanwhile, is possibly the best training partner I have ever had. He is inspiring because of how hard he trains, and he loves to dig in his heels and compete with me. But I have a trick up my sleeve for the run. I actually embrace my darker side.

Initially, the whole squad stays together, but as we hit the hill at the far end, Liam and I start pushing it, and by the time we are turning to come back, the two of us are out ahead. We are halfway home, about four minutes to go, and I'm thinking right, I'm going to push it up another level. You're going to have to see if you can live with this.

This is when my mind can ignore the physical pain. If I was mentally in a better place, I wouldn't be able to do this. I would feel naturally demoralised by the fact that there is still so far to go. But now I get angrier and angrier each time Liam tries to go with me.

I up the pace again and I feel Liam try to go with it. Then I go again, and I know that's the end of it, but I won't slow down. I go and go and go until the end. I finish the run in less than nine minutes. No one else has done that all summer.

And a few minutes after everyone has got back, Blackie does exactly what I thought he would do. He tells us to go again.

Most of the guys groan oh my God, you're kidding. But I just set off at pace, adding Blackie to my list of things to be angry about. And then I allow my mind to drop back into my own world – and I finish in under nine minutes again.

● ● ●

The team sheet for Newcastle–Leeds, a Premiership home game on a nice sunny day, is very special. We have started the 2002–03 season badly, we have lost three on the trot, and today we have a lineup that includes

J. Wilkinson at ten and M. Wilkinson at twelve. M. Wilkinson is Mark – or Sparks. The pride I feel for Sparks is immense.

Way back when we were at school, I was small, so I was a back, and he was big, so he was a forward. That's the way it always went. He was never able to find his niche as easily as I did. Mine just fell into place. And I had guidance from Dave, Rob, Steve Bates, Clive. I've worked hard, but compared to Sparks, who's worked hard too, I've had it on a platter.

Here at Newcastle, he has been on the conditioning staff for three and a bit years, working on the sidelines so all these guys can go out and do what he has always wanted to do. At Northern, a talented local club, for whom he played at weekends, they'd never settle him. One week they'd say we're playing you at six, and the next week he'd be playing at twelve. Maybe it was his own fault for having such a wide range of skills.

At Newcastle, he sometimes trained with the team, filling in when they needed someone to train with them. Then, when the second team were missing someone, they'd say why don't you play on the weekend? And he'd come in with no preparation and no understanding of the moves or the calls.

Unbelievably, despite all this, he was able to make his point in the only way that really matters, on the rugby field, and he earned himself a professional playing contract.

So now we start together for the first time since we were schoolboys. Sparks's greatest strength is probably his ability to take the ball to the line and sling incredibly hard, long and accurate passes with either hand. This is a joy to play with. He puts the ball wherever I want it. He is happy to step in and take the pressure at ten when required, so I can work out wide with more time to organise and threaten. Not surprisingly, we have an immediate understanding of what each other is doing, an understanding built up over years of hanging around together.

We win 27–20. And, for me, playing with Sparks ranks above playing with the Lions or playing with England. It is undoubtedly the best feeling I have ever experienced on the rugby pitch.

● ● ●

Few people realise exactly how good a kicker Sparks is. He's got long legs, kicks incredibly high and reminds me of a punter in American football. Rob Andrew certainly doesn't get it until we play Grenoble away and he picks Sparks at full-back. He has never played full-back before, but that sort of thing never seems to bother him. Not on the surface, anyway.

The day before the game, we go down to the ground to do some kicking practice – Sparks, Liam Botham, Rob and me – and within seconds of getting there, Liam and I get our boots on and start kicking together. We know the unwritten rule, which Sparks does not, that you kick in pairs, and the last one not in a pair has to kick with Rob. It's like being stuck with the teacher at school. Sparks gives us a look as if to say yeah, nice one, guys.

Liam and I hear Rob talking to Sparks about these long clearance kicks he wants him to do from the back. So Sparks, adrenalin-fuelled, launches a couple of big kicks. Then he really gets hold of a massive tight spiral. He connects so well that it has already cleared Rob before it has reached the top of its flight. Rob turns and hares off after it, sprinting, head down, but it hangs in the air so long that when it comes down, it hits Rob on the back of the head and knocks him straight to the deck.

Liam cracks up. Sparks can't contain his hysterical laughter, although he knows it's probably not too smart to be laughing at the coach. But at least he's made his point – he can kick.

If any doubt remains, it is buried at the opening of the new Hilton Hotel on the quayside in Newcastle. I'm there with Tom May and Sparks, and the idea is for us to kick rugby balls over the top of the new building.

We are all wearing trainers, so we can't quite get the power. I get a couple of spiral bombs to land on top of the roof, which I'm quite pleased about. We are just about to finish when Sparks launches a huge spiral. It doesn't just clear the hotel, it bounces all the way down the long bank on the other side and into the river Tyne. It's a massive kick. I wish I could kick as far as my brother can.

●　●　●

Playing with England, meanwhile, means returning to a steady building process. We have a massive autumn series pending. New Zealand, whom we haven't played since the World Cup, followed by Australia and South Africa. The big three.

Each match marks a significant breakthrough. First, we edge New Zealand by three points, a real statement. Now there's no one we haven't beaten.

We are 12 points behind Australia with 56 minutes gone, and our ability to adapt, our knowledge of how to construct scores and win games is tested to the full. Clive has been telling us it takes just 20 seconds to score. So we don't panic, we start chipping away at the gap with penalties, and then, when we are within striking distance of the win, we launch Ben Cohen for his second try. It may have helped me if he'd touched down under the posts, rather than leaving me the kick from a little left, but it wins us the game, 32–31. The point is these lessons are making sense to us. The win is our reward for our learning. Belief is building.

And finally, South Africa. I don't survive long because Butch James dislocates my shoulder. James is a hard, physical player. Like me, if he sees a chance to catch you, he'll do it, and he likes to catch you high around the ball. He hits me on the side of the arm, just as I've released a pass, driving my shoulder upwards. It's a good shot. I don't realise how good because he also catches me on the chin. I'm so dazed, it's only in the next phase of play, when I try throwing a pass, that I realise something's not right.

Pasky comes on, moves the shoulder round a bit and delivers the sound of a joint popping back into place.

Sorry, he says, you need to come off.

That's not all I've endured from the Springboks. I've already taken a late tackle from Jannes Labuschagne, which got him red-carded. Rewind a year and I nearly didn't make it out into the second half because my hip was so sore. And rewind another year and you get the really horrible match where I got double knee-dropped just above the pelvis by Mark Andrews after five minutes, a dangerous foul that was followed up by various Springbok forwards saying: How do you like that, because you've got 75 more minutes of that to come?

In that 2000 game, Neil Back received a head cut so bad that a flap of skin was flopping down over his eye. That was thirty-odd stitches. And I saw Hilly recoiling from a ruck as if he'd been shot, with blood spurting out over his teammates from a head wound. I'm not proud of it, but later in the game, when Mark Andrews ducks into my tackle, I break his nose. Accidentally, of course.

But in 2002, England pass all the tests. South Africa come at us with their most intimidating game and we don't budge, neither do we react. We carry on doing our jobs, building a score, which, on this occasion, finishes 53–3.

● ● ●

The sense of momentum with England carries on into the next Six Nations. We start against France, but Clive plays Charlie Hodgson, a second playmaker who gives them something else to consider in their defensive game plan, outside me at twelve. We then play a good Wales side in Cardiff, and even without being at our best, we win by 17 points.

Against Italy, in Martin Johnson's absence, Clive makes me captain for the first time, which is a massive honour, and we win 40–5. We then play Scotland, another day when Jason is special. We create a decent lead and for the last 20 minutes, let the shackles off, take risks and just embrace what we've been training to do and what we've been practising in the week. It feels great because we know we have earned ourselves another Grand Slam match, another shot at a title we've let slip so many times before.

● ● ●

The first time we lost a Grand Slam, the frustration was intense, and it has just grown every time since then. We know that all the other sides seem to raise their game against England, almost as if the motivation is to spoil our fun. We also know that every time we have failed at the final hurdle, it has been close, less than a score. We haven't been beaten out of sight. I cannot express the intensity of the desire to get across the line this time.

During the week, Clive works on me. Be ruthless, he says. Another message has been pushed my way recently – stop hitting those rucks, stop playing like a flanker – but my mindset is his priority for Ireland. He reminds me of the Wales game in Cardiff. They gave me a rock solid ball to kick off with and that was the reason I couldn't get any height off the restart. Why didn't you just toss the ball off the field and demand another one? Fair point. I didn't even think to challenge it. Don't be nice.

In training, he tells me if you're not happy with the communication or the organisation in the team, just smash the ball directly off the field and tell people to get it right and start again. He wants a bratish edge from me.

He pushes the whole team. Accept nothing less than you deserve. When we arrive in Dublin, we have a clear attitude – we've had enough of losing and not coming through these situations. It can't go on. This one's going to be different.

On the field before the game, I'm fiddling with my tracksuit when Clive is in my ear again. The message is the same. Be ruthless, he says.

In those last few minutes, I'm always nervous. As we're standing in line, waiting for the national anthems, everything is being dragged out and this is making it worse. Johnno has some issue with the officials. I don't really know what's going on and I want us just to get on with it, but Neil Back has a mischievous look on his face and Johnno shouts down the line no one effing move. Under no circumstances are we now going to move a muscle.

It is only later that I discover we were apparently standing in Ireland's preferred spot. That shows the mentality that Clive has driven into us. The drive for skills and performance has now been adopted into the personality we carry around the game. Don't accept anything less than we deserve.

We make a good start, turn the ball over from their scrum and Lawrence scores under their posts. That's a big psychological moment for us. The performance reflects our collective personality, because we don't stop. After the try, we score three points more and then three more again. We're making a statement – we're not here to take any nonsense, we're notching up a few points and we're not stopping.

Soon the pressure is turned round. They attack us and keep on coming, and we let nothing through. We have a commitment to our defence coach, Phil Larder, not to allow the opposition to score any tries, and we hold strong.

Phil has come up with this great new call, 'Hit the Beach', a respectful reference to the Normandy landings, a massive call to arms. It means that for the next 30 seconds, two minutes, minute, 10 seconds, however long it takes, everyone has to armour up and die for the cause, because we know the next short period will be crucial. On this occasion, we just hold out and don't have to hit the beach.

I make a number of tackles, one after another, in quick succession around the pitch. This is rugby at its simplest for me. People make the mistake of thinking passing and tackling are the basics of the game. The truth is that it all begins with the desire to give absolutely everything you have for however long it takes. I've long known that my greatest quality is nothing to do with tackling or kicking, passing or running. It's my refusal ever to give up. Never stop working for the cause.

By the time I have to go off with a blood wound, we have a healthy lead. In the changing room under the stand, Simon Kemp, the doctor, puts some stitches in my mouth and I try not to cool down, or lose focus. When I come out, we are another seven points ahead.

But we keep resisting them. The shout goes round the pitch – no fucking tries! No fucking tries! We are going to win the Grand Slam, but we're not relaxing. We want to keep making the statement.

And we don't stop making it. Not until the final whistle and the 42–6 scoreline make it for us.

● ● ●

I am due to appear in an adidas ad with David Beckham and word is that they are going to want me to hit a few football free-kicks. And being a perfectionist and not wanting to let myself down, I make sure I get my preparation in early.

So the day before, I turn up to training at Kingston Park with the usual kit plus a bag of footballs. To my great fortune, Newcastle United's reserves have been playing a match, so the goals are set up on the main pitch, and after training I go out to practise. Jamie Noon and Dave Walder join me for a kick-around, but they don't last long. I don't want to look anything but natural in the ad, so I practise free-kicks for an hour and a half.

The next day, very early, I arrive for the shoot near Manchester. Two Hollywood-style trailers, one for each of us, have our names on the door. I've not had anything like that before. I suspect that David's trailer is superior to mine, although that might be because my name is spelled wrongly. Nearly everyone everywhere still seems to spell Jonny with an 'h'.

They mike us up and, with a bag of balls over our shoulders, David and I head over to the pitches. He seems a relaxed, decent, interesting bloke, and I am fascinated to ask him how do you perform so consistently? How do you manage your career? We exchange views and stories. I really like him.

When we get to the pitches, the guys directing the shoot say right, let's do some kicking.

What about the dialogue? I say. What are our lines?

We've already got all that, is the reply. Nice one; very painless.

I am glad of yesterday's practice because I acquit myself OK. My first shot goes just over the bar. The second hits the underside of the bar and bounces back out. As long as they caught that one on camera, I know there's something of me that looks all right.

But whereas I'm just smashing balls at the goal, David places them left, right and centre. They ask him for one particular shot from a different camera angle and he finishes off by lacing it over the wall and into the top left corner. That's a wow moment. It's like watching Dave Alred.

He doesn't have much trouble with rugby goalkicks, either. I talk him through the routine and then put a ball down for him in front of the posts about 15 metres out, thinking it'll be OK for the cameras from here. But he smashes it straight through the middle and about 25 metres beyond. We move back bit by bit and he continues to do the same thing. The guy has incredibly well-educated feet.

I like doing this. If I wasn't here, I'd be kicking anyway, but here I'm getting a glimmer of the Hollywood experience and, as much as I am supposed to be one of the stars of the day, there's a part of me that still feels like a little kid hanging around with someone I've always wanted to get to know.

Quite soon, though, David has to go. There's a Manchester United function he has to attend and a David Beckham lookalike takes over for the rest of the day.

Funnily enough, there is no Jonny Wilkinson lookalike here, although I am aware one exists because once, when I gave my consent for a character in a kids' novel to be called Jonny Wilkinson, it turned out that the book publishers got the lookalike to attend the launch party. Apparently, he turned up wearing full England kit and merrily signed autographs.

I know this because I started getting letters from angry parents who felt their kids had been duped. I'm not sure why this was my fault, but I sent these kids genuine autographs in return.

But I hate to leave a negative impression. I got a fairly strong letter from two girls in Leicester recently. We asked for your autograph when we saw you before the game and you ignored us, they said. How could you do that?

I wrote back: You have to understand that before the game is very different from after the game. It is a very tense time, I have to prepare, I have to get mentally into the right zone, so I can't stand around and sign autographs.

I sent them some autographs and they wrote back to say thank you. We appreciate the situation, they said, and we understand.

I want to do the right thing. Once a game is finished, I'll stay and I won't stop signing until the last person has gone.

● ● ●

We arrive in New Zealand with the World Cup looming ever closer and, as proof of our credentials, an eleven-match unbeaten record that stretches back for more than a year.

In Wellington, two things in particular come to my attention. One is the stern advice of our medics. After a long flight like that, I always want to go out and take some exercise, and because they know exactly what I'm like, they insist I go easy and don't kick for too long, because jet-lagged muscles are prone to pulls and tears.

The other is the rugby media here, which is so different – not that I read it, I'm past that, but you can't avoid it. It's everywhere. And they want to talk about how good their team is, how great their players are, and how much they want them to win. I get the feeling that they are rugby supporters first and journalists second. It seems they'd rather write a story about winning than losing. Compared to the English attitude, it's pretty refreshing!

And they hype up their own players and spend the entire time ripping into us. They're calling us 'Dad's Army', which is hilarious and focuses attention on Dorian West, who is our oldest squad member and a definite Captain Mainwaring candidate.

In an unusual break with tradition, I treat myself to a day off during Test week. My days off on tour usually involve kicking for most of the morning, getting back to the hotel and then shutting myself away because I'm just so stressed and hyped up I feel I need a break and a bit of time to myself.

Here though, I join the others on a trip to the *Lord of the Rings* set. For some reason, I'm introduced as the team captain, a misapprehension I'm unable to shift while we watch a battle scene being filmed or when I'm introduced to Viggo Mortensen and some of the other cast. We have a great day. I barely think about the Saturday Test match. Stress and hype leave me briefly alone. It's certainly a pleasant break, although I'm still not sure this day-out thing is going to catch on.

The day before the game, the anxieties are back in force. I go to the Wellington stadium, known as the Cake Tin, for my kicking practice. I throw a bit of grass in the air, it disappears behind my back and then materialises again in front of my face. In other words, the wind in here is impossible to read.

● ● ●

Back at the Cake Tin a day later, our winning streak is under threat. We have our noses ahead. We also have Lawrence and Neil Back in the sin-bin at the same time, and we are defending a five-yard scrum, six against eight.

The call goes up – Hit the Beach. Johnno shouts it, everyone shouts it. Hit the Beach! Hit the Beach! Whatever we do, we're going to get through these next few minutes without giving anything away.

What follows is awesome. Our scrum doesn't take a step backwards, but it has to be reset. The same happens again. Still not a step back. This happens four times and four times we hold out. A monumental effort.

I kick four of my goals and a drop goal, but it is in those moments in that scrum that we win the game.

It is a huge achievement. The last time an England team beat New Zealand on their home turf was over thirty years ago. But the changing room afterwards does not reflect this. The celebrations are a little muted. There's no conscious decision to play it cool. It's just that, despite everything we have just been through, most of the team are actually quite disappointed with our performance. The result's not enough now. We've just won in New Zealand but we feel we could've done better.

The New Zealand media see it differently. They just rip straight back into us. They don't seem to want to go deep into the defeat. They're more interested in pointing out how big and lumpy and old we are, and what on earth have we been doing in training to look like this.

As we leave their country, we are being labelled 'white orcs on steroids'. I love that.

● ● ●

We sign off for the season against Australia and, as a statement before the World Cup, this game is possibly the best we have ever played.

There is something in our history together, and the momentum of our victories, that works as a kind of glue. We are held together and, on the pitch, the togetherness keeps us safe.

All the repetition in training and our collective experience on the pitch means that instinct takes care of us. We know our jobs and our roles and when it doesn't quite go as expected, we just alter and shift a little. We hang in the game because we have a structure for our game-breakers to come in when the time is right.

It feels as though we are permanently moving forward and waiting. The team performance becomes a springboard from which any player can launch at any time. In defence, the support is like a white wall round each player; in attack, it is the decoy runners, the unselfish options. It means that week in, week out, we're seeing the best of each other. Whose turn will it be today to bring out the brilliance?

Last week it was the forwards. Today it is Will Greenwood and Ben Cohen. But you feel right now, it could be anyone.

CHAPTER 13

AS preparation for the World Cup, we meet at Pennyhill for three weeks' pure, hard physical training. The hotel have effectively built us our own gym in a marquee by the training field, and a heavy routine gets under way – 6.30am starts, training, two-hour afternoon sleeps, then more training. I roomshare with Noonie and we create our own DIY recovery facilities in the room, pouring endless bags of ice into our bath – anything to help us for the next session.

We do plenty of speed/endurance training, which is perfect for me – sprint as far as you can around the field for a minute, sit down and rest for two-and-a-half minutes, and then go again. We have to do five of these. Some people pace themselves, but I'm used to the Blackie way and I see no alternative to going full out. So I charge ahead of everyone at a ridiculous speed and then die as the final seconds of the minute elapse.

I like leading the way. It's kind of my obligation. Josh Lewsey isn't far behind and Noonie is good, too. Noonie is definitely quicker than I am, although I may have the upper hand in endurance.

The forwards take little pleasure from all this, and they get their revenge on the rowing machine. You have to row 500 metres and then run round the field. I couldn't be less suited to rowing and, despite my greatest efforts, I am almost always the last off the machine. When I begin to run, I feel like someone has stolen my legs. I detest the rowing. I hate not being able to compete.

I have a problem with a nerve that runs through my quad, creating a hot-needle feeling down my leg. It's a slight injury risk so, on the last day of one week, when they are doing another tough speed/endurance drill, I sit out and watch training from the physio bed by the posts, feeling really bad because I'm not going through what everyone else is going through.

The next day is gorgeous and sunny. I have a meeting to go to with Tim and he arrives to pick me up.

Sorry, I say, there's something I need to do first, and I'm going to need your help.

We go down to the pitch and I put out the cones. I want to do the exact same training session I missed the day before. I have to do it. So Tim has to play the coach, running up and down the pitch, sweating in his suit, holding the stopwatch. I make him do this.

We are in the middle of this when the sprinklers come on and Tim gets soaked. He is not too impressed. I guess this kind of thing doesn't appear in the agents-players handbook. He says what are we doing?

On days off back at Newcastle, I'm getting further help from Blackie. The results of the Team Fitness Test are the ones that really matter and we know the score: completing the lung-busting course in under 197 seconds is considered world-class, under 205 seconds is excellent, under 210 seconds is good and over 215 is average. One hot morning, I set my personal best. I do a

194 seconds. That's the best I will ever do and a squad record for years to come.

Three times during the camp, Clive gives out a bottle of wine as a kind of prize to a player whom he judges to have made a difference or performed seriously well. On the last day of the camp, he says he is giving the last one to someone who has been constantly pushing themselves harder and harder, and one or two heads turn in my direction.

The wine has a face value of about £900 and, to be honest, it is wasted on me. The accolade, though, is not. I have a few Man of the Match bottles back home, but this is one I really treasure. To me, working hard every second of every day is what is important in team sport. So this award has real value. I owe it to Blackie and I owe it to my obsessive drive.

But not everyone is a winner round here. As the squad gets cut, I say goodbye to Jamie Noon and Dave Walder. I was so hoping to have these two great players and great friends from Newcastle in Australia with me. They deserve it, but I know that they would have been good for me too.

● ● ●

The real trophy, though, remains a long way away. It feels as though we have been building up towards this World Cup for months, but on 1 October, we finally leave Pennyhill for Australia, and I have a fax fresh from Blackie safely tucked away.

The fax contains the famous speech from General Patton, which reads like this:

I have personally benefited from the passion of this oratory at numerous times throughout my life. I hope it has the same effect for you:
  • Today you must do more than is required of you.

- Never think that you have done enough or that your job is finished.
- There's always something that can be done, something that can help to ensure victory.
- You can't let others be responsible for getting you started.
- You must be a self-starter.
- You must possess that spark of individual initiative that sets the leader apart from the led.
- Self-motivation is the key to being one step ahead of everyone else and standing head and shoulders above the crowd.
- Once you get going don't stop.
- Always be on the lookout for the chance to do something better.
- Never stop trying.
- Fill yourself with the warrior spirit – and send that warrior into action.

That is certainly something to occupy my mind as we head to Perth. I actually love long-distance flights. I look forward to them. There is no video analysis to be done. I can't practise my kicking or my passing. There is nothing I can do towards helping win a rugby game. Just put on the TV and, for what will be the last opportunity for a long time, properly relax.

We are heading to Australia as favourites and that's not a false tag. It's a title we have earned and, for now, it doesn't feel bad.

● ● ●

At the other end, the intensity and the pressure are immediate. Just like 1999. I try briefly to get away from it by going for walks with Hilly, but seven weeks out from the World Cup final, supporters are already gathering. It is such a big affair.

Every day, I write an entry in a kicking diary. This is on Dave's advice. Write down what you've done, he says, then you can look back at it and remind yourself how much good work you have stored away. So every day I write down the length of the session, the conditions, the number of punts off each foot, the number of goalkicks, drop goals and drop-kick restarts I do, and how well they all go.

On Day One, I take it easy as advised: one hour. Day Two: one hour 20–30 minutes. After that, I'm generally between one and a half and two hours a day. On Day Eight, two days before our opening game against Georgia, I can practise in the Subiaco Stadium, where the match will be played, and I'm up to two hours 40.

The Georgia game is a good start, but the minute it's over, I am aware again of an uncomfortable edge, a feeling that I cannot escape. South Africa are next, a completely different story. The pressure is on. We need this game. It's billed as the group decider. We have all seen this day coming ever since the draw was made, and the tension simply builds all week.

Rudi Straeuli, the Springbok coach, tells the media that he thinks I am putting myself under too much pressure, but he doesn't know me, he doesn't know the deal or how I operate. Anxiety has always been there in me, but no matter how painful it can be, I know it's what gives me the edge. It's the anxieties that keep me buzzing.

Nevertheless, by the time we get to the stadium, the anxieties are already so great that I'm back in an old frame of mind – if I get through this, I need two weeks' rest. It's been hinted that I might be rested against Samoa next week. That'd be perfect.

The game itself is tentative, edgy, and we struggle to get the scoreboard moving. I don't help by kicking two balls down the left, straight into touch. And

Will Greenwood doesn't help when the Springboks miss a penalty. Our strategy when facing penalty kicks at goal is for me to stand by the 22 so that if they miss, we can take the 22 drop-out before they have the chance to reset themselves. But Will catches the penalty and flings the ball straight out to me.

I feel like shouting at him Guscott-style, what the fuck are you doing?

The look on his face shows he realises his mistake. He forgot to touch it down. In other words, he has thrown a forward pass and thus conceded a five-yard scrum.

He shows good mental strength to put the slip-up behind him. He even makes amends with a try later. England win 25–6. Not a fantastic performance but it's the win that counts. My prize is to be selected afterwards for a drugs test.

Providing a urine sample on demand has never come easily to me, especially after a game when you are already badly dehydrated. I use all the techniques I can muster – a long shower, a flushing toilet, running taps. Eventually, I am facing this big metal urinal with a 50-year-old doping officer standing as close as he can to directly in front of me without being in the line of fire. He is only doing his job to the letter by insisting he sees exactly what is happening as I produce my urine sample. But protocol, right now, seems particularly strict. Lift your shirt up, he says, lift it right up. Pull your trousers down, all the way to your knees.

I am really hoping that there is no one outside listening to this. I am now sweating almost as much as I did during the match. At least I have got a week off to relax.

● ● ●

The next week, I get two telephone calls of note.

For the first one, my phone indicates unknown number. These are often media related so I tend to ignore them, but I give this one a go. It's Dave. Dave who? David Beckham. He has rung to chat and wish me luck. I like that.

The second is from Mum and Dad. My grandmother, a truly amazing woman, has died.

If there is anything that can make you feel you are all those miles away from home, this is it. I feel guilty that I'm not able to do anything or help the rest of the family. Here I am on this selfish pursuit. The World Cup, suddenly and quite rightly, doesn't seem such a big thing after all.

My state of mind is not improved when Clive comes to speak to me. I expect this to be the chat when he explains why he is resting me. But he says I want you to play number ten this week.

That means my whole mindset has got to change. I feel the pressure back on immediately. I go from being relaxed to feeling trapped, claustrophobic almost. My whole week changes shape.

● ● ●

Before every game, I have a very specific warm-up routine. I'll do my kicking with Dave, go back into the changing room, then come out and warm-up with the team. Ten minutes before kick-off, as the boys are returning to the changing room, just to finish off with a confidence booster, I'll kick one more goal from straight in front of the posts, 30 metres out.

Before the Samoa game, I line up my last kick and leak it out to the left. Immediately, I demand the ball back. This one smashes against the left upright. That's two misses from two and I can hear murmurs from in the stands. Again, I demand the ball back and this one creeps inside the post. My head now is spinning. I'm going into this game and I'm not kicking straight.

There is no more time. I have to get into the changing room. I'm trying to think about the whole game, but my kicking is so key to my confidence. Everyone's talking to me about the game and what are we going to do at the first kick-off? But my eyes have glazed over. I'm just thinking what's the first kick going to be like?

From the moment we kick off, Samoa run it everywhere. Side to side, fast, relentless, I don't know where they get it from. They score an awesome try. We struggle to find our rhythm.

We win a penalty, an easy kick to keep our score moving. It's humid, hot. The stadium roof has been shut and we've been chasing hard for almost a full 40 minutes. I'm pouring with sweat. My strike on the ball feels good. I look up and have to clear a bead of sweat from my eye to see it smash off the post. It's my first miss of the tournament and it feels awful.

At half-time we are 16–13 down. We are still behind with 15 minutes to go. We have to sort this out quickly.

From a lineout, I see that their winger is up flat and their full-back is tucked in. I get the message out to Iain Balshaw. Tell Balsh to expect a DA.

Named after Dave Alred, who invented it, a DA is a cross-kick move. As our lineout forms, Balsh tries to stay unnoticed as he drifts wider. We win the lineout, I take the ball up a bit to draw the defence and then kick it flat right over their winger's head with my right foot. I watch, breath baited, as Balsh drops a gear and uses that trademark acceleration of which I am so envious. He takes it and we are at last ahead.

In the changing room afterwards, I know for certain that I do now have a weekend off. I feel finished right here; that was enough.

● ● ●

The crowds are starting to swell and the media scrutiny seems relentless. When England move now, particularly through airports, Phil Keith-Roach, our scrum coach, has been assigned to me, almost like a minder. When we are in the hotel, though, my instinct is to allow myself to get boxed into my own room.

I think Dave Reddin has sensed this because he suggests a day out. We are now on the Gold Coast. The squad is preparing for the Uruguay game, which I am definitely not playing in. So Dave suggests driving up the coast. We'll find a beach and just have a mess around up there.

Normally, I'd find it easy to say no. If it was let's go to a bar or out for a meal, that would be a no. I can find some kicking or another rugby reason not to go. But I have played enough football-tennis with Dave to trust him, and he has played enough with me to know where I'm likely to be susceptible. A beach and a ball. Easy decision.

We go with two of the guys with whom I feel most at ease, Hilly and Krajicek, in an open Jeep, and I sit in the back for the whole journey. Miles away, we find a beautiful beach, and we do little but run up and down it smashing footballs around. Throughout the whole of the World Cup, this is probably as close as I come to relaxing.

● ● ●

The boys do a good job against Uruguay. Afterwards, the non-playing members of the squad head back to the hotel. The radio on the bus is loud and tuned into the Wales–New Zealand game, the loser of which will be our quarter-final opponents.

Usually, I can't stand watching or listening to live rugby if the match has a knock-on affect for us. But the radio is so loud, there is no escape, and what's going on is unbelievable. We are fully expecting to play Wales in the next round, but with an hour gone, they are in the lead. We've already started to do a bit of homework on the Welsh, although we have beaten them twice this year already. We haven't considered the All Blacks.

So it is more than a small relief when New Zealand sneak through with some late tries. The next day, though, when we start watching the video analysis in the team room, the rugby that we see from the Welsh is so good that it is actually greeted with applause. I am so impressed that, after the meeting, I ask to see some of it again.

All of a sudden, the World Cup temperature has risen. We are starting to hit some media criticism for our form. But we've taken such a bashing over the last five years of our journey here, mainly for our Grand Slam losses, that we're just too strong and thick-skinned as a group for it to matter any more. We're very tight, very resilient. With the confidence from everything we've been through, we feel it's coming – the momentum of earlier in the year will click back in again.

Clive wants to see me. He arranges a meeting in the evening in the team room. He says some great things. He says how much he needs me to be directing the game, but his point reiterates the message from the Six Nations and throughout this World Cup – keep out of the rucks. We can't have you with your head in a ruck because then there's no one to drive the game.

But I sometimes find that difficult. If I pass the ball and our ball-carrier gets tackled, if I am our closest man, I find it difficult to stand away and not clear out the tackler. It's in my nature to help a teammate. But Clive's serious about this. OK, I say, I'll try to avoid the rucks.

My kicking diary shows some good work for the week but it also shows that the pressure is starting to tell. Ideally, I would be tapering down with shorter sessions as we approach the games. However, four days before the game, I spend two hours out there kicking after team training. Three days before the game and it's down to one hour 45, but then two days before the game, on our day off, I get tight and allow myself to panic over every little miss hit, and I'm up to two and a half hours to find the reassurance I need.

We go into the game expecting to click, but what we get is the opposite. We actually get what's probably been on the cards for a while.

●　●　●

The first 40 minutes against Wales are horrible. Absolutely horrible. The biggest crisis of our World Cup.

Everything we do is contrary to everything we've worked on for so long. Ever since 1999, we've worked on width and using the whole of the pitch so there are options left and right, inside and outside, options to kick, guys running lines, everything was taken care of. But here, at times, you could throw a blanket over the entire team. We are that tight, everyone is around the ball, which means we're predictable in attack and therefore easy to defend. And it's worse when we turn the ball over.

We get stuck in our own half, and people are saying to me we need to get down their end. And that's great, but where do you want me to kick it? They've got four players waiting for the kick and we're so tight, who's going to chase it?

We end up with our kicking being punished. We kick it long, straight to Shane Williams, who doesn't need a second invitation to run it back. Having Ben Kay completely on his own in acres of space, trying to cover against

Williams, doesn't quite work for us, and our frantic scramble defence only delays the inevitable and it's Stephen Jones who goes over.

It's frustrating, exasperating and so desperate that it comes down to survival. Sod the number on your back, just hang in there and stop them from scoring. The carefully laid plans, the urging of Clive, are no longer the priority. Suddenly, I'm not thinking like a number ten. I'm thinking like someone who has got to chip in and get their hands dirty.

Wales score again, we are 10–3 down and I can feel dreams fading away. Standing under the posts, watching the conversion, rifling through my mind is the thought what if we can't rescue this? How are we going to be viewed back home? Are people going to say you've had a good year and were just unlucky? Or are we going to get ripped to pieces? And would I ever let myself get over the disappointment?

Half-times with the England team have become a military process, with almost every minute accounted for. You go in, get a drink, change your shirt and shorts. There is specific time allocated to talk to individual coaches and then, at the end, from a board in the room, Clive presents in bullet points a summary of whatever he and his staff feel is required.

But here, 10–3 down, it's difficult not to look around as if to ask what the hell is going on? Why is this happening?

But you have to resist that. Relax, just relax. Resist panic mode.

Clive has his say. More width, don't get sucked into rucks, we don't need so many people clearing out the ball. And he brings Mike Catt in at twelve.

Bringing in Catty is a massively good call. This game is going to be won by decision-making and there is now another guy out there thinking like a number ten, who also has a great kicking game.

So we come out and slowly start to chip away at the lead. When Jason sets up a try for Will Greenwood, we slowly start to quell their spirit. Catty is outstanding, absolutely brilliant. We haul our way back and only when we pull away do I finally feel confidence coming back.

In the dying moments, we are at last where we want to be – more than a score ahead. As the buzzer sounds to signal that time is up, I receive the ball from a ruck on the left, about 35 metres out, and I decide to go for it. I hit my favourite drop goal of the tournament and that, for me, serves as a way of putting a lid on a truly horrible experience.

The inquest, though, is just about to begin. We all know we are going to take a hammering in the media. I attend the press conference with Clive afterwards and he gets the question: Aren't you concerned that Jonny is playing like an extra flanker?

Clive's response is strong. He talks about my work rate, and says that without it we might have lost the game. Just hearing that makes a massive difference to me.

● ● ●

In Sydney two days later, in the Manly Pacific Hotel, we have a crucial meeting. It's not quite a crisis meeting but not far off.

We are getting closer and closer to our goal, but we've stopped playing. Pretty much from 1999, we've tried to take the game to the opposition and, when necessary, switched into three-point mode. But here, we've been starting in three-point mode. We're almost ensuring that these games become tight, edgy affairs when they might not actually need to be. We've been safe and conservative. We've not committed to playing like us. The same approach just won't cut it from here on in.

The agreement is this. We have to go out and win these games, rather than trying to protect a lead before we've even got one. And, it seems, this is what everyone wants to hear. This is how we'd all rather play anyway.

Personally, though, I am feeling the pressure. And my real concern is that the media view of the way I am playing is the view held inside the camp. I need to know. Are the guys in the team blaming me like the outside world is?

When Johnno asks me, in the way that Johnno does — Wilko, are you all right? — I tell him. We may not be playing the way we play as a team, we may not have our same structure, but it just seems the blame is all coming down to me. Whatever happens on the field, it's me who takes the shit.

Johnno is so matter of fact. He says he understands the flak I'm taking. He says the whole team needs to get the feeling back. It's never one person's fault, and in this case, it's certainly not mine.

It makes a world of difference to hear this. I feel the support, too, from Catty, Lawrence and Hilly, and the effect is instantaneous. It gives me the energy to get back out on the field.

When we head for training, the sun is out and there is a buzz about the squad. It's exciting to feel we're back on track, and Mark 'Ronnie' Regan feels one of his trademark tricks is called for.

Sometimes Ronnie's gags are welcome and sometimes not. We have a game, the Circle Game, which is very basic. You make a circle by touching together your thumb and forefinger, and if you can distract someone into staring at the circle, you are allowed to punch them on the arm. Ronnie loves the Circle Game. He once famously put the circle in front of Phil Greening's face when they were opposite each other in a scrum. His masterstroke was lying down in the hotel toilets, putting each arm under the door of two neighbouring cubicles in which two England players were sitting and showing them the circle that way.

This time he pulls another trick. He slides in behind Simon Kemp and rips down the doctor's shorts. The doc is left in front of about twenty newspaper photographers with his shorts round his ankles and it's just too funny a sight not to laugh. This is rare, but today Ronnie's trademark joke actually works a treat.

● ● ●

Compared with the Samoa game, my warm-up for the semi-final goes well.

Part of the routine is to hit goalkicks from the goal-line, aiming at the single post. It helps me to visualise the exact line of the flight of the ball. Here in the Telstra Stadium, I hit one, it strikes the central part of the post and doubles back to me along the exact same path. I barely have to move to catch it. I want to laugh about that, but I've got just over half an hour until kick-off in one of the biggest games of my life. I need to get my brain into gear.

After all the criticism of the last few weeks, our forwards are now fired up, and against France, at last, it clicks. We concede an unfortunate early try, but after that we just kill it. We prepared for, and longed for, a dry day and it pours down. Our pack, however, are so dominant and they push forward so well that even in these difficult conditions, I can more or less pick and choose what I want to do and when.

And when we drive forward so effectively, France have to put more and more forwards into the mauls to stop us. This means their backs have no inside support in defence, their wingers are forced to come up and help and it frees up the back field. Now we can kick into space and turn them.

We get lineouts in return, we win them and we drive them. Our forwards smash rucks and dominate the physical battle, they pretty much ensure the victory is ours. I drop three goals near their line, we keep the scoreboard ticking; with 25 minutes to go, we are already more than a score ahead.

And right at the end, as the clock is running down, standing on halfway as we reset a scrum, I glance at the scoreboard, which reads 24–7, and I spare myself a thought. At some point, Jonny, you've got to start embracing these situations. We've come back and as a team we have attacked it together; individually, you've had pressure on your shoulders and you've kicked all 24 points. We've now made it to the World Cup final. Just for once, give yourself a break. Even if it ends here, you've done OK.

● ● ●

We play Australia in the final and so, of course, the scale of the Australian media coverage rockets. My problem is trying to avoid the damn stuff. I don't know how they do it, but some of the guys sit there at breakfast and read it all. They consume stories about themselves or other people whether they're rubbish or not. It must just mess your head around.

Without wishing to appear rude, I try to sit somewhere slightly apart from them, like at the end of the table, and just keep my head down. I don't want to see the press, but it's all there, under my nose. I see they've got a picture of me on the front page, or the back, or both, and I don't want to look, but at the same time, I've just got to know what it says about me. What's the headline? I get annoyed at myself for taking a glimpse but I can't help myself. And whatever I see, good or bad, it just adds to the pressure.

It's impossible to relax. The team room in the Manly Pacific, where I spend a fair bit of time, has a beautiful view of the beach and the ocean. But every time I look out, I see people in their hundreds, almost all in England shirts, on the street below. It makes you realise there's so much to lose.

Every day when we go for training, we walk through reception, out of the hotel and straight on to the coach, and the fans are there, all cheering and shouting and trying to pat you on the back. And when we get back, it's the same. It might be three days until the game, but I can't escape. I feel as if every day is match day. Increasingly, they chant my name, and although I love the support, it makes me feel under more pressure, thinking of all those people I could let down.

I don't actually enjoy the chanting. It's draining everything I have. And it feels so uncomfortable with the team. This isn't what I wanted. I didn't want it to be about me. I feel as though I'm cheating them.

On the Wednesday before the game, I'm in my last press conference before the final, probably the biggest I've ever sat in, and I hear about what's being said and what's being written. The journalists want to know if I am concerned about what Australia are going to do to stop me. What tactics might they use to take you out of the game? Their questions criticise the type of rugby we've been playing. They don't realise this is a complete misunderstanding. Against France, we were dying for dry conditions so we could run the ball.

I walk away from the top table at the end, nervous and caught up in it all, and a guy walks up to me and says good luck for the final. He puts his hand out to shake mine.

Thanks very much, I say, returning the handshake. And at that moment, another guy next to him takes our picture with a professional-looking camera. It is only then that I register his white T-shirt, which has a picture of me in my kicking stance and a red circle with a line through it over the top and the words 'Say no to kicking rugby'.

There are two different worlds operating here. There are the people writing about it and then there are the people living it. The intensity of the environment makes the gap so obvious, and there is simply no way to make the media understand what we're going through.

But subconsciously, I take some of the press-conference questions back to my room with me, and I wonder will they try to take me out of the game?

On our day off, some of the boys go down on the beach that we can see from the team room. I'd love to join them, but there's no way. There are too many people with cameras and too many of them are press. I don't want to give them the pictures they want. I might be making my life harder, but I refuse to let them win.

So I take off with my dad. I meet him in the parking lot under the hotel, where he is waiting with his Australian mate Scotty and Scotty's young son Ben, and we drive half an hour up the coast to a small cove. Not many people there, and none of them would know to shout my name. We have a picnic and mess about with a football. Just briefly, I have escaped.

The following day, I try another escape with Bilks and manage to sneak on to the beach unnoticed. I wear a hat and sunglasses, and sit up against a wall, watching people walk past, not relaxing for a second, in constant fear that the next passer-by in an England shirt will be the one who blows my cover.

It's not that I'm trying to avoid having to talk to people. I'm merely trying to avoid this constant reminder of what lies ahead. I just want to think about something else for a few hours.

The thing is, this is my goal. This is what I wrote down when I was ten, and all those other times. But I can't remember the last time I smiled properly, and enjoyed it. I'm trying my best to embrace this amazing opportunity but I'm not even close.

● ● ●

On the day of the final, I lie on my bed in the hotel reading a book by Michael Connelly, *Angels Flight*, which Blackie sent me. I've been speaking to Blackie regularly. He knew I'd be struggling this week.

I look at the clock next to me and think to myself I've got four hours till we meet as a team and leave for the Telstra Stadium. Four hours is good, four hours is a lot of time. I feel like I could stay here all day, never leave this room.

I get back to my book. I check the clock, read for a bit, check the clock, read for a bit. In bursts of a minute or two's reading, I escape, and then it all comes back. The final.

The clock says three hours to go. A part of me is thinking I want it to stay paused on this moment for the next two years, ten years, twenty years. I want it to stay at three hours to go because I don't want to go any nearer to this game. And another part of me says I just want the time to disappear, I want to be on the field now. It's a constant battle between wanting the moment I've trained for all my life to be here, and wanting it never to arrive.

I make my phone calls, the ones I make before every game I play – to Mum and Dad, Sparks and Blackie. I talk about the game and how I feel, how I'm going to draw on a life's work in about eighty-five minutes of rugby.

Increasingly, I understand that in this game, there is no running away.

● ● ●

Three hours later, the CD player on the way to the Telstra Stadium isn't working properly. Mike Tindall always puts together a CD for the journey. He times it to finish with carefully chosen songs as we are approaching the stadium. Our stadium arrival song in Australia has been Eminem's 'Lose Yourself', which is about 'one shot, one opportunity'. On this occasion, though, the CD keeps skipping or sticking, and so we arrive instead to the sound of Dorian West's favourite, The Clash and 'Rock the Casbah'. Slightly different era, that. The boys are split on whether to find this amusing or to remain in 'biggest game of our lives' mindset.

I have a slight feeling of inevitability about it, and it's the same later when we are standing in the tunnel, looking at Johnno, waiting for him to give his last address before we run out on to the pitch. This team has been together for five years, through thick and thin. We've stood together through strikes, through horrendous defeats and through glorious victories, whether we've been slagged off or praised. It seems now that this journey has always been bringing us here, so it doesn't matter what music we have on the coach, and that's where Johnno is when he turns to speak.

Usually, he'll say something strong, punctuated with horrendous swearing and powerful messages. This time, we might all be as nervous as hell, but we all know what we've been through. He knows that and he stops, looks at us and says nothing. There's no need.

The game starts badly for us. Australia put a high cross-field kick in to the goal area and Lote Tuqiri, with a big height advantage over Jason Robinson, takes it in the air and scores. It is astonishing that this ploy, which works so well, is never used again.

We edge our way and start accumulating points. I see a hole in their defence as Lawrence muscles through the contact; he offers it to me on the inside and I'm clear. I have two options. Move it on outside to Jason, who could dart over in the corner, or inside to Ben Cohen, who could go in under the posts. I can't see if Ben is being chased down by cover defence, so I go wider to Jason, knowing that with a half-decent pass he'll get in. We get the try but I'm not sure if Ben will ever forgive me for the choice I took.

We carry on accumulating and at half-time our lead is 14–5. Gradually, they begin to claw themselves back into it, and we are locked at 14–11. It doesn't feel like anyone is going to score another try. In the last minute,

Australia are awarded another random penalty from a scrum. Elton Flatley has a chance to level the scores. The pressure on this kick is remarkable, and Flatley shows stupendous mental strength to come through it. The problem then is that it lumbers us with extra time.

I've never experienced extra time before. We don't have a routine for the five-minute break while we're waiting. We don't go into the changing room, but stay on the field. It's a bit like being in junior rugby again and I'm half expecting a plate of oranges to turn up.

I don't like the atmosphere. Everyone stands around, edgy, nervous, uncertain, looking at each other. Two minutes ago we had the game sewn up; now we are back to square one.

Clive and the coaches go round with drinks. Despite all his powers of foresight, Clive hasn't thought about this one. There is no third change of shirts.

Clive walks over to me, and he seems nervous and tense, too. I am the guy he has spent five years working on to hit drop goals. Initially, when it was contrary to all my instincts, he almost begged me to try them, and ever since I was 20 years old, he has been forcing upon me the idea of taking my chances when they arise. By now, it's been drilled into my core.

Jonny, he says, we need three points, we need a drop goal.

Thanks, Clive. In terms of ten minutes each way of do-or-die, incredibly tight rugby, you couldn't have stated the obvious better if you tried.

Mate, I say to him, choking back the 'No shit, Sherlock' response, I need to go and practise my kicking.

I exit fast to the end of the field. I don't know what the protocol is for this period of time. I don't know if you are allowed to kick. But I hit a couple in front of the posts in readiness. It is 14–14, and we're starting again.

We soon get a penalty, 49 metres out and, there and then, all those late nights at Middlesbrough with Dave Alred become worth it. We are 17–14 up.

We take our lead into the second half of extra time and we do well. We stay in their half, out of range. But then they get another penalty and again Flatley shows nerves of steel to score. We are tied, 17–17.

We now have 95 seconds to score. We already know the plan – kick off long, so that they catch it deep. They won't want to risk setting up the ball deep in their own half, not in penalty range, so they will kick it back.

My restart is taken by Matt Rogers. He smashes the ball off the field and does a reasonable job of it, better than we hoped. We have a lineout 40 metres out, and a drop goal routine called 'Zig-zag' – get the ball to the middle of the field and truck it forward left and right until we're close enough for the three points to be a formality.

As we wait for the lineout, I don't need to say anything to Catty outside me. After over ten years of this, he knows exactly what he has to do.

But so do the Australians.

Everyone now has to execute their roles to perfection. Steve Thompson has to hit his throw, which is called to the back of the lineout, so we can get perfect ball off the top. Matt Dawson fires it to me flat and I feed Catty. He sprints into their defence, gets smashed for his troubles but ensures the ball comes back on our side.

I get myself into position. I feel like I might have to try this now. It's over 40 metres. I tried one from this range earlier and it just missed. I've got a shot at it now, but it's still not ideal.

Then, a big let-off for us. As Daws goes to play the ball, a defender jumps out of the line slightly, Daws dummies and breaks through. At this point, my whole mentality changes. This has gone from a potshot to win us the game, to a sure-fire opportunity. It's no longer let's have a go. It's now, this is it.

He gets brought to ground by the full-back 15 metres out and we edge closer to the line until Neil Back is left standing at scrum half. I'll have a go from here. We've got this close to the line, it's a good shot.

But then Johnno comes running in on the open side. Backy pops it up and he charges into contact taking plenty of Australian defenders with him. And Daws is back on his feet and playing nine.

I'm now in as good a good position as I can hope for, 25 metres out, a little to the left, but with their defence ready to charge down the kick. So eager are they to close me down that they jump the gun and go offside. They put their hands up – they don't want to concede the penalty – and the moment they do that, Daws passes the ball.

The pressure is now reduced. They've backed off. I don't have to worry about charge-downs or trying to get the kick up over raised hands.

In my head now is nothing but my normal routine – go through the process of key focuses. As I drop it, the ball drops very slightly into me, tipping a bit forward. This means that it'll spin a lot quicker, follow its point and I'm not going to kick it a long way. But the trade-off is it's going to be accurate.

The moment I hit it, I know I've given it enough. I look up and I know it's not deviating from its line – it's going straight through the middle.

And then I'm running back, half thinking we've won but also oh God, they've done it to us twice already, they've still got 30 seconds, don't let them take this away from us now. Not again.

Their restart goes to Trevor Woodman, who takes it like a seasoned full-back. We recycle it slowly, all eyes on the clock. Daws goes right to Catty, and this is the moment I could freeze-frame for ever. Catty smashes the ball into the stands and the referee moves to put his whistle to his mouth. The ball is in the air, we are on the brink of achievement, we don't have the victory yet but we know it's coming. This is the milli-second in which I'd like to live my life. Stop the clocks.

CHAPTER 14

IF you are a perfectionist and you have set out a goal, it can be a challenging experience when you finally achieve it.

The celebrations after Catty's kick are just incredible. I find myself running around in a circle, jumping up and down with Will Greenwood, shouting World Cup! World Cup!

A tidal wave of hugging and emotional outpouring is unleashed. Every single player and coach in the squad is out there on the field, totally consumed by the moment – apart from Mark Regan, that is, who has seen this as a very opportune moment to pull down Simon Shaw's tracksuit bottoms.

We do our laps of the pitch and I eventually find myself alongside Johnno, who drapes a long arm around my shoulder. Mate, he says, looking down to me, it's all been worth it, hasn't it?

After all those times of asking – Wilko, are you all right? – this seems to supply an answer. It seems to tie up the loose ends, to seal all those meetings, all those words on the pitch, all those experiences together. For once, I'm able to say you know what, I'm pretty damn good.

And I am, but it's not that simple. It never is.

I am now a World Cup winner. The stadium is an expression of everything I wanted. People are supporting me, cheering me, giving me their respect. But what happens afterwards? What happens when we all leave here? What happens when I wake up tomorrow?

The problem with reaching the peak of your tallest mountain is that there is only one way to go, and that is down the other side. Here I am, celebrating the achievement of my life's goals and yet I can't stop thinking it can only be downhill from here.

The next morning, I go down to breakfast and Neil Back is reading the papers. Of all the days to look at what's been written, I guess this should be it, but I can't. I go straight back to looking the other way.

●　●　●

I didn't read a single paper in Australia, so I have no idea what to expect when we get back home. But not even the guys who did read the papers expected anything like this. At Heathrow, after our early morning arrival, we wait in the pre-arrivals area and the security people tell us there are quite a few people out there.

Then we go through the doors and it's mayhem. Thousands upon thousands of people cheer us through. It is absolutely unbelievable, incredible, even a touch frightening. I had no idea it had got like this back here.

Yet I can't help but feel hugely embarrassed by it. I hear my name being chanted over and over by the supporters, and it feels great but terrible at the same time. I don't merit this treatment. I am so aware of all the mistakes I made in Australia and the way the guys cleared them up for me on the field. I can bring to mind instantly everything I did that was not good enough, yet so much extra attention is directed at me. I feel like a fraud.

● ● ●

Incredible though the reception is, I just need to get back playing. Most people might think it'd be nice to take it easy for a bit, but I don't want to. I want the opposite. I don't want to feel I am coming down the other side of this glorious mountain. It's like I'm riding a very big and dangerous wave and to stop and take too much pleasure in it all will bring me crashing down too hard. I want to stay on that wave, and to do that I need to play.

Four days after getting back, hidden away at the top of the clubhouse at Kingston Park, I watch Newcastle play Wasps. And I'm thinking I need to be on that field. I need to get back because I've got stuff to be getting on with. I'm scared. Time is going by and I'm already losing what I had and where I was.

For the sake of a quick, easy exit, I leave the match just before the final whistle, but when I get home, I find I have company. It didn't take the press long to discover where I live, and now I cannot go back to my house in Slaley without a reception of a car or three and some big paparazzi-type lenses waiting for me.

To get to my house, you have to go over a cattle grid and up a private driveway. A couple of times, they've parked right in front of the house, and Sparks has explained nicely that it's private property and they really ought to get moving. So now they park behind the cattle grid instead.

Our mate Chris Machin is currently living with us, and the three of us put into play a carefully planned operation, although there is probably a lot more fun in the execution than in anything it actually achieves. The next day, I return home from training, wearing a distinctive beanie hat and coat. A little later, Sparks leaves the house with Chris, who is now wearing the beanie and pretty much the same clothes I arrived in. They turn right out of the drive in his car and are followed for a few kilometres. Meanwhile, I leave the house in my car, head in the opposite direction and set about getting on with my life unperturbed. Nice bit of teamwork.

But on occasions, I do feel I'm being chased, which in a car isn't too smart. Sparks tends to take the wheel and I duck down low in the passenger seat, insisting that he cuts corners and hides in country lane laybys or people's driveways until the trouble passes. It's not simply that I don't want to have my picture taken; I don't want to give them a victory over me.

●　●　●

The aftermath of the World Cup continues long and hard and there are some truly amazing experiences.

We have the open-topped bus tour through London. We go to Buckingham Palace. A reception is held in Downing Street. The Buckingham Palace trip is particularly special, even if my abiding memory of it may turn out to be the fact that Ronnie Regan took time out to lie on one of the Queen's carpets in order to distract Simon Shaw into looking at his finger circle.

From the Downing Street reception, I get a taxi back up the A1 to Newcastle and I am on the phone to my friend Mike Latter when the car suddenly starts fishtailing at 70mph. It's only when I am looking up the middle of the motorway out of the backseat window that the panic really sets in. The car careers off the road and into a ditch. Both the driver and I are unhurt. The car is a write-off.

Sorry, Mike, I explain, bit of a car-crash situation going on here, mate. I'll probably have to phone you back.

A few days later, out of the blue, I receive a letter from Elton Flatley. It's a lovely note – congratulations on your victory in Sydney and well played, but we'll get you next time. I treasure that.

Everything right now seems a little surreal. It culminates at the BBC Sports Personality of the Year award, back in London.

I know I have a chance of winning because I'm on the shortlist, but I don't take it seriously. If it's someone from our team, it simply has to be Johnno. They do the top-three countdown and name Paula Radcliffe in third. But then Johnno is announced in second.

I don't believe it, because then they announce the winner and it's me. I make my way to the stage, terrified I'm going to trip over, and the first thing I say to Johnno is you should have won this, mate, not me. It shouldn't be me.

Just enjoy it, he says to me. Johnno, being Johnno, doesn't give a toss.

Of course, the award is an enormous honour. When I was a youngster, I craved adulation, but this experience here is not right. This is the ultimate example of me, an individual, being picked out from the team. To stand up here on stage beside my team captain, who led by example and took care of his entire squad and has just received second prize – it's just not right.

As the programme credits roll, this is what is going through my mind. I'm a fraud. This entire audience of hugely successful people are on their feet and the applause seems to go on for ever. I stare gormlessly at the camera, realising how tough it is to look cool and natural when you are really trying hard to do so. And there's another question in my head. How the hell am I going to meet the eyes of all the other boys after this?

CHAPTER 15

AT last, five weeks after the World Cup final and three days after Christmas, the wait is over. Newcastle versus Northampton Saints at home. I am able to be a rugby player again.

The pressure I put on myself is massive. My last game was a World Cup final and my performance here has to be at the same level. It's what I feel everyone is expecting of me. The way I see it is this. If I don't come up with the goods and prove myself to be worth all the praise, I'll lose this perfect situation for which I've worked so hard. I have defined myself as the guy who helped England to win the World Cup. Now I have to hang on to that reputation.

But then something else happens.

We are in the second half of a tight game when their centre, Jon Clarke, dummies and breaks our defence down the shortside, giving them a simple two-on-one. I've already seen the danger and am hurtling across from the openside, thinking I can catch him blind, unload into him without him expecting it. Uncontrollable aggression surges through my veins. These are the kind of chances I'm driving myself hard to take. I want to make the sort of impact that will change the game.

As I go in to smash him, at the very last moment, he steps in towards me. Basically, he catches me before I catch him and hits my head, compressing it hard against the top of my shoulder. After all the stingers over the years, after all the tests, the different diagnoses, the pinched nerves, trapped nerves and worn discs, it all finally gives out in one massive collision. The ultimate stinger. It's like I can hear a siren going off in my head, a blaring alarm. I can't hear a word anybody is saying to me. And with every ring of the alarm, a massive pulse of searing hot pain shoots down my right arm, which I cannot move at all.

After 30 seconds, there is no lifting of the pain. Two or three minutes later, I still can't get even a twitch from my fingers. I leave the field, but an hour later, still in the physio room, no strength has returned and I'm starting to panic. I'm suffering from a kind of paralysis. I'm told that in seven to ten days' time the power will come back, and so I wait. But after ten days, two weeks, I'm no better. It's lucky I drive an automatic car because to put my right arm on the steering wheel, I need to lift it up with the left arm. Then it just drops down again, completely lifeless.

So we convene a meeting – the England physios, the Newcastle physios, my dad, a surgeon and me. We talk about the options. Option One is to leave it as it is and, with no guarantee, hope that the strength will come back. But the way it's gone so far, that could possibly signal the end of my career. Option Two is surgery. Plenty can be done, but only when they see the damage to the nerve will they know the extent of the problem. At worst, the nerve is severed and that, for sure, is the end of my rugby career.

The decision isn't hard. I can't not have the surgery. And not for a second do I believe that my career is finished.

● ● ●

On Sunday, 15 February, England will play Italy in Rome and it will be the first game in the Five or Six Nations Championship that I have not started since February 1999.

Three days earlier, Mum picks me up from Newcastle General Hospital and a sneaky member of the paparazzi in the car park snaps me hunched over in pain. Not without a touch of vanity, I had prepared for the off-chance of this happening and taken off my neck brace. I don't want the whole thing to look too serious.

The worst news is averted. The operation indicated that an old, undiscovered fracture of the C4 vertebra was the problem. I am convinced that this takes me back all the way to 1997 and that Under-21s game at Headingley, although it could also be the London Irish game in 2001. Then again, it could be any of the other fifty or sixty stingers of my career. The point is that where the fracture healed, a bony spur – an osteophyte – had grown out of that vertebra and was pushing firmly against the nerve. The stinger against Saints had jammed it so far into the nerve that no impulses could get through.

So they took out the osteophyte and cleaned around it. Now it was a case of resting and waiting for the nerve to regenerate. No one can put a timescale on that – it'll do it at its own speed.

Later that day, I have had enough of this rest business. While making sure I am supporting my head, obviously, I have the brace off again and am doing a forty-minute aerobic session on an exercise bike at Slaley Hall. I can't stand not doing anything and feeling like I'm losing fitness.

● ● ●

Frustrated at the incredibly slow pace of recovery, I need to get away. Somewhere far away like Mauritius, but somehow word gets out. Paparazzi are everywhere and a picture duly appears in one of the English papers of me sat hunched over on a beach.

To make a point, the Mauritius photograph is compared with another, taken two years previously in Majorca, and to give credence to this then-and-now story, a 'specialist' is quoted in the paper, declaring that this picture shows me to have around 29 per cent body fat. By definition therefore I have suddenly become clinically obese.

I've been training hard since the day I was released from hospital, and am still pretty fit. I'm probably on about 10 per cent body fat, which is about 2 per cent higher than when I'm playing. The pictures focus mainly on my now withered right arm and shoulder and are a bit shocking even to me, but unless this is where I'm hiding the extra 19 per cent body fat, I think the 'specialist' nutritionist may have been having an off day.

This incident shows how much things have changed. I have never sought publicity, never been to a premier of a film, a dinner or a public event with the intention of boosting my public profile. I've been meticulous about that. That is a world I find really quite intimidating. It seems to be an environment where you actually have no say in how you are portrayed. To someone who wants to control everything, that is a living hell. But even avoiding all that, privacy has become a massive challenge for me. Against my wishes, I have become the business of other people.

So, back home, it's easy to say no when *Hello!* magazine comes knocking. They want the full Jonny-at-home photoshoot, probably lying back on various bits of furniture while wearing leather trousers and an open white linen shirt with the cuffs undone under a nice waistcoat. I don't even need to know what money is being offered. It's just not my thing.

Among the many other offers that come my way are the chance to endorse a range of Jonny dolls and the opportunity to appear with Keith Harris and Orville the duck, whom I used to watch as a boy, in a supermarket ad. These are not for me, either.

Hello! are very keen and offer £1 million. The answer is still no – not my style, not how I want to live my life, I'm not going to change my mind. But I make the *Hello!* cover nevertheless. They run a stock picture of me and concoct a story out of a bunch of old interviews. I guess you discover sooner or later that you can try to compete on that territory, but you will never really win.

● ● ●

I like the fact that fans write to me, and I am so keen to respect the effort they make and the support they give that, for some time now, I have had my mum helping me deal with the post. I try to answer genuine letters, enclosing a signed photo with a personalised message. What I do not appreciate so much is seeing the signed photo then being flogged on eBay. Sometimes you can even see that the personalised message has been scrubbed out in order to make it more widely marketable.

I am just getting my head round the whole eBay phenomenon. I've seen shirts on offer with the Jonny Wilkinson signature so badly forged; they haven't even tried to copy the genuine article. 'Johnny' spelled with an 'h' is a bit of a giveaway. I'm starting to receive letters from people who have bought a signed Wilkinson shirt at an auction, but found the signature wasn't mine.

How do you police this? How do you get a grip on it?

The problem is twofold. One, honest people find they are buying signed photos and shirts that aren't genuine. Two, I support five children's charities, which I care about passionately, and if the marketplace is being flooded with fakes, the value of the genuine items will go down and my ability to raise money for these charities is reduced with it.

Sometimes, when I'm signing autographs, someone will give me a photograph of myself to sign, and then hand me a whole lot more and ask me to sign those, too. I suspect I know where those are going, so I say yes to just the one. A minute later, I'll have a kid standing there holding out a load of the same pictures, and I'll say who d'you want me to sign these to? And he'll say I don't know. That guy over there just asked me to do this.

So, reluctantly, I've decided to stop signing England shirts. As a result, I get letters from people who are disappointed. One even threatened to take the story to the media. I say to them all I'll sign anything else, a Newcastle shirt, a Lions shirt, a ball, anything. I just need to be in a position to work out what signed shirts are out there and where they are coming from. That's why I won't sign.

The answer comes from Bren, my godfather, who has offered to help with this. Bren found a company in Chester called Sporting Icons, which was selling fakes of my signature. He got in touch with the police, who put him on to the Trading Standards department at Chester Council. They were interested in the case but progress was slow, so Bren played a masterstroke. He told them that there appears to be a considerable amount of fake Manchester United memorabilia for sale there, too. The case suddenly became more important and kicked into action. Watch this space.

● ● ●

I decide to address formally the process of re-evaluation. In a new notebook, under the title 'Onwards and Upwards [Blackie's favourite phrase] the next step', I write down my new goals.

First, under Goals – Personal:

1 Come back physically stronger, more powerful and in better shape than ever before.

2 Become the fittest player in world rugby, and continue to increase the gap between me and the next fittest player.

3 Lead the world of sport in use of speed and movement.

4 Improve all skills to lead world by a ridiculously inappropriate amount.

5 Continue to ENJOY playing more and more.

The next subtitle is Goals – Sparks:

1 Play alongside Sparks on a consistent basis.

2 Help Sparks to be the player and success that he wants to be.

3 Create a successful business environment or company together.

Then Long-term Goals – Personal:

1 Win the World Cup again.

2 Be selected for the British Lions 2005 tour and return as part of a successful team.

3 Continue to be the best-prepared rugby player in the world at any time.

4 Maintain a consistency of world-leading performance.

5 Reach the 100 Test mark.

6 Be the world's highest Test and points scorer.

7 Win more Grand Slams.

Then Team Goals – Newcastle Falcons:

1 Win the League.

2 Win it again.

3 Win the domestic Cup.

4 Win the European Cup.

5 Lead and effectively be the force of the club, along with Steve Black.

Then Other Goals Personal To Me:

1 Always be able to sign off the video from 24 hour surveillance camera.

2 Become a better, more developed, more mature person.

3 Learn fully the guitar and piano.

4 Become fluent in French.

5 Maintain all my values regardless.

● ● ●

I may now have goals. Naturally, I also have an intense anxiety about whether I can get to where I want to go. And as is my way, I decide to tackle that anxiety, to contain my fears, by working hard and inviting obsession to kick in.

I manage to construct a daily schedule whereby I'm in the gym for rehab at 9am. I'll also do a fitness session with Blackie and, from the end of February, when I find I can just about kick well enough, I fit in a separate kicking session, too. Basically, I train pretty much non-stop from nine till five every day.

My pledge is to come back better and I won't let it go, even if it means being distinctly economical with the truth with the people who are trying to help me. Blackie doesn't know that besides his fitness sessions, I am doing a whole lot more. And when he asks how long I've been kicking, I give him a number that might be missing a digit or so in a key place. Likewise, the physios don't know how much I'm doing with Blackie, and when my schedule dictates that I have a day off to take it easy, I go and kick at Darsley Hall, Newcastle United's indoor facility, so no one has a clue where I am.

The medics at Newcastle all tell me take it easy, don't do too much. And I say OK and then carry on doing the opposite.

The results aren't good. I get chronic tennis elbow in both arms and I have trouble with diet. The food I eat never seems to suffice. I eat and eat and eat but nothing fills me up. And I cannot sleep. If I go to bed at midnight, I wake up at four or five in the morning. If I stay up later and go to bed about one, I'm awake at five or six.

Deep down, I'm simply stressed and angry with what is happening to me. Most of the energy I'm burning is pure worry and that's what is waking me up so early, too. But I can't stop. My frustration and anxiety used to be channelled into rugby; this is the outlet it has settled upon instead. It's my way of keeping sane, although it also has adverse results. I am extremely fit but also unhealthy.

When I go to watch our home games, my regime is particularly strict. I go to Kingston Park and straight to the gym underneath the stand to get a session done. Then I change into my suit to watch the game, often in a box with some of our corporate sponsors, and at half-time, I'm back down to the gym for ten minutes' gym work and then back up again to watch the second half in my tracksuit. As soon as the second half finishes, I'm off down to the gym again.

That's my way and the regime doesn't drop for away games. It's just simpler. I need to be in the gym when the game is going on. That way I still feel part of it and I don't feel so much as though I'm being left behind.

People want to know if I'm going to be back and fit in time for the England summer tour to New Zealand and Australia. I have a breakfast meeting with Clive, but have to tell him I'm not ready. If there was any chance, I'd be there like a shot. Clive doesn't push it. Put rugby and England on hold a little longer.

CHAPTER 16

THERE'S a scene in the *Bourne Identity* series where the Matt Damon character explains how he can go into a bar and tell you immediately how many people are in there, which ones have got a gun, whether they are right- or left-handed and where the best escape routes are. I think I have now developed the same technique.

I can go into a café or a restaurant and immediately sense who has noticed me, who is likely to recognise me, who is carrying a camera, who is pretending to text on their phone but is actually using it to take my picture, where the best seat is so I don't get boxed in and what is my best exit option if a hasty departure becomes necessary.

Don't misunderstand me. I love having the opportunity to speak to rugby supporters, to talk about the game and the World Cup and all these fantastic things. And I think the passion and values of the supporters are really special. The energy that kids seem to have for the game, and the spirit they have to listen and learn, makes me feel that the future is in good hands. It's just that in public, non-rugby settings, I get embarrassed, and turn inward. Off the field, you see, I'm really no performer.

I have started to be apprehensive about being in those places where I can't control the situation. So I tend not to go to restaurants in town any more. It's a good thing I love country pub food, and around my way, a few places suit me perfectly – the Black Bull in Corbridge, the Travellers' Rest in Slaley, the Wellington in Riding Mill. I can go to any of these places and the people look after me brilliantly. They hide me at a table round the side or in the corner without the slightest fuss.

It's worse if I go to the cinema, a sports event or a concert. In those environments you're kind of stuck. I get very self-conscious, and feel like a sitting duck. When I do go to the cinema, I walk down the aisle head down, hat on, relieved if I can make it to my seat without hearing my name mentioned behind me. And during the film, in the dark, I'll be thinking mostly about my exit strategy at the end.

When Sparks and I go to see *The Last Samurai* at the Warner Bros in Newcastle, the whispering starts immediately we join the ticket queue. I notice one person lean in towards their friend's ear and say something. That person spends about ten seconds pretending to look around the cinema before turning round to stare straight into my face. Others are doing it, too, and in the end it just gets ridiculous and we just can't relax, so we go. We leave the cinema and go home.

It's Sparks and my other friends I feel most sorry for because it impacts on their lives, too. But Sparks just says OK let's go. He makes it really easy for me.

One of the worst situations occurs when I walk into a bar. It's the first bar I've been to for months and I have barely made it inside before the DJ announces my arrival to the entire club. My immediate reaction is a quick 180 degree turn and bolt for the door.

But the all-time most awkward situation for an introverted person like me was waiting to board an EasyJet flight to Newcastle. There is simply no match for this one. I am on the transfer bus to a plane that seems to be parked miles away. I sit in the corner of the bus with my beanie hat pulled low, feigning being totally engrossed in a book that I'm not really reading. I'm staring at the words while concentrating on every little sound around me. That's when it begins. One guy says that's that rugby bloke.

Oh shit, I think. I start praying that maybe there's another rugby player aboard. No such luck. I chance a look to ascertain if I have indeed been rumbled, and what I see is a twelve-strong stag party. It's barely ten in the morning but these boys have started proceedings early. They start to chant my name at me, loudly, and when we get on the plane, they don't stop. So everyone gets a look. And now I have my own special version of fear of flying.

And because of all this, I end up spending time elsewhere, away from public settings, in the countryside or just kicking on the Slaley Hall football field. That's not even kicking to get better. It's just doing something enjoyable when I know that, all being well, nobody else is going to be there.

● ● ●

For the start of the new season, I have finally been given the all-clear. I've got about 70–75 per cent of my power back on my right side and that is, officially, just about enough.

We go to Ireland for our pre-season tour. The first game is at Connacht, and I'm asked to pose for a photo on the halfway line with Eric Elwood and his family before the match, because it is his last season and he has been a great Connacht player. I respect Eric hugely, but I don't know why I need to be in his picture. I feel uneasy about it because the guy has been a legend in his career, and he's played for so much longer than I have and been through more hardships and come through them all. I feel my past invading my present.

I don't feel too comfortable with my kicking, either, and I start ringing Dave. I'm not sure about this, Dave, I say. Trust yourself, he says, it'll come.

I feel a huge sense of the unknown about my whole game. It seems I am the big story – Jonny's Big Comeback – and I feel that pressure, but I'm missing the old sense of familiarity. When I last played rugby, I'd strung together three Test matches on a full Lions tour, more than fifty games for England and God knows how many for Newcastle, and so I'd developed momentum. Instinct and innate confidence told me that experience would carry me through, even on the not-so-good days. Now I haven't got a clue where I stand.

Rob Andrew keeps telling me it's going to be six to nine months before I start feeling like I'm back where I was, but I think that's bullshit. He doesn't know how hard I've been working. And I pride myself on being the exception to this kind of accepted wisdom.

Actually, I have no idea how right he is.

We start off the league season against Worcester and we win pretty well. I feel I've lost a bit of the feeling I had for where the defence is and where my teammates are. But everyone is happy to put the responsibility straight back on me and, as ever, I am all too keen to step up and take it.

I am also starting to feel an intense pain in my right bicep, which gets worse and worse with every tackle. We look for ways to protect it. We try strapping, padding, everything, and I try to use a different part of my shoulder to make the hits, but nothing helps.

Then we come up with a new solution – bubble wrap. We wrap it, layer it thick and tape it over the top. Being me, I decide to test it hard immediately. I make one big tackle on the training pitch and I drop to the ground in agony.

● ● ●

I haven't played rugby for England for nearly eleven months, but now I'm the captain. Andy Robinson was appointed head coach after Clive resigned, and he asked me to do the job. Of course, I feel immense pride, but I also have to face a press conference.

Beforehand, the England press chief, a guy I've got to know really well, Richard Prescott, says here are a few things, so you can be prepared, and he puts down a bundle of press cuttings, the kind of newspaper stuff I haven't read for a couple of years. I start to read and am immediately staring at them in horror. Is this really what people are saying about me?

What is he captain for? That's the tone of it. If he's captain, that means he's got to play, but he's not even the best number ten. He's not playing very well, he shouldn't be playing.

This is a nightmare, like someone's implanted a virus in your mind that's going to breed and breed. Richard says that not everyone's writing this stuff. Really just one guy, Stuart Barnes, is driving this agenda, but I should be prepared.

It's difficult not to take it personally. The words jump off the page as though they are being said with venom. It's been written for the public, yes of course it has, but deep down it feels as if the writers would like to know that I've read it, too.

It's so strange. I'm trying to be the best I can be, get back all the match fitness I need and contribute to the teams I play in. I'm definitely not trying to stop anyone else playing for England, and I'm definitely not out there saying I'm the best, you should pick me, forget about so-and-so. The thought that I'm in the team when I don't deserve to be, and I'm trading on some former glory, to me that concept is horrendous, absolutely horrendous.

●   ●   ●

In a tight match against Saracens, I hit a last-second drop goal to draw the game, and the media is rampant with 'Jonny Does It Again' stories. They couldn't be further from the truth. I feel frustrated as hell with my game, and the pain in my arm is becoming unbearable.

I line up a tackle on Hugh Vyvyan, their number eight. He used to play for Newcastle so he knows full well how I love to go in for the big hit. At the last minute, as I launch forward, he sticks his head down low and hits the exact spot on my arm. The sudden flash of pain is worse than anything I've ever experienced. I feel physically sick.

I stutter through the rest of the game, fiercely protecting the arm, but there is no longer any hiding the fact that something is clearly wrong.

Rob asks me to come to a meeting and states the obvious. You can't go on like this. This is so tough. I've barely been back. I am England captain and I am having to make my own decision to step away from it all again to get myself right.

So I'm back to the medics and specialists, the numerous tests and the X-rays. We get to the bottom of the problem, which stems from the muscle wastage as a result of the neck injury. The sheer number of hits and bruises on the exact same spot means that blood has been pooling on the bone beneath the muscle, and started depositing bits of calcium. The tiny shards of bone deposits within the blood have joined together and moulded on

Left: My first England cap and the realisation of a massive dream.

RUGBY FOOTBALL UNION
The Lloyds & TSB International **TSB**
ENGLAND v IRELAND

SAT 04 APR 1998   Kick Off 02:00 PM   04 04 98   W9 26 227

WEST STAND GATES 3 & E,F

WILKINSON J   TEAM Entrance W9   Row 26   Seat 227
LOWER   £0.00   COMP   **A**

NO REFUND WILL BE MADE ON RETURNED TICKETS

The Lloyds TSB International **TSB**

The Rugby Football Union gratefully acknowledges the support of Lloyds

This team was accurate at ... Thursday, 2/4/1998

15	Matt Perry (Bath)	Full Back	Ciaran Cla... (Terenure ...)	
14	Mike Catt (Bath)	Right Wing	Richard Walla...	
13	Will Greenwood (Leicester Tigers)	Centre	Kevin Maggs (Bristol)	13
12	Jeremy Guscott (Bath)	Centre	Mark McCall (London Irish)	12
11	Austin Healey (Leicester Tigers)	Left Wing	Denis Hickie (St. Mary's College)	11
10	Paul Grayson (Northampton)	Stand-Off	Eric Elwood (Galwegians)	10
9	Matt Dawson (Northampton)	Scrum-Half	Conor McGuinness (St. Mary's College)	9
1	Jason Leonard (NEC Harlequins)	Prop	Reggie Corrigan (Greystones)	1
2	Richard Cockerill (Leicester Tigers)	Hooker	Keith Wood (Harlequins) CAPTAIN	2
3	Darren Garforth (Leicester Tigers)	Prop	Paul Wallace (Saracens)	3
4	Martin Johnson (Leicester Tigers)	Lock	Paddy Johns (Saracens)	4
5	Garath Archer (Newcastle Falcons)	Lock	Malcolm O'Kelly (London Irish)	5
6	Lawrence Dallaglio (Wasps) CAPTAIN	Flanker	David Corkery (Bristol)	6
7	Neil Back (Leicester Tigers)	Flanker	Andrew Ward (Ballynahinch)	7
8	Tony Diprose (Saracens)	No. 8	Victor Costello (St. Mary's College)	8

Replacements
16 Phil de Glanville (Bath)
17 Jonny Wilkinson (Newcastle Falcons)
18 Scott Benton (Gloucester)
19 Dean Ryan (Newcastle Falcons)
20 Danny Grewcock (Saracens)
21 Graham Rowntree (Leicester Tigers)
22 Dorian West (Leicester Tigers)

Replacements from
Kilian Keane (Garryowen)
David Humphreys (Dungannon)
Brian O'Meara (Cork Constitution)
Michael Galwey (Shannon)
Eric Miller (Saracens)
Nick Popplewell (Newcastle Falcons)
Peter Clohessy (Young Munster)
Ross Nesdale (Newcastle Falcons)

Score	Tries	Cons.	Penalties	Drop Goals

Referee
Derek Bevan (Wales)

Touch Judges
Joel Dumé (France)
Didier Méné (France)

Left: An England team full of legends, and me.

GARY M. PRIOR/GETTY IMAGES

DAVID ROGERS/GETTY IMAGES

Above: My first touch as an England player ... and as a winger.

Left: Playing 12 against Scott Gibbs and Blackie's Wales at Wembley.

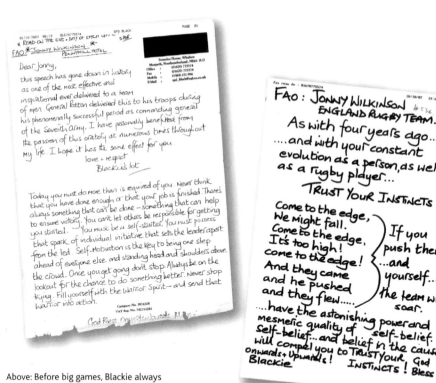

Dear Jonny,

this speech has gone down in history as one of the most effective and inspirational ever delivered to a team of men. General Patton delivered this to his troops during his phenomenally successful period as commanding general of the Seventh Army. I have personally benefited from the passion of this oratory at numerous times throughout my life. I hope it has the same effect for you.

love + respect
Blackie's lot

Today you must do more than is required of you. Never think that you have done enough or that your job is finished. There's always something that can be done – something that can help to ensure victory. You can't let others be responsible for getting you started. – You must be a self-starter. You must possess that spark of individual initiative that sets the leader apart from the led. Self-Motivation is the key to being one step ahead of everyone else and standing head and shoulders above the crowd. Once you get going don't stop. Always be on the lookout for the chance to do something better. Never stop trying. Fill yourself with the Warrior Spirit — and send that warrior into action.

God Bless. Onwards + Upwards. Blackie

FAO: JONNY WILKINSON #536
ENGLAND RUGBY TEAM.

Fax reçu de : 01670775574   18/18/07 19:18 Pg: 1

As with four years ago....
....and with your constant evolution as a person, as well as a rugby player...

TRUST YOUR INSTINCTS

Come to the edge,
We might fall.
Come to the edge,
It's too high!
Come to the edge!
And they came
and he pushed
and they flew.....

} If you push them ...and yourself... the team will soar.

....have the astonishing power and mesmeric quality of self-belief. Self-belief... and belief in the cause will compel you to TRUST your INSTINCTS! God Bless Blackie Onwards + Upwards!

Above: Before big games, Blackie always knows the right things to say and the right words to say them with.

Right: Blackie. He is, has always been and I know will always be there for me.

Far right: I owe my performances to Blackie, he really is just that good.

Below: In the gym with Blackie and Sparks. A very common theme during my life.

CHRISTOPHER FURLONG/GETTY IMAGES

MARC ASPLAND/THE TIMES

JED WEE/NEWSCASTLE RFC

Perfect technique
... Dave's that is.

Above: Dave gets another taste of my frustration.

Below: The best kicking coach in the world or not,
Dave always has time for a joke.

Above: I have really leaned on
Dave when the pressure hits
home. Here before the South
Africa pool game in 2003.

Left: An amazing feeling to win the Tetley's Bitter Cup. Even better to do it in the last minute.

Below left: I learned so much from playing alongside Inga.

Bottom left: Desperation stuff with one of the hardest and most courageous in the game, Jamie Noon.

Below top: Trying out some of the Blackie footwork.

Below middle: Another of those comebacks. This time down in Gloucester.

Below bottom: A rare show of emotion as I land a last-minute drop goal to seal a game at Kingston Park.

Top left: Getting an offload away and getting smashed for my troubles in Bloemfontein, 2000.

Top right: One from the corner in the RWC 1999.

Middle left: Here I am making a break against France in a very baggy version of an England shirt.

Middle right: World Cup 1999 and the big one against a very good All Black team.

Left: The Centenary Test in 1999 versus Australia, and legends Tim Horan and George Gregan.

NICK WILSON/GETTY IMAGES

WILLIAM WEST/AFP/GETTY IMAGES

GETTY IMAGES

Top left: Lions, 2005. Trying to get free but there was always a Kiwi defender, or two, nearby.

Top right: Blackie was the Lions' fitness conditioner and we really hammered the footwork drills. Here it is paying off.

Above: It's not often you get a shot on the great Richie McCaw, so I gave this one everything.

Left: Bagging a five-pointer in the deciding Third Test in Sydney.

Below: Lions tours are a good place to make some real team men. Here are two of the best, Brian O'Driscoll and Rob Henderson.

SCOTT BARBOUR/GETTY IMAGES

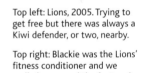

DAVID ROGERS/GETTY IMAGES

Above: When future teammate and inspirational Toulon captain Joe Van Niekerk runs, he runs hard.

Right: Defence was our team's number one priority under coach Phil Larder. I loved that approach.

Below left: Bloody, battered and really, really happy. A Grand Slam will do that to you.

Below right: I get to lead the team against Italy in 2003. There is no bigger honour.

Left: Mike Tindall helps me deal with the swirling wind during our victory over New Zealand in Wellington.

DAVID ROGERS/GETTY IMAGES

Below: One of my favourite matches on tour in Australia, 2003. A tough place to go and win, but we did it.

DAVID ROGERS/GETTY IMAGES

Below: I never stopped thinking about rugby and goals as a kid. I never stopped as an adult either.

Movies, Sport,

Favourite movies Predator, Platoon, Leader, Good morning Vietnam, Asterix in Britain.

Favourite sport Rugby, 2nd Cricket, 3rd Football fourth hockey.

I am now at Pierpoint School and playing fly half for the U13. Our kit

G.Hastings

Penalty

to the humerus. The medical term for this is myositis osificans. The result is that, whenever I take impact on the arm, the muscle is being shredded over these pointed bone deposits, causing more bleeding and inflammation. The remedy is largely pharmaceutical plus, sadly, another two months off.

The thought just destroys me. I have two teams that I am part of and yet absent from. At Newcastle, I can't train, just spectate. I don't feel part of the club. And England is even worse.

● ● ●

England's big games of the autumn season are against South Africa and Australia. Before the South Africa game, I sit in the Twickenham physio room, just around from the changing room, listening to the noise of studs on the floor, the players shouting, people vomiting in the bin, the sound of pre-match anxiety and energy. They are sounds I know so well and I naturally feel the buzz and the energy, but I'm sitting here in a suit, with nowhere to release it.

I am England captain, but today Jason Robinson is doing my job for me. Being here like this is just horrendous.

Andy Robinson suggested that I should be down at Pennyhill during the week. It would be good for the troops' morale, we agreed, and also sensible for me to keep in close proximity to the squad, so that when I'm fit, I can click straight back into it.

The problem is I haven't been involved in the England set-up for almost a year. I don't feel massively part of it, so trying to come in and have this rousing effect isn't easy. If I was on the field with them, it would be totally different, but I feel a bit false, a bit of a pretender, and I suspect that comes across to the others.

Before the game starts, I go out to my seat in the coaches' area, and it's nice to sample the atmosphere of the big game build-up. Normally at this point, when I'm playing, I am so completely absorbed in my preparation, I don't register anything that's going on. It is interesting to see what actually happens. But the moment I sit down, the cameras turn round to find me. And then there I am, my face up on the big screen.

When the game starts, the cameras keep panning back to me, but only, it seems, when Charlie Hodgson does something. Today, he does a lot. He runs the game brilliantly and I am genuinely happy for him – fantastic bloke, great player. He deserves all the praise. The cameras constantly seek my reaction, but I'm not an extrovert, or demonstrative, so I'm not going to be jumping around, like Clive used to, because Charlie's just scored ... again.

As England's victory becomes increasingly assured, I find myself sinking deeper and deeper. Eventually, I desperately want to go home so I can try to work out why I'm hurting so much inside.

I'm not really convinced I deserve the captaincy anyway, but it's so hard to sit there and take a game like this. I'd like to be an absolute saint and say I am 100 per cent, unconditionally happy for the guys. But I can't help thinking what does it mean for me? If the team is playing so well without me, where do I stand as England captain? To be honest, I feel a little embarrassed.

The following week, because the South Africa game confused the hell out of me, I try a change of tack. Around the players, far from helping, I feel a bit of a hindrance. So I keep more of a distance from the team. I don't go in the changing room beforehand. I go to the gym instead. I can't do a work-out because of my injury, so I talk to Calvin Morriss, one of the fitness coaches, and shoot a few basketballs around with my one good arm.

Walking up to my seat, the fans are so warm and friendly, but when they barrage you with comments such as don't worry, Jonny, we still love you, or you'll get your place back soon, it doesn't exactly help.

After the game, which we lose, narrowly, I do go into the changing room, just briefly. I want to commiserate with the guys and let them know how much I respect them and all their efforts. We had come so close to a great autumn. But it doesn't feel quite my place to be here among these players who have given everything and are now shattered and beaten up inside. I'm not remotely convinced I deserve to be here. It's simple. What I need to do is change that fact. I need to play some more rugby.

● ● ●

If you are stuck in hospital and cannot move, and the nurses need to prevent bedsores, you are sometimes given silicon padding. This bedsore technology saves my career. Silicon padding works wonders for my arm. Unlike bubble wrap, which seemed to intensify any impact, the silicon soaks it up.

With rest, intensive medicine, numerous blood and urine tests and the new silicon padding, I am back on the bench for Newcastle in December. I get an hour of a game against Leeds, which we win, and my full comeback is against Sale and Charlie Hodgson, which causes a predictable stir. We snatch victory right at the end when I score a last-minute try under the posts. So all is going well. What a great feeling to get through a game without any pain.

Perpignan is next, in the Heineken Cup, and disaster strikes. We are a little behind, and I try to make an outside break round one of their forwards, who just manages to grab the back of my collar. As he does so, the studs of my right boot are stuck firmly in the turf, and as I'm pulled back over my right knee, I hear a big pop come from the inside of it.

Clearly, something's happened, yet the pain is only a throb, nothing major. I don't know much about knees. Knees are my strong point. When the physio suggests I get up and try a little jog, the knee wavers left and right as if the upper and lower leg are merely balancing on top of each other. There is no stability whatsoever.

I watch the rest of the game from the bench, feeling desperately low. Why me? Why me again? And how many weeks or months of rugby am I going to miss this time?

By the end of the game, the pain is worse, and Martin Brewer, the physio, is a bit more urgent about it. So Andy Buist, another knee-injury victim, is kicked off the physio bed and told to sit on the side so I can take his place.

From there, we are kindly taken to a local hospital, which is closed for the night but the Perpignan doctor gets opened especially for me. The scan shows a tear in my right medial ligament, grade 2/3 – no surgery required but a good eight to twelve weeks out. In that moment, another Six Nations campaign is completely wiped out.

Two days later, we discover that Andy Buist is far worse. He has anterior cruciate ligament damage – surgery definitely required and six to nine months out. Buisty is younger than I am, but he doesn't have his foot in the door or special treatment, like I do, and he certainly has a far harder road back.

Not only am I struggling with another injury, but I am horrified that I kicked him off the physio bed like that. My self-importance needs reassessing. I can look in the mirror and see it. Everything right now is about me, and even if it is mostly based around fear, I don't like what I see.

● ● ●

On the phone to Andy Robinson, I explain the situation, and he agrees and, as ever, he seems to understand. For the Six Nations, I won't come down and hang around the team any more. I just can't be that close to it.

What I don't say is that me being around the England team wasn't helping Charlie Hodgson, either. He was feeling added pressure and responsibility, which was completely unfair and made it harder for him to relax into the role. I would probably have felt exactly the same. As soon as I got wind of that, I knew I had to stop going down.

I make one exception, though, when England spend a day training with the Leeds Rhinos. I love rugby league and these guys have just won the Superleague Grand Final. The opportunity to meet players like Kevin Sinfield and Keith Senior is not to be missed.

What really strikes me is the quality of the coaching. A whole morning's session is spent working on how to catch and pass – not lineouts or scrums, which may take place twice or twelve times in a game, but this very basic skill. We catch and pass throughout every single game we ever play, and simply take it for granted.

For passing, they accentuate the use of the high leading elbow, which gives you a barrier against defenders who are aiming to smash you, and a sharp limb, which is harder to smash against.

For catching, they accentuate the position of the hands round the ball, so you are immediately ready to deliver the next pass. They get us throwing rubber rings to each other to work on how to move our hands to get them in the optimal position.

This is all coaching from the school of Dave Alred and Blackie. It's not a case of you need to work on your basic skills. It's more this is how you do it. It's not you need to improve your performance in this area. It's this is how to improve it.

I just wish I was able to make use of all this by actually playing.

● ● ●

By mid-March, the Six Nations campaign is nearly over, and on the horizon is the British Lions tour of New Zealand, led by Clive Woodward. I want to be on that plane.

First, I need rugby, regular week-in, week-out rugby. Rob Andrew tells me that he doesn't think I need any time on the bench as I did last time. He says I'm going to put you straight back in.

This is music to my ears. I didn't much like being on the bench. I start against Quins down at The Stoop, and it feels pretty good, great to be back. I love the energy and buzz of it, until just after the half hour, when it happens again.

Quins make a break and feed inside to their prop. Coming across, I fly in and smash him on to his back and immediately try to contest for the ball. Simultaneously, someone tries to clear me out of the ruck, but slightly from the side, and I feel the same right knee and the same popping sensation. My head is sticking out from the ruck, our bench are only 10 metres away and I just yell at them. I think I've done it again.

I have now played seven games at the start of the season, one and half after my arm injury and less than a half after the knee. I am soon back on the bench, reeling with sheer disbelief. This is plainly ridiculous. There is no suggestion whatsoever that I have come back too quickly. If anything, I'm two weeks behind schedule. It is pure bad luck.

So I have to start at the beginning again. Scan, six weeks out, a slow start, rehab. I find quite quickly I can get running again in straight lines, which gives me a slight lift. And the sympathy around me actually buoys me up this time. I find I can function off this how-unlucky-am-I identity.

Then I get a call from Clive. He wants to take me to New Zealand but he won't name me in the squad. If I can get fit, though, I'm going.

But the person who really keeps me inspired is Blackie. With Blackie, I work from a different identity altogether, the one where I work so hard I can tell myself that I'm working harder than anyone else. That's the identity I love.

When we can't work my leg, we put everything into the upper body. I shuttle from the gym at Blackie's house to his son's commercial gym near the coast, where they have some great machines – upper-body grinders, the Grappling Rope Machine and the fearsome Dyno, a hydraulic contraption where the harder you push, the more it resists.

Whenever it seems I might be getting a bit lost, Blackie instinctively finds a way to re-engage me and bring the very best of me back to the fore.

●　●　●

I have been injured so much that, for Newcastle, Sparks has actually started to take my place on the field. When anybody else steps in, I can't contain that selfish nagging fear. I can't help but wonder what does this mean for me? Will I get my place back? But I purely and genuinely want Sparks to do well. I feel this so strongly I become like a parent, and find it almost impossible to watch him. Playing on the same team as Sparks has been the best experience of my career. I find it devastating that his real breakthrough has coincided with my eternal life in rehab.

When I'm finally fit again, I'm on the bench for a game against Northampton Saints and Sparks is playing at ten. I get on for an hour, and we are involved constantly together. We lose the match by a point but I love the game.

We finish the season away at Gloucester, one of the most atmospheric and vibrant grounds in the country, where the fans pride themselves on the coolness of their welcome to the visiting teams. But when I go out on the field this time, I get a warm round of applause.

Please no, please don't applaud me. Please don't treat me like an old friend, please don't give me any charity. I feel intensely awkward. I'd rather be abused than cheered. All my playing life, I have wanted to win respect, but I never wanted it this way. I want to earn it.

Fortunately, I play well. I'm right in the thick of the game throughout. We lose but I play the full 80 minutes. I have now strung together two and a half games of rugby and it might just be enough to make me a British Lion again.

CHAPTER 17

I make my first mistake as a new Lion before I have even checked in.

Before leaving for New Zealand, the 2005 Lions meet at our team base in the Vale of Glamorgan Hotel outside Cardiff. When you arrive in a new environment, as this is, among different people, it's important to make a good first impression, and naturally you feel a sense of trepidation. My slight problem here is that I have been away from the game for so long that I don't know a lot of the players, and worse, I haven't even played against them. I used to be an avid rugby watcher and do loads of video analysis. I used to know pretty much every player inside out. But in all those months out injured, I found I couldn't bear to watch any more, so I just switched off from it all.

I am still at the hotel check-in desk when a guy next to me says hi Jonny, how are you doing? I glance at him and say fine, thank you very much. I'm not rude or dismissive. I'm trying to be polite, the way I always am with supporters. It's only later that I realise I have just fobbed off Eddie

O'Sullivan, the Ireland coach, who is the backs coach on this Lions tour.

My first Lions roommate is Shane Horgan and this is a particularly good start. He has an awesome sense of humour, and our connection is boosted every evening when we religiously settle down for *Celebrity Love Island*.

As a squad, we are faced with a new innovation for the Lions – a Test match before we have even left home. We are, almost by definition, a bit short on preparation, having only just come together. We're a bit like the Barbarians, but without the luxury of lack of expectation.

The Argentina side we play may not be quite full strength but they are a good team, very good at disrupting and challenging for the ball in the tackle, especially out wide, good at turning over our ball and kicking a lot of goals. That puts pressure on a team that isn't ready for it yet, and I end up, on the buzzer, with a 40 metre kick from the left to tie the scores.

The ball goes over, thank goodness, but that was an unsteady start. Despite some good moments, we need to find some chemistry.

I am not exactly sure what to make of this. Was it a good day or a bad day? The word afterwards is that this was a good way to start. We have a frame of reference, something to build on.

● ● ●

We fly to Auckland, which is our base, and we haven't been there long before Clive says to me come on, let's go out for a drink. We go to the bar just over from our hotel for a Diet Coke and a chat.

Clive tells me I feel you need to get the enjoyment back into your rugby.

This is a pretty astute assessment. Maybe he can tell simply from my body language that my purpose has changed. Before 2003, and all the way to the World Cup, I was on a mission with my rugby, on a journey somewhere.

I was trying to fulfil my goals and scale the mountains of the international game. The enjoyment then was in the pursuit of that fulfilment. Now, it's a very different game I'm playing. After all the injuries, I'm just trying to hang on, wanting to get back and keep going in my perfect-world rugby. And it's a fight, a battle for the game and for my career, and Clive is right. There is very little enjoyment in this for me.

I tell him yes I know, but I basically don't feel like I'm ever going to be the sort of person who can smile while I'm playing. It's just too serious for me. There's too much riding on it.

Clive says OK, but on the same note, it would be great if you could really try to enjoy this for what it is. Away from the rugby, get out of the hotel and do something different. There are a lot of activities organised for the players. Don't be afraid to take a day off here and there to engage in some of it.

But I can't seem to do much of that, either. My kind of release is getting out of the hotel in the evening, walking across the port to a newsagent's where I can browse round the shop, buy myself a couple of Diet Cokes and some snacks and then get back to my room to chill and watch a film.

For some people, these tours have a slight holiday element. They find time for a little bit of holiday besides playing rugby. For me, even when I'm on holiday, I still train like mad. But when proper rugby and matches are involved, like now, I can't take holiday time. I can't justify it to myself. There's always something I can be doing to improve, to help me make these games go right.

Nevertheless, I know that Clive is absolutely right.

● ● ●

The set-up Clive has created here is certainly impressive. We've got iPods with specific tour songs loaded, we've got a wealth of information about

227

everyone in the squad, which I should probably have read earlier, the kit is brilliantly done, and we've got a code of conduct. And we haven't got just security, we've got three great guys from the SBS. We cannot be accused of lacking attention to detail in our preparation.

What I find different here from the old Clive is the extent to which we are going out to make friends with the local media. Previously, with England, we were constantly labelled as boring or overrated, we were nicknamed Dad's Army or Orcs on Steroids and we laughed at it. We didn't give a shit.

Here, though, there is a change of tune. We are giving the media more time, letting them get to know the Lions and our ethos, and really trying to get them and the locals on our side. I don't recognise that from Clive.

My experience is that it's a mighty tough battle to try to win over the opposition press. I think it doesn't matter how nice you are, they'll still write whatever they want to write. And if we manage to come over as nice blokes, is that going to make any difference to the rugby?

There's only one way to gain respect here and it's not by being nice guys. It's by playing hard and competing out on the field.

● ● ●

So much for good intentions. We have been in New Zealand a month when we line up for the first Test in Christchurch. The rain is so bad it's bordering on the conditions of Scotland 2000, and the gulf between the sides is so great that although we lose 21–3, we should go down by 35 points.

I am selected at inside centre with Brian O'Driscoll, our captain, outside me, but he lasts barely a minute before he is off with a dislocated shoulder. Inside me is Stephen Jones, another player I have a huge amount of respect for, but we've only played in this combination for part of one game, against

Wellington. I was excited about playing twelve. I've always enjoyed being a decision-maker in that position, with a little more time to organise moves. But here, that is barely a factor. Here, defence is the main aim.

But under pressure, we don't react as a team; we react individually. We get sucked into the ball. At times, you could throw a blanket over almost our entire team. We don't defend with any structure, so we get pulled apart. And New Zealand play so well that, on occasions, it seems like a team run for them. We fall for everything they do. We are cannon fodder.

I find myself trying desperately to spot where the real danger areas are for us, and a few times I end up as the last man in defence with four or five black shirts in front of me. That's when you resort to running in and trying to pick off the pass receiver. You need to stop him, man and ball, but it's so helpless I get frustrated and very fired up. I start looking for big hits everywhere, whether they are on or not, to try to change the game. I don't know how else we are going to achieve anything. But that's last resort stuff. Out on the field, I feel insignificant because there's nothing I can do to help. And I've never really felt like that before.

● ● ●

When you do your press interviews before a Test match, you always say how confident you are. You let the media guys know that if we play to our best, we've got a good chance of winning. Before the second Lions Test, in Wellington, I do say all that, but for the very first time in my career, I'm not sure if I really believe it.

We are about to play a team who are really firing. They have just beaten us 21–3, this time it's going to be a dry game, and the Lions have found no chemistry at all.

Mum and Dad are in Wellington and when I hook up with them, that's exactly what I tell them. It's a strange situation to be in, thinking that unless something miraculous happens to a number of parts of our game, we are going to find this very difficult.

With England, we always had confidence in our basic structure, so that even if we played absolute rubbish, we could battle to the end of the game and either hang on to a lead or fight for the winning score. We don't seem to have that here.

On the 2001 Lions tour, we had chemistry and just clicked. We don't appear to have that here, either.

We've had six and a half weeks to get to a level where we can beat the All Blacks on their home soil, but found no answer to the question of how to make the best use of that time. We've still not achieved the deep-down, real understanding of what we're doing. No one is quite sure who is leading the charge. Between the four home nations, we've mixed things up and we're not really sure what we're supposed to end up with.

So the second Test is even worse. We score first but then find ourselves facing a team so tight and so together that we'd need an extra two or three players on the pitch to stop them. When the All Blacks have finished with us, they are 48–18 ahead and after attempting to seek out more and more game-changing tackles, I have been taken off with concussion.

I have also been re-acquainted with a horrible old sensation – the burning pain of a stinger that I'd hoped I'd left behind with my neck operation. This one goes down my left side, like a red-hot cord being pulled tight inside my arm; and in bed that night, when I turn over, I pinch the nerve again and wake up feeling the red-hot rawness over again. This is not good in any way.

During the week, the slightest twitch triggers it off. And that's me, out of the last Test, a touchline bystander, watching the tour on its last lap of pain.

● ● ●

During the last week of the Lions tour, I phone Inga, who is now an Aucklander, and am invited for an evening with his family. We go out for dinner and have a lovely evening. Afterwards, Inga drives me back, and as we sit parked outside the Lions team hotel, I have the chance to ask his advice, as I've been wanting to do.

I tell him I'm really struggling here. I'm not enjoying this any more. I feel like I'm just trying to survive. Rugby, for me, used to be about what you can do and what you can achieve, but now it's about trying to come back and meet expectation, and then carry on keeping your head above water to the end of your career.

It's Inga I want to say this to because he's the guy who had the smile on his face when he played. And he was different from me. He could try something on the pitch and if it didn't go well, he could handle it. Some of what he did was jaw-droppingly good, but he didn't feel a need to be perfect. And although he may not have had goalkicking duties, he still bore enormous pressure because Newcastle used to rely on him so much every week.

My world is now just confusing and frustrating. I'm used to chasing goals. And I'm used to a set-up where day after day, game after game, you just get in there, stick at it and things more or less turn out OK. Now I'm seeing it from a totally different point of view, and there doesn't seem to be a moment when I sit in the changing room and smile reflectively upon my day's work. So I'd value Inga's opinion.

He tells me you can't go on like this. This is no good, this whole no enjoyment side of things. You can't afford to play rugby like that. He says to have faith in my ability and that I've got to go out there and show it to people and celebrate it with the way I perform on the pitch. That is what rugby is for, a celebration of your skills and a chance to demonstrate what you are all about.

The thing is, I'm a perfectionist with an obsessive mentality, and after feeling like I had it all with the 2003 World Cup victory, I'm left with a fear of losing everything I've achieved. I'm never going to change anything.

CHAPTER 18

ON holiday in Majorca, before I go to the beach each day, Chris Machin does his reconnaissance patrol. I've never asked him to do it, but he's simply good at looking out for me. He walks up and down the entire beach a few times and then gives me his report. There's a suspicious situation over that way, there's a camera over there and there's a guy with a long lens in the bushes next to the rocks, who has been taking photos.

Unfortunately, people are making money from waiting for me on the beaches. This is my holiday, my annual break with Sparks and some of the boys. We've been coming to Majorca for years, since Sparks and I were three and four, and it now requires a Machin patrol before we can properly chill. I can measure out the changes in my life by my Majorcan holidays. Step by step, my Majorcas have changed every single year.

On certain beaches in some of the busier resorts, we used to have competitions between the group of us – Sparks, Mach, Ian Peel, the Newcastle captain, Pete Murphy and me – on the inflatable doughnut rings pulled along by a speedboat. We had to queue for the ride, and in 2002, it started to get a little awkward. Wearing just a pair of shorts, I felt self-conscious when a load of people I didn't know started to stare. Worse still, I worried about what they thought of me. For some reason, their judgement of me really mattered.

Then, in 2003, pre-World Cup, the first of the cameras started turning up. Strangers stared more, alerting other people to me. I'd still stand in the doughnut queue, but I'd take off my shirt at the last minute, stand with my arms folded looking away from the crowd and then dive straight into the sea and hide as soon as the boat pulled up nearby.

Last year, I just didn't bother to go.

Now I'm back, but we go to some other quieter beaches, really beautiful beaches that are frequented by Germans and Spanish, who are not so big on rugby. But we still need Machin's patrol and, for me, the doughnutting is finished. If the boys want to go to the doughnut beach, they go without me.

● ● ●

Majorca has been great for me in many ways, one of those being that it provided me with the opportunity to meet Shelley. We've been in the same group of friends since 2003, but it's now, on holiday in 2005, that we properly get to know each other. Sun, sea and sand provide the perfect setting in which to discover the truly best parts about someone, and it has become undoubtedly our favourite place to spend time.

During this particular trip, a group of us decided to venture out to a pretty town called Deia. Our aim was to find a brand new beach on which we could eat our freshly packed picnic. In the end, we found a beautiful but stony one with an enormous rock protruding from the sea for jumping off. The next day, Mach brings home a copy of the *Sun* and opens it up to find, clearly displayed in three photographs, snaps of Shelley, some of the boys and me. Although they managed to find us at our idyllic hideaway, they didn't get a photo from the right angle to show the nasty Eighties ponytail I was sporting that day as a joke.

The *Daily Mail* went one better and there, on page 3, is a big picture of us all playing cricket in the shallow surf. Shelley, fielding at silly mid-on, I believe, seems to have acquired a speech bubble saying 'Hands off him, he's mine!' Another of our group, Anette, also has a speech bubble, which says 'No, he's mine! I saw him first!'

This is a good early lesson for Shelley, allowing her to see the reality of life in the public eye. It was also a good one in collateral damage for Anette, who was simply offering up her own version of Norwegian left-arm medium pace.

● ● ●

I'm still not signing my name on England shirts, but progress has been made and Trading Standards officers have been round to my house to see me.

They have recently made a raid on Sporting Icons, a high-street shop in Chester. Apparently, so many items were seized, there was enough to fill two transit vans. And they found a bunch of photos of me signed, another batch unsigned and a felt-tip pen on the desk with the lid off.

They want to show me some of the stuff to verify whether the signatures are genuine and I am slightly concerned that, when I see them, I may not be able to tell. But I should not have worried. Unless I signed these while drunk, with my wrong hand and my eyes closed, then there's very little chance of them being my handiwork. It is just ridiculous.

● ● ●

A new season approaches and, as with every new season, I go into it with fresh hope and the same uncontrollable ambition.

For our pre-season, Newcastle go on a mini-tour to Japan. Not long after arrival, I do a kicking session at the end of which I get my weirdest autograph request to date. I have, in the past, been sent pictures of some guy posing naked with my head superimposed onto his shoulders, and asked to sign them. I have been sent pictures of other people to sign – Iain Balshaw, Josh Lewsey and even Michael Owen. Here in Tokyo, though, at the end of this kicking session, I am asked to sign someone's dog. I refuse to sign the dog. I don't think I could ever sign a living creature, and anyway its hair is too long. I don't see how I would ever get the writing to line up.

That night, though, is notable. We go out as a squad for an evening of exploring the city and end up in a trans-sexual bar. Interesting. Then, early the next morning, we are woken up by the sensation of our hotel shaking due to what we later discover is a full-on earthquake. And then, most significant for me, by breakfast time I am carrying a shocking stomach pain that I cannot shake off.

I shuffle down to the dining room half bent over, feeling terrible. That morning I just about struggle through a press conference with John Kirwan, the Japan national team coach, who is a hero of mine, but afterwards it is clear I need to get to the local hospital.

There they do a scan and the diagnosis is that I have 'compacted stool'. I am fairly hesitant to explain to my teammates the news that this is what I have been making such a song and dance about.

However, the tablets I've been given don't work. Two hours later I'm back in hospital asking for further help. They do a CT scan and then tell me look, we're really sorry, we've misdiagnosed it completely. You've got appendicitis.

● ● ●

By the start of the league season, though, I am just about recovered. A course of antibiotics was deemed a preferable solution to surgery for my appendix and I am now ready to start the new season where we are away at Sale.

We play well, so well that the last play of the game is a kick from the left corner to win it. This is what all the training is for. These are the moments that will stick with me for the rest of my life. So the pain of missing is desperate. I hate missing it. I want to rewind time; I want to take it again. I stay outside on the field for as long as I can in silent protest, but the truth that I can never seem to accept is that it's done and that's it. Move on.

After the game, I travel down to London to meet Shelley. This is the first time I have seen her since Majorca, yet the thought of that final kick remains twisting and turning in my mind. As soon as I'm back in Newcastle, I'm outside at Kingston Park, putting myself through an impromptu, soul-purging kicking session, taking every single kick from the left-hand corner.

After that, I go straight to tell Martin Brewer that I've got that pain in my appendix again.

● ● ●

No messing about this time, the appendix is swiftly removed. A month of the season is lost, but I recover quickly and soon I'm starting again – again.

I feel so proud to be a part of this Newcastle team. We have developed a pattern – begin the season well, start to struggle as the winter weather kicks in, improve with the arrival of spring and the dry running conditions. When we are struggling, some snap decisions are made and some new signings arrive, and we get the impression that it isn't always Rob Andrew who has the final say on who comes in. I start to wonder if it isn't down to Dave Thompson, the owner, and whom he has been reading most about on the internet.

The issue is we never really have size in the forwards, so we have to find other ways to compete in the winter months. The result is a training regime run by Blackie that is about as impressive as any I've ever been a part of. All of us love the training. Speed, movement and skills are emphasised, and having a structure that means the number on your back becomes largely irrelevant.

When we get it right, it feels great. We play Leicester at Welford Road, a really tough place to go, and I just about survive a tackle from their scrum half, Harry Ellis, where he dives at me while I am taking a clearance kick and flies in at my planted leg. But the point is that we earn ourselves a draw yet we play so well we know we should have won.

Harry's hit on me could easily have broken my leg but my studs released their grip on the turf, thank goodness, and I went flying instead. It's nice to escape an injury for a change because there is an autumn international series on the horizon and I am determined to carry on this run of games. In fact, I am so determined that I choose to ignore the growing pain in my groin.

I start to feel a wrench there whenever I begin my kicking, but I don't want to get it checked, so I don't tell Martin Brewer about it, or Blackie or Sparks. I don't want them to tell me I need a rest. The way I see it, the problem might go away of its own accord. When I kick, especially on my right foot, the first few are really sore and then, after eight or nine, it's not so bad.

We play Gloucester and then London Irish, but the groin pain isn't easing. In fact, it has become permanent. Time to bite the bullet, and suddenly another entire autumn series disappears before my eyes. Mentally, I am finding this really hard.

● ● ●

The diagnosis is not great. I've retorn everything that was repaired in my first groin operation five years ago. On top of that, I have torn a big part of my adductor muscle. I need another hernia repair operation plus a tenotomy, which involves cutting the adductor cleanly so that it can reheal perfectly.

The tenotomy is the most painful operation I have ever had. When I come round from the anaesthetic, I literally fight off the nurses because I am half-conscious and in complete agony.

What do I do now? Focus on the Six Nations. That is my target, but even that will be tough. Maybe not the start of the Six Nations; maybe I can get back halfway through. My goals are slipping. Everything is slipping.

I have the operation in mid-November and, in the new year, start training with Newcastle again, but it's a case of one step forward, two steps back. As soon as I try any sideways or unpredictable movements, I feel the groin tear slightly and have to wait for that to heal before I can train again.

This starts to form a cycle and is desperately frustrating. One day, when I'm back training with the team at Darsley, I break the line with just scrum half Lee Dixon to beat, but as soon as I side-step I feel it go. I just hand the ball to Dicko and walk to the end of the hall, sit down next to the ice bucket, grab a load of ice and start icing it. It's no longer a surprise. It's not even anything to make a song and dance about. It's just a case of there it goes again, that's another two- or three-week step backwards. The Six Nations slip out of the frame of possibility.

So I go for more scans and discover a big hole in my adductor muscle. The best hope I have of playing any rugby before the end of the season is to undergo an intensive course of herbal injections – three at a time, every other day, high up on the inside of the groin. Painful and unpleasant. Plus another occasional injection to draw out blood from the hole in the adductor.

Improvement is negligible and it's getting to the stage where I can't see light at the end of the tunnel. It's now clear that I might never find my way back to where I want to be.

● ● ●

When I am fit enough to kick, I go for sessions on my own at Darsley and I am so desperate to get it right, so driven by the annoyance and fear of not getting it perfect, that the anger I feel inside begins to express itself physically.

I don't know what it is, but my frustration is so intense I start shouting at the walls, screaming obscenities. But I punish myself for my mistakes too. When my left foot lets me down, I stamp down hard on it. At one stage, I am so livid that, before I know it, I am sinking my teeth into my hand, trying to bite right through the skin between my thumb and index finger. It immediately starts bruising, the pain is intense.

Imperfection, knowing that I still can't master what I am doing after all the time I've spent on it, all the effort, all the sacrifices and the heartache – it just makes me so angry at myself. In my mind, I have visualised perfect outcomes of every kick, but when my practice doesn't match that, I have to take it out on something, so I start tearing my T-shirt apart. This becomes habitual; I start getting through way too many T-shirts. I'll be alone in Darsley, wearing half a T-shirt, my voice either hoarse or completely gone because of all the yelling, and a bruised left foot – all purely because I have let frustration get the better of me again.

By the end of a long kicking session, I will invariably have found my way back to an acceptable skill level, and with my sanity thus restored, I look at myself and wonder: what the hell am I doing?

● ● ●

I have now been injured pretty much solidly for two years, and could hardly be further from fulfilling my life goals. Everything feels so far away now. Toby Flood is playing ten at Newcastle, Charlie Hodgson for England, and they are good players playing good rugby. I could not feel farther from the field. I no longer feel needed or valued. Everything I have done and become is fading and I am failing in every way. My natural instinct is always to attack the situation, but the enjoyment and desire just isn't there any more. My mind is fighting me.

The frustration is finally starting to take a serious toll. Sleeping is a problem. Graeme Wilkes, the Newcastle doctor, gives me the sleeping tablets I ask for but they don't seem to work.

For the first time ever, I seem to have lost the drive. Motivation has fizzled out. My fiercely obsessive mind, which has always given me the upper hand on the pitch, has latched on to this negativity and turned on me in a bad way. The negative thoughts won't stop. My obsessiveness, my most powerful asset, has become my undoing.

My mind is way too active to allow me to sleep, but then I don't feel I can get up and face the day. I don't want to face the pressures I put on myself, or the expectations that I feel are constantly placed on me, which I know I can't meet. I feel torn in half.

I don't know what to do. I start turning up late for rehab sessions; some of them I miss entirely. I never would have stood for this sort of behaviour before.

And I can't escape. There's simply no way I can concentrate enough to read a book. The thought of the effort it would take I find depressing. And when I watch TV, I take nothing in. I can watch a two-hour DVD and all I see is the outside of the screen and some flashing images on it. I don't even know what the storyline is.

My mind is totally preoccupied with anything it can find that is negative and destructive; and it causes me to feel panic and my heart to beat quicker. My obsessiveness has vacated rugby completely and started to drive my thoughts downwards, tossing endless dark, nasty images through my head.

● ● ●

To try a new tack with my groin problem, I go for a week's residency at the Olympic Medical Institute, a specialist centre attached to Northwick Park Hospital in north London.

One of the exercises is to run against a strong current in the pool. The idea is to run for as long as you can, and if you don't run hard, you just get swept to the back of the pool. This is the kind of a challenge I usually relish. The old me would be asking what the record was then flick on the Tunnel Vision switch and drop into that zone where pain and tiredness get blanked out – like training with Blackie, or the England cone test. It's what I do, my way of showing the world that I'm too strong, too hungry and too proud ever to be beaten.

But I don't really want to be here in this pool, and I am acutely aware of every kind of tiredness. On the side of the pool, the phyios and trainers bark all the usual motivational stuff at me. Come on! You can do it! That sort of thing. Who are these people? I don't know these people. They don't know what I'm going through. They don't care.

I fight the current as hard as I can, but I get pushed to the back. I try again. Same thing.

This isn't me. It's like someone else is doing it. It's like so many people I've watched over the years who have looked for excuses to give up. Here, I guess, I'm doing the same.

And I'm compounding the problem. Every time I try to fight the current, I say to myself come on, you can do this. But I know deep down that the message is an empty one and I do even worse, and that makes me feel even more pathetic.

Suddenly, I stop. I give up. I can't do it. I have hit the wall — breaking point. I have barely completed one and a half days out of seven, and I've been late for pretty much every session. I can't be here for another second.

I get out the pool. I apologise to the staff at the hospital. Sorry, it's nothing to do with you guys, I just can't do this. I get in the car and drive home.

● ● ●

On the way back up to Newcastle, I phone Graeme Wilkes and apologise to him, too. Besides all this inner turmoil, I still feel I have let people down.

I have a meeting with Graeme when I get back and he and the physios are positive with me. They say we'll work on something else instead. We'll give you some other rehab. But I'm not helping them. I don't get out of bed in the morning. I sleep three or four hours and wake up with pounding-heartbeat panic attacks and a sense of urgency that something has gone badly wrong. But nothing has gone wrong. It's just another day when I'm injured.

In one rehab session in the gym, I'm doing some lifting with the dumbbells on a Swiss ball. The dumbbells feel really, really heavy. Around me, the gym is full of jolly people, laughing and chatting, and I'm struggling with these dumbbells and questioning it all. What is it I am trying to achieve by lifting bits of iron in the air like this? How can all these other people be so happy?

I put down the dumbbells and walk out.

The next day, I go to see Graeme Wilkes again but this time I let it all go. I don't talk to him about my groin. I tell him about my head.

Graeme is a fantastic guy, a very good doctor and the right person to be saying this to. He says what I realise I need to hear, that I have an illness. It's like any other injury but this one is in my head rather than in my leg or my arm or anywhere else.

He is very, very good to me. He explains that my illness is controlling everything else and working on the groin injury is far secondary to sorting out my head. There is no point in my groin getting better if I don't sort out my head anyway, because that issue is much more severe.

● ● ●

Merely to know that I have an illness that is not abnormal is like a first weight off my shoulders.

Graeme refers me to a specialist, but the connection isn't quite right. I need to feel completely comfortable to deal with this.

Not long afterwards, I am at a dinner in London. I don't normally do dinners, especially not the way I'm feeling right now, but I have been asked to attend almost as a secret, to present a surprise award to Richard Hill. I love doing that, and Hilly is special to me. I want to be at this dinner.

In the midst of the evening, I find myself deep in conversation with another player, whom I have known for a long time, and because I am acutely aware of what is happening to me, I am on the brink of sharing my story with people, putting little feelers out in conversation. When I mention that I'm struggling a bit, a door swings open. This player opens up and tells me he had massive problems, too. Here is the proof that, thank God, I am not completely alone.

He tells me his story and I latch on to every detail. I feel great respect for him, to know that he has dealt with this for so much longer than I have. So I tell him my story, and he gives me the London telephone number of an American therapist, David Carter.* He tells me that David is the guy he spoke to, a great guy, funny but engaging. For me, he says, it really worked, so just try it. And that's how I start.

Back home in Slaley, I ring David, although I feel hesitant. One of the first things he says to me is you just need to realise you've got an illness. He informs me that this illness is the cause of the depression and the panic attacks, and it has a cure. You're not doomed, he says.

I enjoy hearing him say that. I need to know I'm going to stop feeling like this, I say to him. I need to know that I'll get back to being my normal self again.

After that, I speak with David regularly, once a week for about an hour, always on the phone, David in his London office and me from the home phone in Slaley. I often ask for a second weekly appointment, and I take notes, furiously. The irony is not lost on me. It may have been my obsessive nature that drove me to my low point, but I intend to be extremely obsessive about finding my way out.

For instance, one time David gives me an exercise — write down every new thought topic that I'm obsessing about, how it's affecting me and how I could look at it differently. So I do, spending a day and a half on it, and when we are next on the phone, I tell him I've done a hell of a lot. So we spend

---

* This is not his real name, which has been changed for reasons of privacy.

the entire hour going through it, and as the session comes to an end, we've covered two pages. What, I ask him, am I supposed to do with the other six?

After just a few sessions, it's clear to me that this is big, way bigger than winning the World Cup or trying to be the best player in the world. But this is what I'm made for, isn't it? Back against the wall, facing a huge challenge that look insurmountable. That's how I see it. I'll just have to give it everything, the way I used to love to do.

● ● ●

At the end of the season, my groin allows me back. I play three games, two halves as a substitute followed by 70 minutes in a good final-match victory over Leeds at Kingston Park.

Out there on the field is the only time I seem able to live in the moment. It allows me to escape from everything and I grab these playing experiences keenly. They are so important to me that I don't want to let them go, and I try to hang on to them for as long as I can. So after the games, in the changing rooms, I sit there, still in my rugby boots, while everyone else changes.

Playing rugby makes me feel a bit better about myself; it gives me back a bit of self-worth. And sitting there in my kit extends the feeling. I know that changing means having to face up to what I know is waiting for me. It's like taking off the cloak of invincibility and going back to reality.

It's probably not hugely healthy to do this. I know that. I know it's going back to my old values, my old self. But until I have found the new identity, I can still derive great comfort from the old one.

● ● ●

When I talk to David, he often says oh yeah, I know what that feels like, I used to do that, too. Often, when someone tells me their story, I feel like it could never be as bad as what I'm going through. But some of David's stories make mine pale into insignificance. I really try to listen to him and learn. I have to retrain my brain to see things in a more helpful way.

For many years, life has been relatively simple, one season blending into another, an upward curve of playing rugby and gradually accruing more success. My identity was written in facts – this many wins, this many caps, this many points, these awards, this World Cup, these Lions tours – and these facts produced evidence to show that my values were right and were never to be messed with.

And my values were so dogmatic, so set in black and white. I decided what was right and what was wrong, what was professional behaviour and what was not, who deserved to win and who didn't. I could go out on the field and say I'm better than these other guys because I've worked harder, given more, care about it more.

But in this state I can't work harder and I can't be the best, and two years of that pushed me to breaking point. Under the scrutiny of my own values system, I was faring terribly.

I explain to David my anxieties about losing everything I had worked so hard to achieve. I tell him my fear of not playing any more, and he mentions a great quote, from the founder of Buddhism. 'The secret of health for both mind and body is not to mourn for the past, worry about the future, or anticipate troubles, but to live in the present moment wisely and earnestly.'

This shocks me. What an incredible thought. And it makes so much sense to me, especially when I think about playing rugby. Before games, I am dying from thoughts of what might happen and what might go wrong and my need for it to go perfectly. Afterwards, I'm no better. I can destroy myself with ceaseless reflections on what I could have done better and how that might have changed the course of the game.

I tell David I want to know more about this and he gives me some reading. I speak to Blackie and find, not surprisingly, that he knows all about it.

David starts throwing in other references. He talks about Gandhi, Jesus and other iconic figures – not preaching, just telling me about their philosophies and how these incredible people, these powerful leaders, have been dealing with the same stuff as I'm now facing for thousands of years.

And I consume it all hungrily. It's clear to me that I have to be honest with myself, and acknowledge that I have to look beyond rugby and achievements and facts that you can find in a stats book. I am being forced to find something deeper. This is a massive turning point for my life, the start of my spiritual journey.

Increasingly, I am inspired by Buddhist philosophy. I want to understand more about who I am and why I seem to be fighting against the world I live in instead of working with it. In order to do that, I realise I need to learn more empathy, and be more flexible with my views and my values. My whole life has revolved around piling on layers of achievements, trying to be the best, wanting people to respect me the most and seeking perfection. I figured all these things would protect me and make me strong, but ultimately they have made me so much weaker. I find a connection with Buddhist philosophy. Just shed the layers, go back to the beginning, stop viewing everything I do in comparison to others.

I won't kid myself. I know that I will always be as nervous as hell before a game and as frustrated as hell after it. But at least I can see a way to a healthy perception of the world and my place within it. I can now see that there is something far deeper, more important and more lasting than the game or myself.

* * *

I am now treating two injuries simultaneously. My head and my groin. I might have been able to make contributions to three end-of-season games, but the groin is a managed injury rather than a mended one.

We arrange for me to go to see a specialist in Bergen in Norway called Peter Sorensen, but first we have to do some filming for him. He wants to analyse my movement, to see me running up and down in straight lines. That is fair enough, except what he wants is to see me running almost entirely naked, wearing nothing but a pair of pants and some trainers. I travel out to Bergen and show the video to Sorensen and, within seconds, he knows more or less what the problem is.

He asks me some questions about key repetitive movements. He asks me to go through the goalkicking movement again and identifies the problem. As he sees it, to ensure that my follow-through and my body weight shift is in a straight line, I am deliberately preventing my body from rotating. By doing that, I am keeping my right adductor really tight, to fight against the body's natural urge to rotate.

The problem is that my glute muscle which works antagonistically to the adductor has now been rendered useless and has switched off. It should be working with the adductor, as a pair, but the adductor muscle is taking all the workload and getting hugely tired, and that is why it keeps giving out.

Sorensen is a genius. He explains: The solution is to get your glute muscle working again properly. This is key to my recovery.

● ● ●

My conversations with David guide me in the right direction, but there is no overnight quick-fix solution to depression. There is no eureka moment when I think I've cracked it.

I experience some big highs, but there are some heavy losses on the journey, too, when I feel I'm sinking even lower. In Majorca, on what should be a holiday, I struggle badly. I go for hour-long walks round the streets with my mobile phone clamped to my ear and David on the other end.

But I also know that I am achieving something. I'm finding a deeper understanding that I consider to be my spirituality, and that is more important than my achievements on a rugby pitch. And I do just start to feel a real strength for once, as though I'm finding a little bit more of myself again.

As the new season approaches, I have a better idea of how to manage myself, how to control my obsessive switch. I know that as soon as the game approaches, or when I hit the field, I can flick the switch on and be my old self, the person who can't stand losing and will go to every extreme to help his team win. But I have to learn to switch it off when I leave the field. I have to be able to say to myself you know what, there's something deeper than the game. Leave the regrets behind.

The World Cup in 2003 was my moment of perfection, the realisation of all my goals. Since then, I've been trying to cling on to who I was and what I had. Now I have a different view of perfection, one that lies within intentions, not outcomes. I cannot let outcomes define me, for good or for bad.

Of course, all that is easier said than done, but at least I know what I want to do.

CHAPTER 19

THE start of the 2006–07 season is another fresh start. What is this, the sixth?

I go into it with so many new and important messages of my own, but a familiar one from the outside is take it easy. The Newcastle coaches and physios have been telling me that almost ever since I arrived here. Try not to over-stretch my body. Don't overtrain. This time I have to listen and be more responsible.

Easier said than done. That is one hell of a challenge. I derive strength from pushing the boundaries. I'm the guy who believes that if I train harder, I'll be better. Generally, my rule of thumb is if they give you a training session, do it and then do some more, stretch it further. And here I am, having to take it easy.

It plays with my peace of mind. For every game I ever play, my intention is to prepare exhaustively. I want to know that I have every single base covered, every box ticked. Only when I have ticked them all do I have the mental equilibrium to go into a game. Now I have to change my entire game plan.

OK, I say, I'll try it. But it feels so uncomfortable.

Pre-season goes well. Then in our first Guinness Premiership game of the season we play Northampton Saints away and lose by two points. I hate that. But I am playing again. This is what I'm supposed to be doing, right?

Next up it's Worcester at home and it happens again. Which part of the body? A knee. Left knee. Even as it happens, I am making my own diagnosis because I have done this before now with the right knee. Twice.

It's all so mundane. We knock on and I dive on the ball. I don't even need to do this because the referee is in the process of blowing his whistle anyway. Meanwhile, Andy Buist is tackled off the ball, and he lands on me. Andy is a big second row (ironically enough he is the guy I chucked off the physio bed a while back), and that's when I hear the pop. It's exactly the same pop I have heard before, and I lie there with this harsh ache, this deep throbbing pain, thinking I know where we are. This is my left medial. What grade is the tear? Probably two or three, which means no surgery and eight to twelve weeks out.

In the medical room under the stadium, lying on the physio bed, I can hear the oohs and aahs of the crowd as the game carries on without me. There's nothing much anyone can say or do. Sparks and Shelley come in to see me. How does it feel? Is there anything you need? Anything we can do? But they pretty much know the answers. Everyone does. They can tell by my face.

It's not as though I'm a boxer who's been knocked out for the first time. I'm used to picking myself up off the canvas. Yes, I'm pissed off, hugely. But after so many injuries, I'm just a bit exhausted by it all. I'm not asking 'why me?' any more. I'm asking what am I going to do about it? How am I going to respond and get fit again?

It's not the pain that's hurting; it's knowing what lies ahead. Two or three days later, back home, the weird, depressing, fleeting excitement of the injury is gone and I have a ten-week recovery plan staring me in the face. And again, I can contribute nothing to my rugby club. After a week or so, I will start to filter back in to the club, where I will be forced to watch other people doing what I want to do and what I need to be doing – playing rugby, moving forward and improving. I'll watch them training, being part of the team. This is the worst part. It is so tough to deal with.

And yes, I was right. A medial tear, grade two. My way out, as ever, is to draw up a programme. My salvation is my training schedule with Blackie, his son's gym in Tynemouth, his own gym, the upper-body grinders, the grappler and the Dyno, and the thought that if I can build my upper-body strength, when I come back, I'm going to be stronger and my tackling is going to be better. This is the positivity that keeps me functioning. The alternative is to sit around, waiting for the knee to heal, which is apparently what I'm supposed to do now. Don't overtrain, don't overdo it. But I just can't do that. I have to keep moving, or I'm afraid I'll fall apart.

●　●　●

When Matt Burke first arrived at Newcastle a year ago, I was surprised by him and by his training habits.

Back then, I was hugely judgemental. I had views on what was and wasn't good enough, professional enough, what was right and what was wrong. I could not deal with the idea that other players might come to games with what I saw as a lack of commitment or preparation.

When Matt arrived from Australia, outstanding full-back, 81 caps, a guy I had heard so much about, I was really excited. But I noticed that he wasn't doing that much kicking, or all the training, and I concluded that he was obviously not the guy I thought he was.

But my new spiritual pathway has opened my eyes and helped me to take a different viewpoint. I have tried to be more empathetic towards other people, less judgemental, more understanding, and now I start to see the situation for what it really is. Matt has had goodness knows how many operations and problems with his body, and what he has been doing is learning from these issues. He has been carefully managing himself, and his abilities, working in a hugely professional way. Everything is directed towards getting on to the pitch at the weekend, with confidence, and playing like a god out there.

He is an example to me, much more professional than I am. He provides another great lesson about my old dogmatic take on life and how flawed it is.

● ● ●

Every game I play now is viewed as a 'comeback'. That's what the media, the club programme, the people who ask if I'm playing again call it.

What I'd like would be to play a game without that attention or those expectations. I do all that training and preparation, but a part of me still doesn't quite know what it's going to be like. I don't have the reassurance of repetition, playing week in week out, and so knowing that I can do this. It's eight weeks since the Worcester game and we're playing Bristol. I'm feeling nervous about it and everyone is watching me, watching another comeback. I'd like to play this game without anyone in the stands or the pressbox, but that's not the way it works. I'm the guy who kicked the drop goal that won the World Cup, and now I'm the guy who can't play without getting injured, so people come to watch. They want to see if I can still do those drop goals and whether I'm going to get injured again. That's two reasons to see me now.

A feeling comes from within the club – Jonny's back, throw Jonny in and we should be all right. That's a further weight of expectation.

For me, the picture has changed significantly. I no longer have a list of life goals, and I no longer have that ambition to be the best player in the world. 'Best in the world' is subjective. It's just an opinion and everyone is entitled to their own. But I'm not interested in dealing with opinions. Rather than being the best in other people's minds, I now want to be the best I can be in my own. That doesn't mean I expect anything less from myself, quite the opposite. There might be expectation from outside with every comeback, but it will never match the almighty pressure from within.

The game actually goes really well, and my enjoyment of it is helped massively by the Bristol full-back. At least, I think it's the full-back, because he hits me so fast and hard I haven't exactly got time to check. Midway through the game, I take a high ball. I don't think anyone's chasing, so I take it standing still. The guy I haven't seen absolutely smashes me. It's a good hit, really good, and I'm winded, so I wander over to the wing, trying to look nonchalant, just for a brief recovery. Now the adrenalin is really pumping.

It's funny that, in rugby, people try to target players in the opposition without knowing what reaction that's going to provoke. You hope that if you smash someone, he'll take the hit, feel the pain, decide he doesn't like it and withdraw into his shell. With me, an attempted hit has always been like stoking the fire, and if you actually get me, well, that means trouble. I enjoy feeling that there's no other option but to fire back. So I take a hit like this one and think right, now I'm ready. I don't mind it at all.

Thereafter, I really fling myself around. I enjoy the game, we win comfortably and I get man-of-the-match, which is nice, although I'm sure they are just being charitable. Afterwards, I am reacquainted with that bashed-about feeling. It's a satisfying feeling that lets you know you've put your body on the line. It feels good, although it certainly hurts.

I have a shower and get changed, feeling a bit dodgy. My stomach still hurts. The next day, we are preparing for a Guy Fawkes party at home, nothing big, just a few of the guys coming round, and I'm feeling worse and worse, hobbling round the house and garden, looking for wood and anything else I can throw on our bonfire.

The day after that, I can only just drive my car. I literally creep into the club and shuffle down to the physio room to tell Martin Brewer about the hit I took in the game and that I'm still struggling. Within no time, I'm off for a scan, and another doctor, with furrowed brow, is clearly trying to work out how to break the bad news. This time it's the kidney. The kidney! I've never heard of a kidney injury.

It's bad, I'm told. The kidney has ruptured and if it had ruptured a couple of millimetres more, it would have started to leak all those toxins into my body. It would have started to poison me and I would have had major problems, emergency surgery time.

The reason I haven't heard of this kind of thing in rugby is because this is an injury you get in car accidents, not rugby matches. If you crash your car and your lower abdomen thumps against the bottom of the steering wheel, your kidney can rebound so hard into the ribcage that it can get punctured by your floating rib. At least, so I am informed – which says even more about the quality of the tackle on me.

So I have effectively been in a car crash. This is so ridiculous. What's wrong with my body? At the club, I'm back to being the centre of attention for all the wrong reasons. This time my contribution lasted just 85 minutes. It's horrendous.

Martin tells me to do nothing for three weeks. Nothing at all. Just a little bit of walking. Other than that, absolutely nothing.

For my new spiritual self, I need to look beyond the injury and make the most of the opportunity that life has afforded me. This is an invitation to clear out, get away from the club, get away from it all. So Shelley and I take off as soon as we can for Thailand. Courtesy of a friend, we go to a stunning villa right on Kata Beach. It's beautiful, luxurious, really hot, and we have a housemaid. I follow Martin's instructions to the letter. For about ten days.

After ten days, I'm hot, feeling OK and itching to get going. I can't sit around doing nothing. I get moody and irritable. So I try some exercise in the pool. Shelley asks me what on earth I think I'm doing, and I tell her I'm just testing it out. She says I'm not supposed to, but I carry on testing it out. Shelley tells me to stop, but I don't.

Deep-water running is good exercise. You are effectively cycling in the water, and it tires your body without putting too much strain on it. That's what I tell myself. I set myself sessions of thirty lengths, once or twice a day. I know this isn't the deal. I know I'm not supposed to overtrain. But rehab, training – this is my drug and I need it.

When we get back home, I see Martin and tell him I lasted two and a half weeks before starting to exercise. He gives me a right bollocking. I don't know what he'd have said if I'd told him the truth.

● ● ●

Sometimes, I think I'm starting to get the hang of this business of being a public figure, but at the BBC Sports Personality of the Year awards, waiting to go on with Nick Faldo, I feel completely the opposite. I used to be terrified of audience participation. When I was a kid and we'd go to the pantomime, I used to squirm in terror at the thought that I might be picked to go up on stage. This is no different.

I have done quite a few of these events now. The first time I really got exposed to a new branch of celebrity was at the 2004 National Television Awards when I found myself in an environment so foreign, it would have been like one of these soap stars walking into a rugby dressing room. Strangely, I suddenly wished I'd paid more attention to the gossip magazines because then I'd have known who these people were. I had to present an award, which put me totally out of my comfort zone, and straight afterwards I went backstage to be greeted by the cast of *Coronation Street*, but I didn't know a single one of their names.

The same year, I was presented with a prize at the GQ Men of the Year Awards, and despite receiving it from Boris Becker, who is one of my big idols, I felt massively uncomfortable. One of the awards was presented by Katie Price and Peter Andre, and I thought I must be lost, I am definitely lost. As soon as dinner was finished, I had no hesitation in deciding that it was time to go.

Some TV shoots and posing in public places have made me cringe with awkwardness. Hackett, with whom I loved working, got me pretending to kick a ball over some famous London landmarks – wearing wellington boots. That barely compared with another Hackett photo-shoot, which involved me sitting on one of the lions outside Buckingham Palace. That was another shocker.

Now, at the BBC Sports Personality of the Year night, Nick Faldo and I are about to present Team of the Year to St Helens rugby league club, and I'm feeling more uncomfortable than ever. We are backstage, waiting to go on, and as we wait we listen to David Walliams and Matt Lucas, who are on stage presenting another award, and they are being hilarious. They are absolutely killing it out there.

When they come off, we spend a minute with them and they make me crack up, but I think their humour has a strange effect on Faldo, because he turns to me and says maybe we should do something funny, too.

Be funny on stage! What is Faldo thinking? Spontaneous stand-up comedy in front of this huge crowd plus a TV audience of millions? What the hell does he want me to do? My heartbeat is racing, I can feel my body overheating and I've got such a panic attack going on that I'm actually thinking about saying I can't go through with it and doing a runner.

But I do go through with it and my panic isn't justified. Faldo doesn't try to be too funny. In fact, he's clearly pretty experienced at this and handles it all rather well, managing to exclude me almost completely, thank God.

One thing I do enjoy is meeting Kieron Cunningham, a fantastic player who is built like a huge cube of brick, and some of the other St Helens boys. And I do know for sure that the stage is not a place where I belong.

CHAPTER 20

THERE was a time – and we are talking six, seven, eight years ago – when I would know the dates, times and details of every England squad selection. I would know at roughly what time of a certain day I might get to hear if I was in the squad or not. But those days are long gone. Now I don't know when the England coaches are meeting to talk about selection. It is not even on my radar.

So I'm quite surprised, a couple of days into the new year, when I get a call from Brian Ashton, the new England coach. I haven't played any rugby for over two months, I have only played two and a half games all season and Brian has a question for me – do I feel capable of coming back and playing for England?

The problem is whether I feel right about it or not, whether I feel remotely unsure about meeting the expected standards after over three years away from international rugby and hardly any club rugby in-between – I am never going to say no. I would do anything to represent my country. It's been over three years and I want that wait to end. Yes, Brian, the answer is definitely yes.

At last, I'm at the end of a long journey. That's the bigger picture, but I can give it only the merest glance and then move on. The moment my name appears on the squad list for the Six Nations opener against Scotland, my immediate reaction is to go straight to the checklist in my mind. What do I need to think about? What do I need to work on?

I guess I should sit back and enjoy the moment, enjoy the significance of this journey's end. Many people said I would never play for England again. Yet even now, I guess I don't do enjoyment. That's just the way I am.

So it is with a slight sense of trepidation that I join up with the England squad again. Everything is different now, of course it is. We don't train at Pennyhill, we train in Bath, we stay in a different hotel in Chiswick before the game and the coaching staff are different. Even the kit and the team suits are different.

And, funnily enough, in three years my teammates have changed, too. Magnus Lund I have hardly ever met. The scrum half will be Harry Ellis, and I only really know him as the guy who nearly took off my leg in that club game against Leicester. And Andy Farrell, what an awesome player, but I only know him from watching rugby league on the TV.

Some reassuring old faces are there, too. It's great to see Martin Corry – Cozza – the old warrior, and Jason Robinson, whom I've admired so very much, has come back out of retirement. But no Dave Alred. At least, not officially.

The new England kicking coach is Jon Callard – JC – who is a really good guy. But I've been working with Dave for over a decade. JC understands that completely, and doesn't try to make it his job to change anything I do. He just says I'm here to help you through the kicking sessions, to get the balls back to you, whatever you want. And that is spot on.

But what I really need is Dave.

I ask the management if I can work with Dave and the response is we'll get back to you on that. When they do, the answer is yes, but with certain conditions. You do it on your own pitch and in your own time.

So I feel like a bit of a villain. Dave and I find various pitches around Bath and Bristol to practise on, but we don't have floodlights, and so sometimes we have to be quick before the light fades. It's not ideal.

When we kick at Twickenham, Dave is allowed on the pitch but we have to stay down one end. JC and the other kickers are at the other. We could all be helping each other here, but it's like we've never met.

Something else concerns me. We have a new coach and new players coming in, as well as some old players coming back into the team. It's exciting, a new start, and so expectations are high. People both inside and outside the camp want results fast. They want this new recipe to work immediately. But this is international rugby and that is a big ask.

I have my own issues. Who am I within this team and what is my role? When I last played for England, I was 24 and the youngest in the team. Now I'm 27 and I have 53 caps, so I am indisputably a senior player, and yet I'm also the new boy again. The other guys don't know me very well. The stats show that I have considerable international experience, but for three years my experience at all levels of rugby has been pretty much non-existent. So I have to feel my way through this, and in the Twickenham changing room beforehand, it feels difficult. How vocal should I be? What are the other players expecting of me?

But England–Scotland is a ludicrous game – ludicrous because it goes so well. The game takes a shape I recognise; the right runners run the right lines off me. Within five minutes, I feel I recognise the pace of the game. This actually feels as though I haven't been away for one second.

And then, bang! Simon Taylor's elbow lands square in my jaw. It's accidental, but pretty effective. England are winning, my comeback game is going swimmingly, and I have a hole in the inside of my top lip, which I can fill with my entire tongue. I'm playing international rugby, trying to focus on the game, but thinking that's a big hole in my face. Maybe I should get it stitched.

I do eventually go off, seven minutes before the final whistle. But first, my comeback is crowned by a dubious try. Harry makes a brilliant break from behind a ruck and feeds me inside. I've got about five metres to make, the Scottish defenders show me the right touchline and I dive over, grounding the ball. But even when I touch it down, I'm not sure if it is a try or not. The moment I watch the replay on the big screen, I realise it isn't. The video shows quite clearly that my right foot was in touch before the ball was down. Nevertheless, the try is given. It's a bit of a joke and I try to disguise my surprise. But that wasn't a try.

Yet afterwards, I feel great. I'm sat down under a bright light in the dentist's chair in the physio room, where I have fourteen stitches in my face, and I feel great. That's partly due to the anaesthetic but also because this is the best moment in rugby. The brief aftermath in the changing room when you've won feels good. The pressure of the week is gone, it's been a good day and now I can just sit here and have my face stitched and embrace it. I don't need to worry about the next game. For a few hours, I don't need to worry about anything.

The media want to call it a dream comeback. They want this to be my day, my headlines. So they ask me was that a dream comeback? Could it have gone any better?

But I won't have any of that. I never, ever buy into that, because if you buy into the good headlines too much, you have to buy into the bad ones.

If you're a player, you're just a pawn in that game. You have little choice and less power. You can't change anything, you just get blown around by the wind. All you can do is play the best you can and then afterwards tell it like it is, tell it the way you always tell it. It was the whole team who just beat Scotland, not me.

● ● ●

Dream headlines can be so fleeting. Three weeks later we are facing the most passionate Ireland performance I have ever had the misfortune to come up against. We are blown off the field.

My preparation is not exactly helped by the hamstring I pulled the previous weekend while playing for Newcastle. I spend the whole week unable to do much at all, and I go to bed the night before the game with the words of Simon Kemp in my head: To be honest, I don't think you're going to be able to play, but we'll have a look tomorrow.

I try to convince myself that I am going to play. I need to do that; otherwise mentally, I won't be anywhere near prepared.

The next day, at 9am, I am on a training field behind the match stadium with Pasky, and Simon, doing drills and some sprints, to see if I'm OK to play. Incredibly, I pass my fitness test and so I travel to Croke Park with the rest of the team. We are full of confidence. We followed the Scotland game with an average performance against Italy and we feel we have learned some lessons that we are keen to show against Ireland. But we are physically dominated, and when that happens, all bets are off. It's like playing against a seventeen-man team. We are under siege and we cannot lift the pressure. They are fiercer, more physical, more everything.

So you think, OK, no worries, let's kick it long and get out of here. But where do you put it? They have every single blade of grass covered, which means that every kick becomes a bad kick. We are 23–3 down at half-time. We have to change something. We have to find some kind of an answer.

As soon as we come off I say to Brian I think we need to work out how to change the momentum in this game because we're getting beaten up front.

Brian looks at me but, understandably, he is not happy. This is rubbish, he says. He is talking about the game, not my comments, but then he walks off to talk to his coaches. As a key decision-maker, I was hoping to have a chat about how to change the tactics but it seems that will have to wait.

Some of the guys start saying we need to get down their end, we're playing too much time in our own half. It's not often that I interject but I look across and reply well, tell us how. How are we going to do that?

Silence, but I was being serious. People are happy enough to say what they want, but they're not happy enough to go to the next level. The number ten has to take on that pressure, and afterwards, when it's being analysed, it invariably ends up being his fault. It helps when other players think in greater depth, and take in the bigger picture. It's terrific when players who see the game through your eyes, such as Catty, or Dave Walder at Newcastle, offer up options and solutions. I could do with some of their help right now.

On the board in the dressing room, Brian writes his key messages: 'field position' and 'keep the ball'. This is one step short of writing 'win the match'. The important question is not what we need to do but how we are going to achieve it. What's missing is what often goes missing under pressure – the how to.

That's the point of rugby – we're all interconnected. If we are to kick down their end, we need first to threaten them, to show them that we're capable of attacking from deeper in the field and that we mean it. This will persuade their wingers and full-back that they can't just stay back and leave us space to run into. We need to make sure that we are not committing greater numbers of players to the breakdown than they are, and recycle the ball quicker, which again means their back three can't sit so deep. Then we can kick and our kicking will be effective.

But we don't take the conversation that far and so nothing is changed, which is why the second half is as painful as the first. It isn't helped by Ireland scoring a long interception try just at the end. Standing under the posts, you know this is a disaster, and that you've got to sit in that changing room and deal with it all.

21

THE England summer tour to South Africa is going to be tough. We're going to have a depleted team and I have just been injured, so there is an argument for suggesting that I don't really need to go. It might be better to stay at home and rest. Why not miss it?

That's the advice I am getting from Tim, my dad, Blackie and plenty of others besides. They're playing devil's advocate. Do you really need this?

After the Ireland game, that hamstring counted me out for the rest of the Six Nations. Rest would, indeed, be good for me. But the decision whether or not to go isn't exactly hard. Your decisions speak volumes about you and I don't want to be someone who stands aside because the situation might not be ideal for me. I have an opportunity to play for England. I've never seen myself as above the England team, or in a position to make a call on whether or not I want to be a part of it. So I am on the plane.

And yes, it is tough, but I enjoy it. I enjoy being with a new group of young England players, I enjoy getting to know Dave Strettle and Roy Winters, I enjoy playing outside scrum-half Andy Gomarsall, and in the hotel I enjoy retreating every evening with Matthew Tait, Toby Flood, Jamie Noon and Dan Scarborough for our nightly shot of the TV series *Entourage*.

What I really enjoy is the backs-against-the-wall spirit in training. We all seem to pull together, and then the most god-awful stomach virus starts picking us off, one by one. Strets gets it so badly that it takes all his effort just to crawl to the phone to call the doc. So he has to go to hospital – and the assignment becomes even harder.

We lose the first Test 58–10. The scoreline looks horrible but we play hard and, for periods, we play well. And I get crunched in the worst collision of my career. I try to dive in to stop a certain try, but Roy Winters has the same idea and I get the full weight of Roy's shoulder on my nose and the impact goes through my back so hard that it feels as though my spine inverts and my feet are going to flip over my head.

A week is not long enough to recover from a hit like that, but I'm not only playing in the second Test, I'm captain for the day. Two and a half years after being made captain by Andy Robinson, I finally get to do the job. Again, we are not close on the scoreboard. We lose 55–22, but that scoreline doesn't reflect how we stepped up to the challenge. It doesn't say that we are ahead at half-time.

That's the story of the entire tour. We give a hell of a lot to it and are heavily beaten. There's no denying it, but we can feel kind of proud. Collectively, we met the challenge, we fronted up, and I'm really glad I didn't walk out on the experience.

● ● ●

With the World Cup on the horizon, we know where we stand. We're not kidding ourselves. We're going into this World Cup rather differently from the way we went into the last. In our dressing room at Twickenham, big new signs read 'STW', which we discover stands for 'Shock The World'. But the southern hemisphere teams right now will be anything other than shocked.

We go to Portugal for a training camp, but a nagging feeling persists that we are not fast-forwarding at all, and, in fact, we are trundling along a bit too slowly. Forty-six players are here, which maybe is too many. Time is the crucial factor. We need to start forming bonds with the players we'll be linking with, and putting things in place structurally. We need to complete repetition after repetition. Everything we do has to be so ingrained that, when the pressure comes, we have inbuilt behaviours that we can rely upon. But we don't seem to be getting it quite right. With this many players, we are working more on selection than fine-tuning.

Mentally, I am not in the best place, either. After all the injuries and my time away, I'm not totally convinced that I deserve a place among this group of players. In our World Cup warm-up matches we beat Wales well, but lose twice to France. We will be travelling to this World Cup in different circumstances from those of four years ago. That much is clear.

● ● ●

The day before we leave for France, the general opinion of England's chances at the World Cup is summed up at the Scrum In The Park event. This is an open day, a celebration, a meet-the-fans occasion, at which we are also expected to do some media interviews. The questions are not forgiving.

Is it a bit unrealistic to think you can win this? I come up with an answer and move on. Being a player, this kind of attitude makes no sense to me.

Next question: would getting into the quarter-finals be a good result for England? I come up with another answer and move on.

Another question: you're eighth in the world at the moment, in world rankings. How high do you think you can finish? I come up with another answer and move on. I am trying to be polite and positive.

Another one: you haven't won many games recently, so isn't the World Cup a bit unrealistic? Thanks.

No one actually says come on, admit it, you're no good and you're going to lose, which maybe shows great restraint, but they have all as good as said so anyway. It's as if I'm being accused of lying, and I find this tiring. It makes me feel hot inside. I don't understand this negative mentality. This is a squad that has faced some of the most ruthless environments in world rugby. Just because we've had a couple of difficult results doesn't mean we have to set our sights low.

More important issues are afoot. I meet Adrian Edmondson, which is a complete pleasure because I am a massive *Young Ones* fan and he is a huge England fan, and he also says he's looking forward to the World Cup. And that's great. So there are some positive people around here after all.

Then we spot Jessie Wallace, better known to *Eastenders* fans as Kat Slater. Shelley and her sister Tracey are certainly *Eastenders* fans and Shelley literally makes me ask Jessie if we can have a picture taken with her. So I do and the result is preserved on Tracey's phone – a picture of the three of them with me in the background looking like some sort of goofy stalker.

● ● ●

When we leave for the World Cup in France, comparisons are inevitably made to four years ago. Back then, we were favourites and we were OK with that; I felt we had earned the right to the tag. This time, we are firmly assured of the fact that people have written us off, and we are fine with that, too. It's nice to sneak in under the radar, although, being England, that is never completely an option. But the atmosphere is good. People expect us to fail and we'd like to prove them wrong; it's just another motivation.

On the flight, I look around at this squad that is expected to achieve nothing: Martin Corry, Phil Vickery, Lawrence Dallaglio, Jason Robinson, Mike Catt, Josh Lewsey, Simon Shaw, Ben Kay to name just a few. Is this what you call no-hopers? Are these guys who can be written off? All I feel is confidence when I look at them. I know that, on the field, they will cover my back and I will do everything I can to cover theirs.

We move into our base for the first month of the competition, the Trianon Palace Hotel in Versailles. It is what it says it is — a palace. It oozes elegance, style and indulgence, and it is a minute's walk from the stunning Palace of Versailles itself. This is not the sort of place you come to fail.

Day One of training. The mood is fantastic, the sun is out, there is a freshness of attitude. It feels like a good start to our campaign.

For me, though, this feeling doesn't last long. We work on our attack and defence in a game of fairly light two-handed touch. This is a training game based around people learning their running lines and positional responsibilities with the ball, and working hard on communication and togetherness in defence.

Steve Borthwick tries to run through a hole and I step in to help Phil Vickery, who stretches out to stop Steve and in doing so brings him to the ground. My momentum means that I have to hurdle the two of them but my right foot lands on Steve's shin, and as the weight comes down on it, my ankle rolls over flat against the ground. It's agony, but the physios haven't seen me. I'm lying on the ground and I yell out to Barney, the physio, to get over here and help me, my language loud and colourful.

Of all my many injuries, few have been as painful as this one. I am taken to a physio bed in the small changing room next to the pitch. Ice is wrapped round my ankle, which is already swelling. I feel strangely numb, certain that my World Cup is over, and yet I also know how this plays out. I use all that I have learned so far along my spiritual path to tell myself: Control what you can control. Let the rest just take its course and maybe just dare to think really positively. And that way I seem to feel a hell of a lot better.

Barney, at whom I've been yelling, takes me to hospital for a scan and the results show torn ligaments on the outside of the ankle and bruising on the inside. In fact, the bruising is so intense that no one can see that I have a tear on the inside of the ankle too, but that is by the by.

Back at the Trianon, Pasky gives me hope. He is maybe the one guy you want to see in these situations. He is so positive; he really cares. So when Pasky says to me there is the chance it could come right, I realise I have a fight on my hands, and I know I'll win it. I want to hug him. We'll give it as good a shot as possible, he says. We're just going to take it day by day, and go really hard at it. Go hard at it? Work hard? This is exactly the kind of challenge I relish.

So this is the deal. I have to ice it every two or three hours, which means setting my alarm two or three times in the night. That's kind of masochistic, but you won't find anyone more willing to undergo this kind of masochism than I am, especially if it means playing for England.

I also have a hand-held machine, called a Scenar, which sends electrical pulses through the foot. So I am now my own little walking physio unit. I have a trolley with my ice and my Scenar, which I push around the Trianon, either to pool sessions with Pasky or to the massage room of Richard Wegrzyk – my old friend Krajicek.

This is another great place to be. Krajicek is an incredibly chilled personality, which goes well with his job, and the atmosphere he creates makes him a magnet before games. On those long waits in the afternoons or mornings of the day before playing, when you want to escape from what's ahead of you for a bit, his massage room is full of players who don't need a massage but just want to hang out or watch a film and feed from his calming energy.

I now have an excuse to live in Krajicek's massage room. Everyone else here is playing a World Cup, but I'm on a totally different timetable playing a totally different game.

I am faced with the kind of challenge I love. Pasky says two weeks, maybe three, to play on it. It's really up to me. I know what I have to do. It's me against myself. I have to drop into the zone and flick the Tunnel Vision switch.

● ● ●

Whether I can move my ankle or not, though, is as good as irrelevant, because on the field, a campaign that started badly is getting worse.

We beat the United States unconvincingly, but our next game, against South Africa, is a shocker. I sit in the stands next to Vicks, who has been suspended, and with Lawrence and the other guys who aren't playing. And it's tough to watch.

I really feel for the boys out there in the thick of it. It just doesn't look right. People don't seem to understand what the others are doing. The players don't seem to be able to connect or adapt to the way the game is playing out. South Africa don't help; for our every mistake, they make us pay.

When you get confusion like this, when players don't know exactly where they're supposed to be, they want to help out in any way possible and, subconsciously, they head to where the action is, focusing on the ball. So you end up with all your players around the ball, which means that, since you have no width to attack with, you are very easy to defend against. It also means you've got nowhere to kick to because you've got no chase options, and it makes you extremely vulnerable if you turn the ball over because you've got no width in your defence.

Catty is at ten and I can see he is feeling the strain more than anyone. I know this because I know exactly what he is going through. When you haven't got any width or options in your attack, you haven't got a chance. He is massively limited in how he can now play his game. I have so much respect and admiration for Catty, and he's struggling so much through no fault of his own. I wish I could help him out.

Then we lose two players – first Jason with a hamstring, but his World Cup is not definitely over; and Noonie with a knee-ligament strain, and his World Cup is unfortunately done. The final score is 36–0 but, if it's possible, it feels even worse. I feel awful for Noonie. He is an astoundingly good professional, incredibly strong, easily one of the most courageous players I've ever played alongside and an absolute belter of a teammate. Great bloke. I feel for him because he's fought so hard for his opportunities, he has finally got himself here, where he deserves to be, in a World Cup, and now this. Poor guy.

The mood afterwards is horrendous. Of course it is. In a small physio room round the corner from the main dressing room, Lawrence, Joe Worsley, Olly Barkley and I try to get our heads round where we go next. We've got to sort something out. Already the feeling is grabbing hold of us that this has got to come from the players, because at this stage, there is simply no other way.

Players start shuffling into the room like defeated soldiers. We commiserate but there's nothing you can say now that's going to make a difference. Everyone is quiet, subdued, empty shells of the people who went out before kick-off. The coaches tell us, basically, that we're down to the 'last-chance saloon'. We can't afford to lose again. We've got to summon everything we've got.

But everyone knows all that. The more important question, as always, is how?

So there we are, in the middle of this sombre team talk, when the door opens and in comes a French guy whom no one has seen before pushing Noonie in a wheelchair. Except it's not a wheelchair. The wheels are really small, more a wheel-trolley. Noonie gestures to the corner where his locker is and they are halfway across the room when the French guy, suddenly aware of the awkward silence, panics, gently releases Noonie and bolts for the door. We are all trying to concentrate on Brian and the messages of doom and gloom but it's impossible to ignore Noonie rolling towards the corner of the room, where he finishes up trapped in-between the benches, unable to move, involuntarily facing completely the wrong way.

Everyone holds their breath, trying not to crack, but some guys start laughing. Make the most of it. The laughter doesn't last long.

● ● ●

No one on that team deserves to face such a scoreline. No one deserves that experience on the field at all. Word is that we have been 'humiliated'. I disagree with that, but frustration in the camp is now tangible.

The frustration is that we – or they, for now – are working hard on the training field, but lack of understanding of what they are trying to do and lack of attention to the finer details means that so much of the hard work counts for so little come match day.

So the England World Cup campaign finally reaches boiling point. Something's got to be done – at least, that's the feeling. At the next squad meeting, a few home truths are finally laid on the line. We don't really know what we're doing out there. That's the message from the players to Brian. Olly Barkley delivers it in the strongest language. He tells Brian that we haven't got a clue.

I sympathise with Brian. As a coach, this cannot be easy to take, but it's not as if we are looking for someone to pin the blame on here. It's purely a case of an England team trying to move forward and put our World Cup back on track. Everyone here hugely respects and likes Brian. What we don't like is being beaten 36–0.

Brian could have gone two ways. He could easily have dug in his heels and refused to listen. But he is not like that. That is not the sort of person he is at all. So he does the opposite. He hears our grievances and he invites us to come up with the solution and wants us to deliver it our way.

This smart bit of player empowerment takes the sting out of the situation. Soon, in a small meeting room next to the lift on the bottom floor of the Trianon, another meeting is under way. The main playmakers, standing around a flip chart, are encouraged to discuss how we want to play. Immediately, there is a connection. I've not played a lot with Olly but he and I seem to share the same vision for the structure. Catty is on board, too. What we want is options everywhere and players to understand their roles.

It has taken a heavy defeat, but we've used that adversity to try to move forward. We have a game plan now, on paper at least. The next question is whether we can play it.

● ● ●

In normal circumstances, Pasky said, we should give my ankle six weeks to recover properly. In these circumstances, we give it nine days before I'm back in training, but I have the most appalling limp. My ankle is strapped so tightly that I can't move my right foot much anyway, and when I jog it looks horrific. Jogging is really painful, and yet the thinking is that I'm going to play at the weekend against Samoa.

My second training session back happens to be one of the few that are open to the media and the supporters. I don't want to make it too obvious that I'm really struggling, so it actually helps that Olly and I miss the start of the training session because the team bus sets off without anyone having done a head count. And when we do get there, I try to hide myself in the middle of the pack as we jog around the field.

However, now we have more of an idea of what we are trying to achieve as a rugby team, the vibe around the squad is more positive. A belief is taking hold that what we are doing could be a catalyst. There is still a lot of stress about, however. There is far too much negativity surrounding every mistake. A session cannot be condemned as 'shit' because a pass or two doesn't go to hand or a ball or two hits the floor. If the World Cup is going to be remotely successful, this is a mind-set we need to change and fast.

Far from shit, I am starting to see the kind of shape we need that will bring the best out of some of England's great players.

● ● ●

Samoa give us a scare. My own jolt comes when Brian Lima, known round the world for his tackling, nearly takes my head off. I am incredibly lucky to duck in time. The pain I felt when I went flying into Roy Winters a few months back would have been nothing compared to this had Lima connected.

But we pull away to win with a little to spare, we follow the same pattern against Tonga and land ourselves an unenviable quarter-final against Australia in Marseille. That's where our stuttering campaign is expected finally to grind to a halt.

The atmosphere in Marseille is a weird mix. The Georgians have just checked out of our hotel and the World Cup, which is possibly why, when Lawrence checks in to his room, he finds vomit all over the walls. I'm woken up one night when the ceiling caves in. And we get a spate of injuries in training.

The media, meanwhile, have written us off, completely and utterly. I'm not reading the papers, but the tone of every comment, every question, is the same. To be honest, I'm not surprised. I don't think anyone is, because we all know only too well that we could soon be going home.

In the hotel, some of the players get their shirts signed, and this tells a story. One of the traditions of a big rugby tour is that, during the final days, the players hand round their shirts for the whole squad to sign, either as a memento, or for a charity auction. But this is happening here even before our quarter-final. We play Australia on Saturday, so we could be home on Sunday. No one wants that, but neither is anyone kidding himself.

My build-up is not helped by the World Cup balls. It isn't that there is anything wrong with them, more the fact that there are inconsistencies within the batch of balls. In any group of balls, for instance, one might fade left, one might draw right slightly, one might go really heavily left and another three might be nice and straight.

Toby Flood and I have worked this out, and it's just common sense that you cannot practise if you don't trust the ball. So during the goalkicking part of every kicking session, we work out which are the straight ones and discard the others. You want to train with the straight ones only. Occasionally, we end up doing our training with just two balls, which is just about manageable. The real problem is the match balls.

For every match, we get six match balls, numbered one to six, and three reserves. The kickers are allowed to practise with them the day before a game. Our day-before practice has thus become an analysis of the nine match balls. Floody, JC and I work out which ball goes where. We smash the balls at goal and quickly agree if they are lefties or righties, how left or how right, or whether they are straight, and on a small piece of paper, we write all this down to commit to memory.

So during games, every time we get a penalty or a conversion, the first thing I do is check the ball to see which number I've got. It's not as if you haven't got enough on your plate already without having to memorise the balls and then worry about which ball you might have to kick with and what the hell it's going to do once it's left your foot. Some of these balls are scary. Over the tournament, the movement on some has been so bad that you are practically aiming to miss. The draw ball – the one that moves right for a left-footer – is controllable. You know where you are with that one. The worst balls are the ones that fade left. This is called an 'escape'. An escape is not a good kick, and controlling an escape is not easy. I hate the balls that escape.

So I take my kicking sheet to bed with me on the night before a match and learn it. I also go over all the game notes I have made to myself in my notepad. The notes are under the titles Defence and Attack, and they consist of everything that we have worked on this week. And beneath them, I write something else.

What I write is so important because the night before the game I feel vulnerable, and the next morning, I feel even worse. I will take any scrap of help I can get to make me feel man enough and good enough to walk out on that field. Thus my messages to myself read like this:

- how far I have come for this
- how much work I have done
- how much pain I have felt
- how hard I am willing to work
- how constantly I go out there, face the pressure and perform.

They counsel me to:

- be the aggressive/competitive kid who scythes people down
- be the obsessive one who aims for perfection every time
- be the guy injured for three and a half years who has learnt how to make time and opportunities count
- take them on and have no regrets
- know that this is definitely my time.

If I read these messages any other day, they would feel strange. The night before a game, they mean the world to me.

● ● ●

Despite everything, something amazing happens out there on that Marseille pitch.

We know what the odds are, but we don't care. Just give it everything, everything you have got. Last-chance saloon, the coaches said, so we come out fighting, and what we come up with is astonishing. We try to do all the right things. We play as much of the game as we can in their half. We fill the whole width of the pitch with players so we have options everywhere. We keep attacking down the blind side where they continue to leave space, and it pays off for us. We get ourselves on the front foot.

Our forwards are awesome. They hit rucks like I have never seen rucks hit before. Ben Kay, Lewis, Andy Sheridan – they are frightening. We dominate the contact area, clearing a way past the ball at every breakdown. We get a clean fast ball and we get it going forward, which is basically what wins games.

We land blow after blow. I can feel our confidence growing. We are hurting them. We build a lead, but Australia do what Australia always do – they compete, they fight back and then Lote Tuqiri scores in the corner, putting them 10–6 ahead.

Yet going behind doesn't seem to phase us. Our forwards drive us on and on. One more penalty and we are a point behind.

The intensity gets to everyone. The referee signals for another penalty and while we are playing the advantage, I take a shot at a 40 metre drop goal. If this doesn't go over, I've always got the penalty. And just as I'm striking the ball, one of the Aussies yells at me: That's all you've got, Wilko! That's all you've got!

But I'm thinking yeah, but it's all we need! It's all we need!

We have the lead again. As the clock ticks, it comes down to trust. If we do our jobs, we will win. And now we believe in each other. Completely. I know I believe in these guys, because I stop looking at the scoreboard clock; 72 minutes are gone, then 79.

Stirling Mortlock, the Australian captain, has a last-minute penalty. We win this match or lose it on this kick. It's a hell of a kick, 45 metres out from the left, and with these balls, I'd hate to be in his shoes.

We win it. We are still alive.

The atmosphere afterwards is incredible. I confess that there were moments when I thought we'd be going home, and in the changing room, everyone is saying the same, laughing, amazed. We're not going home. We're staying. We are here at least until Saturday. I feel immensely proud to be part of a team of men who have done something no one expected. Cozza has so much tape holding him together, he looks like Mumm-Ra the Ever-Living from the cartoons. Lewis is bruised and battered and looks like he's been to war. And Simon Shaw is a bit older than us but consistently world-class. I love playing with that guy.

We are still here at the World Cup. It's so unlikely, it's hilarious. Cozza and Catty – no two guys deserve it more – shrug their shoulders and exchange broad smiles and a look that says what on earth's going on?

The three of us experienced it so differently four years ago, and we are among the last out of the changing room. For me, that is because the changing room in moments like this is one of my favourite places in the world. I don't want to leave. So I take my time. I am so happy for everyone. I am so happy for Catty, again demonstrating what a truly great rugby player he is.

How many times have I come off a rugby field and had people say to me God, you had a great game today? And on how many of those occasions have I thought to myself I didn't really do anything, all I did was make a few decisions and listen to Catty helping me out? Sometimes as a number ten, you feel you are the driver on a long coach journey; with Catty, you occasionally feel someone else coming up and taking over the wheel. We drove well out there today.

● ● ●

I came out to this World Cup desperate to enjoy it and to embrace it differently from the last one, but I can feel myself slipping back and I cannot stop myself. I feel the anxiety more than ever, and the fear, too. I thought I was out of this mould, but the worrying is back. As the magnitude of this

World Cup has risen, and my expectations with it, I am again worrying about things that are out of my control.

After the game, Shelley and I walk down to the beach for a crêpe. That's about as relaxed as I can ever get. While we are there, France complete an unexpected win over the All Blacks in the other quarter-final, an evening game, and now it's England v France in the semi. Marseille is suddenly buzzing with excitement. The roads are full of cars hooting their horns, people on scooters shoot by waving flags, and I become aware that, from their point of view, I am one of the people standing between them and the World Cup.

I think we'd better head back, I tell Shelley. I don't want to be seen out now. I want to get back to the hotel quickly.

So we start walking back, but we don't go back the way we came. We avoid the main roads and the crowds, and find a route back that takes us up some side roads. It takes longer but, more importantly, it's quieter.

At one stage, though, when the crowds and commotion are unavoidable, I find myself ducking behind trees and road signs and clinging to the shadows. This is, of course, quite funny, but I'm nervous about being out in public when we're playing France in the next round. Just get me back to the safety of my hotel room and my collapsed ceiling.

● ● ●

We move to Paris and I can feel the tournament intensifying.

Thursday evenings are a time to look forward to. Floody, Taity and I go out to eat. It has become our weekly fixture. We don't go anywhere smart, just round the corner. This is time out, rare, precious time to switch off from the World Cup, just once a week.

Other than that, I struggle to turn off the switch. I try to distract myself with the ridiculously bad *American Pie* films, the later ones in the series, numbers four to six. Chill and enjoy them, I tell myself, deal with the game later. But it's just so difficult to escape. I disappear into a film for five minutes and then reality comes crashing back. I feel more anxious, more nervous, and have to walk round the room, pacing one part of it and then another.

I try to work it out. Just sit here, stare out of the window, try to meditate, try to find some peace. But when I stare out of the window, everything tells me about this game that's coming. I wish it was here or cancelled, but it's neither, and I just have to wait.

On the eve of the game, I get back to my room after kicking practice to find that a newspaper has been delivered. I haven't ordered it. I'm trying not to see the papers. But the massive picture of my face on the front cover is unavoidable, as is the huge headline in a big tabloid typeface: 'Ayez peur! Ayez très peur!' Be afraid, be very afraid.

And then it all comes rushing back. People are counting on me. I don't want to be the one who fails them.

●　●　●

In the changing room before the semi-final, Catty says to me Wilko, this is your time, buddy.

I understand what he means. We have been in situations like this ever since 1998. We've linked up, helped each other, we know the game in the same way and we both know what to expect in this particular game. It's going to be tight, edgy, intense with lots of emphasis on defence. It needs us to be ahead at the right time, to keep the scoreboard ticking over if we can. But, above all, we need to hang in there to the very end and take our shot if and when we get it. This is the time when I'm supposed to come alive. This is a game for me to finish. That's what Catty is saying, and it's a great compliment to me.

And the game follows the pattern we thought it would. We get a fantastic early lead when Josh scores in the corner within two minutes. Great start. But then it is dogged and tight, and France start working their way back into us. No one wants to make a mistake. Especially the place-kickers.

The French start pulling ahead. Three penalties converted by Lionel Beauxis put them 9–5 up, but we get another precious penalty. As is the way, I grab the ball and immediately look at the number on it – two, one of the ones that leaks left. In this batch of six, there are two balls I do not want to kick, two and six. Six is even worse than two, less of a leaker, more of a blatant slice. So as soon as I see I've got two, I throw it out to the ballboy on the side of the pitch and ask him to throw back his. He sends me back the number six. Surprise, surprise.

I contemplate kicking the number six ball over the stand, but I throw it back to him and get number two back again. All I want to do is hit this kick straight, but I'm swapping balls with a ballboy and trying to work out in my mind how far right I should be hitting it.

I hit the target. We are 9–8 down.

We struggle to get back at them. We struggle to get close. France nearly score but Joe Worsley intervenes with a last-ditch tap tackle. And then, at last, we are down their end again and we have a penalty – 11–9 up. I take my chance with a drop goal – 14–9. And then it's over. The no-hopers are in the final.

• • •

After a game, a lot of the guys recover in the ice bath but I prefer to get on the bike. It's always been my way. So I'm on the bike, in the warm-up room outside the changing room, pedalling away with Calvin Morriss, one of our fitness experts.

I don't want to get out of my kit. It just feels so damn good to win sometimes. I'm back in the moment I'd hang on to for the rest of my life if I could – the transition between winning the last game and not having to think about the next one.

Calvin says that we'll do 10 to 15 minutes on the bikes, but I go on for 25, and every couple of minutes I take up the effort for a 10 second spurt. I don't feel knackered, I'm in my own world and I could go on for much longer. I don't want to stop. I don't want to go and get changed. The quicker I get changed, the quicker we start talking about the preparations for the next game and the quicker this moment subsides. So the more I can hang around the changing room, the longer this feeling exists. The other boys pass me in their suits on their way out, but I carry on pedalling.

Eventually, back at the hotel, I struggle to sleep. After a late-night game, I'm never a good sleeper. Winning a World Cup semi-final doesn't help the process.

I go for a stroll before bed, just to try to tire myself out, but when I do hit the sack, I have a pain in my stomach and my back. I feel the grazes on my knees burning and I cannot lie with the bedsheets touching me. I sleep for an hour.

My mind won't stop racing. What's this week going to be like? What was last week like? What could I have done better in the game? I'm just wired.

At 5.30am, I realise it's a losing battle and go downstairs to the team room with my DVD player and a guitar. I play a bit of Arctic Monkeys – not that anyone would recognise it – and mess around on the guitar, and about an hour later, the door opens and Lewis walks in. Exactly the same deal. That's funny. I know he suffers from night-after games, too.

This is an opportunity to share a special moment. We talk about the game and how we feel. I'm so proud of what we've done. We have dug in our heels and dragged the belief from out of our hearts. And now we have a final to deal with.

●　●　●

The week leading up to the final is not going to be easy. Not so much because we are facing South Africa, who have already beaten us 36–0, but because of where I am in my mind. I know I have slipped backwards.

I'd like to spend the week enjoying the company of my teammates, but being in the team room with them reminds me too much of the game that's coming. So I lock myself away a bit. At least I can control that environment. I ask Shelley to bring me in a load more DVDs. I try to help time disappear by losing myself in anything I can find on the TV. Literally anything will do, although my cause is not exactly helped when Ainsley Harriott starts asking the guests on *Ready Steady Cook* so where will you be watching the big game on Saturday? That'll be the one I'm playing in, then.

I wish my ankle would improve but it remains a compromise. At this stage, it's so stiff that Pasky performs what he calls ankle surfing on it. My foot hangs over the edge of a forgiving surface and he stands on it, bouncing up and down. I'm still having treatment on it every day. Before the Australia game, I took a couple of painkillers, which is hardly ideal. If this was regular-season rugby at home, I simply wouldn't be playing.

The thing is if South Africa are really smart, they will have worked this out. All my career I have kicked with both feet, but in four games here, I have hidden my right foot almost completely. I haven't kicked once on it in training, and in games I have tried it just twice – two drop goal attempts, two misses, one hit the post. If the Springboks have sussed this, they'll know I'm always going to use my left foot, which also means putting all my weight on my bad right foot. Knowing this would definitely help them and hinder me.

● ● ●

On the eve of the game, backs coach Mike Ford slips the same printed sheet under my door that goes to everyone. On it are key thoughts to take into the game, South Africa's strengths and, in big capitals through the middle, COMPETE ON EVERY PLAY. NO SURRENDER! NO SURRENDER! Handwritten on my sheet are the words: Jonny, your game, your tournament, your World Cup! Good luck. MF.

In my notepad, I write more mental reminders to myself:

- I have done this so many times, it is the same each time.
- Believe in who you are and what you are.
- Know what I have learned and what I have been through, and most of all how hard I have worked to be here. I deserve to win.
- This is my time and opportunity.
- Enjoy it. Live it.

The next morning rolls around and I receive a handwritten fax from Blackie entitled 'Onwards and Upwards'. In typical Blackie style, the key word shouts at me in capitals: 'If we all did the things we are capable of doing, we would literally astound ourselves. Today let yourself do all the things of which you are capable, and astound yourself. It is essential that you see yourself as an achiever and as a WINNER! Believe you can do this, and when you think positive, excellent thoughts, you and the team will be propelled towards greatness.'

I tuck the fax away and watch the seconds ticking before we can return to the Stade de France. Once there, I'm caught up in the momentum and turning back is no longer an option. I know the exact timing of a countdown to a game and I manage to fill every minute with preparation work. I do my kicking practice to an exact formula, I return to the changing room and then go back out on to the pitch with the boys. We go through our warm-up routines as a team and then we are back in the changing room again and Vicks is gathering us all together for the last big huddle.

Here, in the Stade de France, I have been so into my pre-match pattern, I haven't had time to think. Until now. Oh shit, this is it. The big one.

In the huddle, minutes before we go out on to the field, Vicks gives us the last big hurrah. The intensity has been building and building. Now it's as high as it gets. We've come so far, he tells us, we're unbreakable, we're like a band of brothers.

As he says 'brothers', Ronnie Regan is so caught up in the mood that he does something only he would do. He thrusts his fist into the middle of the huddle and echoes the words. Yeah, boys! Brothers!

An awkward pause follows. What the hell does he want us to do? Nobody has ever done this fists-in-the-huddle business before, but Ronnie's fist remains firm. Half the team are looking around, thinking someone's got to do something. I do my utmost to avoid looking at Taity because this is a World Cup final for God's sake and there is a good chance that if I catch his eye I could burst out laughing right now.

Ronnie's fist remains remains there, but Vicks picks up where he left off. Eventually, Ronnie meekly withdraws his fist. I make a mental note that, whatever happens in the next eighty minutes, we're going to laugh about this afterwards. But first there is a pretty big game to be played.

These Springboks are one of the best teams I've ever played against. They are enormously tough, ruthless, deadly in the lineout, and they start building an early lead. I try to peg it back with a drop goal, but I'm forced to use my right boot and, although it's on target, my injured foot simply doesn't have the power in it.

We go in 9–3 at half-time, but the second half has barely begun when we have our big moment. Taity makes a scorching break out of nowhere and does what he can do so well, which is beat players for fun. He is brought down a mere five metres from the try line, and from the ensuing ruck, the ball comes out to me. I have just enough time before getting hit to bat it on to Mark Cueto down the left wing, who dives in to score in the corner.

The decision is referred to the video referee. Did he put his foot into touch or not while scoring? I watch it on the big screen with my kicking tee in hand, ready to take the conversion. The decision is long and slow and I cannot work out whether it's a try or not.

The video ref decides not. No try. So we are chasing the game. We get the deficit down to three, but our ill discipline costs us dearly and they land two penalties, which means we are more than a score behind. This is probably the difference for us; against Australia and France, we were always in touch, always close enough to believe that we could hang in there and close the game out when the opportunity came. But here we are more than a score behind and so we have no choice but to force it against a very well-organised defence. And we can't find the opening we so desperately need. We simply don't have that in our armoury, not on this night, not against this side.

We had a chance to make history with a successful defence of the World Cup. Two World Cups in a row. With Cueto's try it could have been different, but the score is in the book. It's 15–6 and, at the last, the World Cup dream is gone.

● ● ●

On the coach on the way back from the Stade, Vicks issues his instructions to the boys for the evening's activities – whatever happens, we all stick together as a team.

Under my rules, I would usually take that to mean you can all stick together and I will chill with you for a bit before sliding out the back door. This time, however, I want, more than anything, to finish it off in style. I want to be with these boys right up until the very end.

My mate Andy Holloway joins us in L'Arc, the bar that has been booked for us. He played rugby this morning for Southend RFC, then managed to leg it from his game to get on a private flight, courtesy of his boss, to be in the Stade for the final. He didn't even have time for a shower. Later, when eventually he crawls back to our hotel, he is utterly unable to locate my room, so he sleeps on the floor in the corridor outside the room he thinks is mine, but which happens to be on the floor below. I don't see him in the morning because he gets off to catch his flight home. And he still hasn't showered.

My own performance is not particularly impressive either, and the reasons are twofold. One, I haven't touched alcohol for two and a half years. Not so much as a beer or a glass of wine at dinner. Two, it's my aim in life to avoid tequila, gin and whisky, but that's all L'Arc seem to have.

I get into a session with Josh. We exchange champagne toasts. We toast world peace, wonky rugby balls and anything else that comes to mind. Andy joins us. Josh has a mate, too, and the toasting goes on and on and on.

I get a bit overexcited and ask the barman if I can spend some time behind the bar. It's my party trick – except no trick is involved. And the princes are here – William and Harry – and they are in fine form. Floody is on fire. Taity is a right mess.

Shelley is having a good time, too, but she has to do a lot of looking after. Me mainly, and Taity. Sure enough, when the inevitable happens and I can stand up no longer, Shelley and her twin sister Tracey (who has come out with us too) start putting the get-me-home process into operation. A couple of the security staff who are with the England team come to our rescue. They wrap a coat round my head, so no one can see who I am, and walk me into a waiting taxi.

By the time we get back to the hotel, I have become a dead weight. They have to carry me in, one under each shoulder, with my feet dragging behind me, laces down.

Brian Ashton is at the bar and sees us making our shambolic way through the foyer. He asks what's happened. Shelley tells him that I've had bad food poisoning. From what I am informed later, he doesn't buy it. There's a surprise.

The poor concierge comes to my rescue. I tell him I'm going to be sick, so he rushes back with a bucket. I take a good look at it, take aim and then manage to vomit right down his arm.

Shelley somehow manages to get me up to my room where I am sick again. And again.

The next day, I'm no better. From mid-afternoon, I'm still vomiting about every twenty-five minutes. A sick bug has been going round and I wonder if maybe that's the problem. So I call Simon Kemp and he comes to my room. He brings me paracetamol and I ask him to bring me my toothpaste from the bathroom to try to remove the nasty taste from my mouth.

Simon, I ask, do you think I've got this sick bug?

No, he says. It's called a hangover. And if you didn't wait four years between drinking sessions, you might be able to recognise it.

● ● ●

That night, as we make our way to the end-of-tournament dinner, I recall the mood on the exact same bus journey four years ago. It's amazing what a difference a couple of penalties and a disallowed try can make.

My phone beeps with a text from my mate, Newcastle full-back Anthony Elliott. It reads simply: great pictures of you, Taity and Floody on the front of the *Sun* today. Must have been an awesome night!

Oh my God! My heart is suddenly racing. This is my worst nightmare coming true. This is what I kept myself tucked away for all those years to avoid. I should never have let my hair down. I can't remember a thing that happened last night. I feel a sense of panic rising within me.

I show Floody and Taity the text. Anthony has sent me the pictures and they sit behind me, all of us staring at my phone as the images slowly download. The tension is unbearable.

The first picture arrives bit by bit, starting from the top. First to appear on the screen is Floody. He is wearing Taity's T-shirt and pouring a bottle of vodka straight down Prince Harry's throat! This is not a good start.

Next up is me. My eyes are gone, looking everywhere but nowhere at the same time. I look a right state but nothing incriminating. Not as bad as Floody. That's OK, then.

And I feel even better when the final member of the Newcastle trio appears at the bottom of the screen. In a fitting end to an amazing six-week competition, full of highs and lows to match any I can recall, Taity has seen off the event in style, barely awake in a silver cowboy hat with hardly any clothes on.

CHAPTER 22

AT Newcastle, I don't think I ever realised how much of a buffer role Rob Andrew played between the management and the club. Rob moved to work at the RFU last year and now we have John Fletcher as our director of rugby. He is really impressive, too. Originally, he was the academy coach, and I have never seen a guy so trusted and respected by his students. I really like working with him; his man-management skills are an inspiration.

We have a great culture here, tight team spirit. This is a club punching above its weight, and the coaches, including Fletch and Peter Walton, a teammate from the early days, are doing everything they can to help players improve and get selected for England. But we are now starting to feel pressure from above – not from Fletch, but even higher – and, as ever, Blackie has been fighting the players' corner.

The lengths Blackie has gone to for us know no boundaries. For a long time we'd been asking for upgraded weights and gym equipment, and eventually Blackie took it upon himself to go out and get it for us. He did motivational speeches for equipment companies and they gave him our new gym equipment in return. He never stopped. He was always there for us, requesting nothing in return but our effort and focus. He lived the dream for us 24/7. His set-up, positivity and energy are the secrets behind my career.

It was at his request that resident artist and maniacal back-rower Ed Williamson painted the wall with words that drive us. 'If it's not true, don't say it. If it's not right, don't do it.'

But now the Blackie days are over. Some tough decisions are being made round here. Blackie wanted to provide the players with an environment to help them get the best out of themselves (energy, spirit and a commitment to getting better every day), but Dave Thompson, the owner, and to be fair the guy who puts the money in, has a different idea of how to do this. I get the impression that Thomo feels it's better done by putting a bit of fear into us – fear of losing our jobs, fear of what's going to happen if we don't win. I think that's more Thomo's way. He likes to show who is in charge.

Blackie would never allow that ethos to be placed upon his players. He knows how we pull together. He knows it always begins with the team and the players. Basically, he just told it how it is, and Thomo chose to tell him that he is no longer needed.

Typical Blackie, his parting shot was humble and thoughtful, and showed where his priorities always lie. He asked Thomo to look after the players and give us an environment in which we can go out and thrive.

There is only one person I would possibly choose to work with in place of Blackie and that's Sparks. So it's a huge relief when Thomo puts him in place, but also an interesting decision because Sparks's and Blackie's philosophies are almost exactly the same. So now I work with Blackie away from the club and I love working with Sparks within it. But with what seems to be unfolding behind the scenes, I do start to fear for the future of the team.

● ● ●

For most of my life as a professional rugby player, I have been advised to lay off the kicking practice a bit. I've been told to spend a little less time out on the pitch and a little more at home with my feet up. And I cannot argue with the advice. My injury record over the years – particularly the groin injury – is proof that there was some mileage in what everyone had been telling me. I just found it hard to accept.

The Newcastle medical team have now got me keeping a diary of how long I kick for and how many kicks I hit each day. They've been threatening me with this for two years, ever since my groin problems, and I've done an expert job of dodging it. Even now, I rarely fill it in honestly, which probably renders it pointless.

Back in those earlier England days, Clive was never afraid to let me know his concerns that I was doing too much. I still get it from Pasky and Simon Kemp. Even Ronan O'Gara, on Lions tours and after England–Ireland games, has told me I might be taking it a few steps too far.

It's not that I don't want to take the advice on board. In fact, deep down I know it holds the key to taking me to the next level. The problem is that my best intentions of finishing up my practice in good time are too easily overpowered by the need for perfection, and by the fear and anxiety that builds in me when things don't go exactly to plan. The way I still see it, the only solution is to stay out practising until I have literally kicked the feeling away.

But now, the current England management have fresh, undeniable evidence with which to confront me.

As the 2008 Six Nations season rolls around, the players are being told to wear a new device, a GPS monitor. This allows the coaches to collect data on each of us, and to see the exact distance we have covered in training, which in turn gives them an idea of how hard we are working.

Where I go wrong is that I forget to take my monitor off when squad training is finished. I keep it on for my kicking training afterwards. This means that for those hours when I'm kicking, every time I jog there and back to collect the balls is notched up as part of my day's work.

In the build-up to the Six Nations, the GPS stats show that I am doing well over seven or eight kilometres a day. Before games, that is too much. The evidence is there before me. Not that I find it any easier to respond to; after all, by my standards, these are already shortened sessions.

The GPS does not just show distance covered, it shows your average and maximum speed. Before the Wales game, the coaches are fascinated to see that my top speed is significantly, astonishingly faster than anyone else's. They call me in. How come? What are you doing that we don't know about?

The answer is that not only did I forget to take my monitor off for kicking training, I forgot to take it off when I was in the car on the way back to the hotel.

● ● ●

At Newcastle, we have a new, world-class prop, who doubles as a useful guitarist. Carl Hayman is the latest member of the band, although I'm not exactly sure that's what you'd call us.

I've been playing the guitar for a few years now, and we have a great recording studio at home. It all came about courtesy of a music company called Roland. I happened to mention in an interview that I was trying to learn the piano. Roland got in touch and offered me a grand piano in exchange for an interview and some photographs for their personal use. Great deal, except the house didn't have room for a grand piano, so I asked for a few other things instead.

So now when we rock out, we do so in style with amps, effects pedals, microphones, a digital piano, a 24-track recording studio and a fully equipped digital drum kit for Sparks. I think the expression is: all the gear, no idea.

Pete Murphy was our lead singer, but when he left Newcastle, we had to find a stand-in. John Stokoe, the club kit man, more than competently took the mic. Toby Flood is our resident bass slapper, and when he is able, Graeme Wilkes, the club doctor, pops along to show us how it's really done. He is a genuinely good pianist.

The type of music favoured by this group with no name is very broad. We like a bit of Motown and have played a whole range from Stones to Oasis, from Arctic Monkeys to Pearl Jam. In fact, we are open to any suggestions, as long as they involve a decent guitar solo for me and something difficult for Sparks to get his head round on the drums. The song 'What You Could Have Won' by Milburn nicely ticks both boxes.

At our height, some of us have made cameo appearances in Graeme's band, The Klack. So yes, I have played live, up at Slaley Hall. Great fun, but boy do I hate performing in public. There's only one public stage I ever want to go out on and it's not this one.

But I love messing around with the guys in our studio. I can get pretty immersed. It is probably the only other environment where I feel the same buzz as when I'm playing rugby or training hard with Blackie.

Carl has introduced a new element. He has started turning up in fancy dress and he insists that we join him. The latest is Carl on rhythm guitar, dressed as a nun, Sparks on drums in an off-grey leather jacket and incredibly low-slung beige slip-ons, looking like a sleazy seventies second-hand car salesman, and me on lead, wearing black cowboy boots, viciously tapered stone-washed jeans, a black playboy vest and a long black wig, all from the charity shop. We make quite a sight now as well as quite a noise.

● ● ●

At last, I can sign England shirts again.

The Sporting Icons case has finally been to court and two of the company's directors have been found guilty, one of cheating customers and the other of supplying forgeries.

I never actually had to appear in court myself, although footballers Steven Gerrard, Jamie Carragher and Ian Rush all gave evidence.

The memorabilia dealers all now know our stance on this business. Since 2003, over 2000 items bearing my fake signature have been removed from eBay, and without one single legal challenge from the seller.

● ● ●

For all the time and work, and all the reading and thinking, that I have put into following my spiritual pathway, I cannot change the core of who I am.

On the morning of the Wales game, before we leave for Twickenham, I find myself caught up in the biggest bout of pre-match nerves I have ever experienced. I am 28 years old, I have 70 odd caps, yet this is as bad as it has ever been.

In my room with an hour to go before the coach leaves for the game, an old thought process rifles through my mind. If you could offer me a way out now, would I take it? Right now, I probably would. I'd probably leg it.

I phone Blackie in a panic. Blackie knows the right messages to give me. He helps calm me down. So I go to the game. I'm ready to play. I don't leg it. I don't even know where those intense nerves suddenly came from.

The game starts well. In the first half, we are really effective. We run the ball well, we feel confident, we make good decisions and build a lead. But in the second half the game changes. Danny Cipriani is off the bench, making his England debut at centre, and I throw him a long pass. There is nowhere for me to kick, so this pass is delivered knowing that it will bring up the Welsh defence and give him better kicking options and plenty of time to execute one of them.

But I overthrow the pass and it goes over Danny's head, bouncing between him and Paul Sackey. Any sort of half-reasonable bounce would have been absolutely fine, but this one goes everywhere. We struggle to control the ball, concede a scrum and, a bit further down the line, they score a try.

We are still ahead, but then Balsh has a kick charged down and another Welsh try goes in. Now the game has genuinely turned and we need people to help manufacture scoring opportunities. But there is a whiff of panic in the air and we have too many players committing themselves to rucks that we have already won when we need them to take responsibility elsewhere. We lose 19–26, and afterwards, the questions from the press to me are all about that pass. I think I can see where this is going.

A week later, against Italy in Rome, Danny unluckily has a kick charged down and a good victory becomes a close one. And then, when we beat France in Paris, Jamie Noon has a great game at thirteen, but I win Man of the Match, and the press ask me was your performance today a kind of response to the criticism you got after the Wales game?

The question is about as pointless as any you could ever get. The stories are already written in the journos heads and they are now just waiting for my permission so that they can go ahead and fill in the blanks. But I won't play the media game; it's like banging your head against a brick wall. I just tell them that I appreciate being given the opportunity to play for England. That might not be what they want but, on my spiritual pathway, it is genuinely how I feel.

But if, in the public eye, I was up again against France, I am apparently down again after Scotland. We go to Murrayfield, where the conditions are terrible, the wind is shocking for the kickers and we struggle to assert any dominance. I don't feel that our structure and game plan are troubling them at all. I try to manufacture something out of nothing but I'm forcing it. It's what I do when I sense we are idling towards defeat. Someone has to step out of a structure that isn't working, put his head above the parapet, and that's what I try to do. What I'm trying to show on the field is that I'd rather take a few risks and win this than do nothing wrong and lose.

So I try to make things work, but they don't. We lose 9–15 and, again, the questions afterwards make it pretty clear who is going to be held responsible.

●　　●　　●

The following Tuesday, four days before the Ireland game, we are training at Bath University. Near the gym, before the team meeting, Brian asks for a word. He tells me he is going to play Danny at ten on Saturday instead of me.

I am not surprised. I knew there was a chance that the coaches would share the same opinion as many in the media and move me. Straightaway I find Danny to say well done, and I mean it. He is a good player with a firm vision of the game. It's thanks to my spiritual development that I am genuinely able to want him to do well.

This is the first time I have been dropped from the England starting XV since the World Cup quarter-final against South Africa in France nine years ago. It is impossible not to take it as a slur on my character. I try not to question it too much. I try to rise above it. But no matter what I have learned about life and how there is something far deeper than rugby, I am still in full competitive mode. Out of the blue, I receive an email from Kris Radlinski, the Wigan rugby league player I admire so much. I barely know him but what he writes is so supportive. I can't believe you've been treated like this, he says. And that's great, yet nevertheless, emotionally, I am still hugely rattled.

Watching from the bench at Twickenham, I am then given further food for thought when England come out and dominate in a way that they didn't in any of our previous games. Ireland just aren't as strong as they were last year at Croke Park, and our guys are able to play with the ball going forward and good powerful options around them.

Why couldn't that have happened when I was there? That is one question I ask myself. But maybe that is actually the point. Maybe it didn't happen because I was there.

Maybe somehow I've been getting in the way of the progress of the England team. Maybe, because of all the attention paid to me and everything else that goes with it, I have been affecting the dynamic of the group of players, so that they have found it hard to be who they are and express themselves to the full.

I feel pretty horrible about all this, but at the same time, I find myself thinking about Mike Catt and how he endured successive spells of being dropped from the England team. Catty would go through periods of more than a year when he wasn't in favour, and he would go back to his club and just get on with his own game. It's all right for that to be the case. At least, that's what I tell myself.

Anyway, it can give me a break. Ever since my neck injury, whenever a glimmer of fitness has returned, England have called me back in. I was called back without having played a game; I was called back in and asked to be captain.

For the first time in a long while, I have the chance to concentrate on myself and my own game. Maybe I can get some games together with Newcastle, get back on my learning curve, stop worrying about what England need from me and just work on getting better day by day with Blackie and Sparks.

* * *

Sometimes, when you are an obsessive perfectionist and never allow yourself to give in, it can backfire. This becomes the case on a road trip to Majorca.

I love soft-top cars, I love driving with the top down, and I'd really like a soft-top in Majorca. So I buy an old, soft-top BMW and persuade Andy Holloway and Pete Murphy to join me on the drive through France to Barcelona. The one rule is that, unless it is raining, we are not allowed to put the roof up. We play endless Oasis and Beatles CDs and we take shifts in the driving seat and it's all great until it gets dark. Our intention is to drive through the night, but I didn't realise how cold it gets, and under no circumstances will I sanction the roof going up.

For whoever's turn it is to do a shift in the back, we have three pillows and a duvet, but even then, it's ridiculously freezing. We put the heaters on full and it makes no difference.

In the morning, we stop in the south of France, near Montpellier, for breakfast and petanque on the beach. None of us has had much sleep. Andy is particularly cranky because it is soon 30 degrees and his head is burning. But he knows the rule. I still won't allow the roof to go up.

● ● ●

When I was young, I had a party trick. I could move my right shoulder out of its joint and then make it go back in, and when it clunked back in, it would make a hell of a noise, and that would make my friends at school recoil. Ugh, they'd exclaim.

If you put that natural defect together with all the years of hard tackling, you get to where I am now. I always used to feel strong in my shoulders, but for a good few years now, I have started to feel some pretty strong pain. It got to the stage where I was feeling it after every game. Just one hit and it was really sore. Recently, it's been taking me until Thursday after a game before I can lift it above my head, and before I'm ready to do anything physical with it in training for the next one. Now it's so bad that the shoulder feels as if it's dropping in and out of position even when I'm just jogging in a warm-up.

The agreed solution is to operate on it during the summer. This means missing the England summer tour to New Zealand, but there is no alternative.

Len Funk, my shoulder specialist, thinks I have a standard labral tear, which consists of a lesion in the cartilage that sits in-between the ball and socket of the shoulder joint. He thinks the operation should take about an hour and that he can put a couple of anchors into the joint to secure it.

When he goes in though, what he finds is rather different. If the cartilage is a clock-face, I have lost the entire amount from two round to ten o'clock. The whole thing has been clean worn away. So the operation takes three and a half hours, he has to put in seven anchors, which he says is a hell of a lot, and it will take five months rather than three to recover fully.

In other words, I have the whole of the summer to myself, and I intend to make the most of this gift. Once I can move my arm backward and forward, I can run, and this becomes the focus of the summer.

This is the new thinking coming in, influenced by the Matt Burke approach. I am no longer setting out to be the strongest and fittest in the world, the best at everything. I discuss it with Blackie. What am I happy with? More to the point, what do I really want to work on? What can I do that would make me better? Let's be ruthless here. Where can we really make a change? Our answer is twofold – sprinting and my spiritual pathway.

So, physically, we work on speed and nothing but speed. We get back to spending all our time together, working on astro-turf, on the track, in various different gyms. Everything physically is entirely concentrated on the one goal.

Mentally, this is a great summer for me, too. When we work out at Blackie's gym, he puts on videos of famous speakers, so I'm training while listening to some hugely impressive people. I discover spiritual and motivational speakers, such as Jim Rohn, Dr Wayne Dyer and Eckhart Tolle, who is rated as the most spiritually influential person in the world. Sometimes this spills over beyond training. Blackie and I sit in his spare room, watching videos of these amazing people, and then afterwards we discuss their message. We talk for hours.

The result is that I find myself in an amazingly good place. I feel a genuine spiritual contentment. It resembles a sense of invincibility because, in this mood, there is no situation I find threatening. I have nothing to fight against. I am working with the world and not against it. I have had time out of England, I have my shoulder back, I feel refreshed, as if the new season represents a brand new start. There may yet be one more World Cup in me; now I can give it all I've got. My last shot.

With my kicking I have a new approach, too. I discuss this a lot with Dave and decide at last to be ruthless. I have to control what I can control and let the rest go. It means focusing on my intentions, honing my mental application, and building faith in myself as opposed to getting too consumed in the stats and the results. In essence, the process takes precedence rather than the outcome.

So my daily kicking sessions become a very concentrated warm-up and then eight shots at goal from wherever I choose. Just eight shots and then I go home. I don't re-do any of them if they go wrong. I don't get second chances in a game, so I start to train that way, too.

By the start of the new season, I feel genuinely fabulous, and the new me is reflected in the new haircut. I always used to have the right haircut, the right image; it was important. But that doesn't seem imperative now. I feel different, I see things differently and I have greater faith in myself. So now my hair is long.

●   ●   ●

The start of the new season is about as enjoyable for me as rugby gets.

My first game is against Northampton and I have a hand in everything we do and sew up the win with a big right-foot drop goal at the end to put us out of reach. We then get completely smashed at Saracens. Still, I score a try at the end and I feel good about my game. Tellingly, I manage to save another Saracens try by running down Kameli Ratuvou, their Fijian winger, just short of the try line and stealing the ball. That's the speed work with Blackie paying off.

I continue on this roll against Bristol. I really feel liberated, as though this is my chance and I'm starting to take it. It all seems to make sense now. I see the game playing out in my mind before it actually happens, and therefore I'm in the right place at the right time. I'm not afraid to try new moves and I haven't missed a goalkick all season. I don't feel I'm going to, either.

But all that is fleeting. We go down to Gloucester and not half an hour into the game I get cleared out from the side of a ruck and my left knee is driven downwards. It feels as though the bottom half of my leg is pointing completely the wrong way. While I'm lying there, I get hit again, which straightens out my leg but feels horrible. I know this one is bad.

I stay down until Martin Brewer is by my side. I can't look at it. I tell him don't touch it. Something is definitely wrong.

But when I do look down, it looks normal. Martin says do you want to get up and have a run? But there's no way I'm doing that. I'm helped off, as usual, by Sparks and then sit below in the changing room, listening to the cheers of the crowd as we slowly lose touch with the Gloucester team. By the end of the game, my knee has swollen up massively. It suddenly looks grotesque and throbs madly.

The next morning, I get a call from Graeme Wilkes, who has the results of the scan. He asks if I'm sitting down. Yes, I reply, surprisingly enough I am.

Unfortunately, it's not good, he tells me. You've dislocated your kneecap, which isn't that uncommon, but your kneecap has sheered away from everything on the inside. It didn't dislocate and come back – it completely tore away.

The reason it felt as though my leg was back-to-front was because the kneecap went round the side of my leg. But in the second impact in that ruck, the kneecap had been pushed to the front again.

Graeme isn't finished. When the kneecap returned to its usual position, a large piece of cartilage, the size of a 50 pence piece, was sheered away from the back of it. This is the worst piece of news by far. The early prognosis is an operation and then four to six months out.

A few days later, I'm in with Rob Gregory, the specialist at the Washington Hospital in Newcastle, who operated on Andy Buist. He explains that it's not straightforward. We can stitch your knee back, he says, but the cartilage is the problem. We can nail the cartilage back in to the kneecap, but whether it takes, whether it rebuilds a blood supply so that it regrows and attaches itself – there is no guarantee.

Basically, if the cartilage doesn't take, my career is over.

I've heard that before, with my neck injury, and my reaction is the same: It'll work out, the cartilage will take. I barely even stop to consider that the three and a half games I have just played may be my last. I am still enthused by how well they went. I'm convinced I'm moving forward, that my whole new approach has made a difference. I may be injured but I know I am a better player now than I have ever been.

● ● ●

Normal service is resumed, but not for long.

A day or so after the operation, I'm round at Blackie's, working out in his gym. My knee is held firmly in a brace, so I'm doing upper-body work, and a bit on my right leg, to keep me feeling positive.

This is all very well for six weeks, but then this long window of rehab seems to offer a good opportunity to sort out a problem with my left shoulder. It requires an operation and, with my shoulder in a sling, I can't work my upper body, either – and that is not good for me. Being completely unable to work out, to channel my energy into improving myself in some way as a rugby player – I hate that.

The achingly slow progress that my knee is making doesn't help much. I work regularly with Salwa, a caring, talented and diligent physio at Newcastle, trying to get the bend back into my knee. There is a certain point beyond which it will not go and it is up to Salwa how far we try to force it, but the pain of doing so is so intense it makes me want to vomit. Every day, I turn pale-faced as I sit on the edge of the physio bed, dangling my legs over the side, while Salwa tries to work the knee-bend a little bit more. It's the most painful rehab I've ever undergone and I make a deal with myself. If I ever have to go through this again, I'll pull the plug and retire there and then.

The daily pain reminds me how big this injury is, as if I needed to be reminded. Usually, with an injury, there is a beginning, when you get yourself sorted and start planning the rehab, the middle, when you just soldier on, and the end, when you're concentrating on the specifics of coming back to play. But after three months, I'm still stuck in the middle part and no end is in sight. No light shines at the end of the tunnel. I'm so far from playing, I can't even jog.

The club, of course, is full of people doing the things I can't do, and I start to feel awkward. I don't go to the meetings, and I find watching the games a depressing reminder of what I'm missing and what has been so natural to me for so long.

So it is a great relief when I am sent, at the suggestion of the England medics, to Vermont to spend three weeks with a knee genius, Bill Knowles, who has already helped mend the knees of Richard Hill and Charlie Hodgson.

You find Bill in Killington, a ski resort at the top of the Green Mountains, ninety minutes from the nearest airport, but, as far as I'm concerned, a million miles from anywhere. Here I find isolation and the chance to immerse myself completely and utterly in my knee.

By day, while Shelley hits the slopes, I work out in Bill's gym, and by night, we can relax. Here, I can push my trolley round the local supermarket and not a soul knows who the hell I am. After a week, Shelley leaves so I can attack completely solo. When I go to watch *Gran Torino* at the Killington cinema, I can relax, knowing that there is no danger of having to leave before the film starts.

I love working with Bill. I love his methods and his positivity. By the end of our time together, I'm playing football-tennis and doing indoor gymnastics around an obstacle course. He makes me feel like an athlete again. He makes me feel that the Six Nations and the 2009 Lions are back within reach.

● ● ●

There's no point in pretending that I'm hugely politically tuned in, but nevertheless, one particular incident at the BBC's Television Centre is not my greatest moment.

I've just come down in the lift with Tim, after a radio interview, and we are exiting through the foyer when Gordon Brown comes past the other way with a small entourage.

Obviously, I don't stop and say hello. I mean, he's the Prime Minister, isn't he? And God knows what kind of pressure he is under. But one of his aides comes after us and asks have you got a couple of minutes for a chat?

Of course, I'd be honoured, I say. The PM asks how are you feeling? How are the injuries? He really makes an effort to engage me and is pleasant and kind.

But then he stops. I'm terrible with awkward silences, and I'm thinking Christ, I need to return the favour, I have to ask him something back. I'm politically out of touch and fishing for something to say to this world-leading politician, who is trying desperately to plot a way out of global financial disaster. So I hit him with the first thing that comes into my head. Have you been busy lately?

Over the Prime Minister's shoulder, I can see Tim's face drop like he's just seen a ghost.

● ● ●

As a statement of loyalty to Newcastle, I agreed to a pay cut of around a third of my salary this year. The idea is that they backload my contract, pay the extra next year and use the extra money this year to bring in new players. What I find distressing, though, is the number and calibre of players going the other way. Dave Walder left a couple of years ago, Matthew Tait and Toby Flood went last summer, and Jamie Noon, Phil Dowson and Tom May are considering their options for next season. Matt Burke went back to Australia a year and a half ago to fast-track rehab of a knee injury, and a few months later, just when he thought he'd be coming back, he was phoned up and told there was no contract for him any more.

I miss the friends who have gone, who shared common cause with me. And I've been away injured so much that I feel I'm losing connection with the players who are left.

Salwa has been informed from on high that she is spending too much time with me and needs to concentrate more on the other players. This doesn't actually make sense, because I go round to see her at her house a lot after work, purely so as not to impinge on her time with everyone else.

So the signs at the club are not good, but I have put so much of my life into the place that I choose to ignore them. However, when I hear that there may be an issue with the club's ability to pay my salary next year, I start to reappraise. I wonder if maybe they don't want me here next year anyway.

From my position on the sidelines, it pains me to watch the things that have made Newcastle such an amazing club to be part of for so long be dismantled bit by bit. Every time one of the coaching staff is sacked, Thomo comes into the team room and starts the meeting. Just a quick word, he'll say, this is what's happened. I've let so-and-so go because I need results. We can't accept not getting results.

This time round it's Fletch and Peter Walton who get the bullet, which is just plain wrong. We aren't a team who are going to get regular results, and I think that Thomo, unfortunately, is missing that fact. Every time he makes one of these decisions, it serves to make us worse. Without the budget and the right signings, Thomo doesn't seem to realise just how well these guys are doing. All he has to do is look at what happens to the guys who have recently left – invariably, they enter a new, more stable environment and begin to shine.

So now, after twelve years at this club, I concede that I must open my mind to opportunities elsewhere. I've never entertained the thought of moving clubs before. I've never asked what could I get from another club that I'm not getting here? That's because I've never allowed myself to look past another question – what more could I give to this club that I'm not giving already? Rather than thinking that this club's not good enough for me, I've never gone beyond: How can I make this club better? I know that some people believe I'm fighting for a losing cause here. Lawrence Dallaglio has said openly that he thinks my career could have been very different if I'd moved clubs, but I actually enjoy the challenge.

But times change, and my conclusion now, after immense discussions, is to find another challenge elsewhere.

● ● ●

Back at Newcastle, I finally get back on the training ground with the team, but again, it is so fleeting. I get through one and a half sessions before I'm back in to see Martin Brewer. I've got this pain, I tell him. I can't even bend my leg. I'm actually finding it hard to walk.

CHRIS MCGRATH/GETTY IMAGES

BOB THOMAS/GETTY IMAGES

Above: Taking on the Australian defence and the powerful Stirling Mortlock.

Left: A massive performance from the boys up front provides me with some shots at goal in the RWC 2003 semi-final against France.

STUART HANNAGAN/GETTY IMAGES

Above: That kick, the one that changed my life in so many ways.

Right: Words cannot describe just how good this moment felt.

RICHARD LANE PHOTOGRAPHY

KIRSTY WIGGLESWORTH/PA ARCHIVE/PRESS ASSOCIATION IMAGES

England Rugby World Cup Squad

Buckingham Palace, December 8, 2003

Jenny

🌹
ENGLAND
RUGBY

CLIVE WOODWARD OBE

You were born NOT to go
into RUCKS!!!
Really looking forward/excited
about seeing you bring the very
best out of PR's back division!!
Enjoy it — say hi to your
Dad when you catch up

Clive

PAUL GILHAM/GETTY IMAGES

DAVID ROGERS/GETTY IMAGES

DAVID ROGERS/GETTY IMAGES

MARC ASPLAND/THE TIMES

Opposite:

Inset: Clive really did know exactly what he was doing. He was fantastic to me. I owe him a lot.

Top: Here's a classic example of somewhere that you never thought you'd end up. It was an amazing privilege to meet Her Majesty The Queen with the team.

Middle left: Here I am flanked by a couple of guys I would lay down and die for: Mike Catt and Richard Hill. You won't find two better people or players.

Middle right: BBC Sports Personality of the Year. I can't even remember what I said in my speech. Thank you for the votes.

Bottom left: The guy behind it all who led from the front in every way. Our inspirational Martin Johnson checking on me one last time.

Bottom right: My close friend and the team's Mr Consistent, Richard Hill, and I on the celebratory trip round London.

Above right: Sometimes you just get the timing right.

Right: Sometimes you don't. The chiropractor Brian Lima is a little high with this one. What a tackler, though.

Below: I loved the contact sessions.

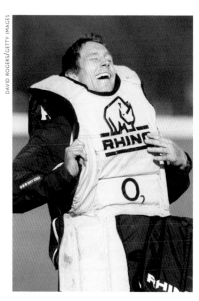

Above left: The final straw, almost. I thought this one had finally got me. The torn and dislocated kneecap was probably the worst of the lot.

Above right: Even worse than the big neck injury I suffered in my first game back after the 2003 World Cup.

Below: I still can't stop myself from flying in.

Neck operation

Fractured shoulder

Haematoma to right arm

Never lost heart

Appendicitis

Lacerated kidney

Torn abductor muscle

Knee ligament damage

Impossible is nothing

Jonny Wilkinson

adidas

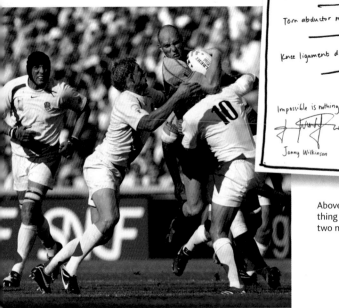

Above: Adidas: always supporting me. The scary thing is, they missed off a shoulder operation and two more torn knee ligaments!

SHAUN BOTTERILL/GETTY IMAGES

Above: Thankfully, this one hits the mark in the RWC 2007 semi-final and we pull away just enough from a French team who were flying high.

Left: What a player, and a truly nice guy too. I give you the legendary Jason Robinson.

Right: The incredibly gifted Matthew Tait. Awesome player, great friend.

Below: Four years on and so close. It was a phenomenal effort from a fabulous group. It still hurts.

DAVID ROGERS/GETTY IMAGES

JAMIE MCDONALD/GETTY IMAGES

Top left: A proud and exciting moment for me, alongside President Mourad Boudjellal, as I sign for French team RC Toulon.

Top right: Wearing the colours with pride, and sporting my new South of France tan.

Middle left: What a pleasure to be on the same field as two of the world's best back-rowers. Joe Van Niekerk and Juan Lobbe.

Above: Le petit General Pierre Mignoni. A true example of what's great about French rugby.

Left: Carl Hayman, Juan Lobbe and myself leap from the white rocks of Cassis.

Right: Shelley and I at her twin sister Tracey's wedding near their family home in Bristol.

Below: A bit of down-time and a laugh with Shelley. She has been absolutely amazing for me. Heaven knows, I can't be easy to live with!

Right: You won't find a more loyal and supportive bunch. Shelley, Mum, Dad and my godparents Bren and Myf at the World Cup in Paris, 2007.

Below: Mame, Bilks and Sparks. I will never be able to thank you enough.

Overleaf:

Top left: Enjoying my international rugby again after a good start to the season in France.

Top right: Harder times, and with them a real challenge for me.

Middle left: The influence of Sonny Bill. I manage to get this one-handed offload away to Nick Easter in the quarter-final versus France.

Middle right: Sending it out wide to Manu and Tinds against the Pumas.

Bottom left: A good opportunity to remind myself that no matter how tough things seem, we are and have been a privileged bunch to be doing what we do for a living. A glorious stage on which to practise my kicking in Queenstown.

Bottom right: A right foot drop goal against Scotland.

He tells me straightaway that playing rugby this week is out of the question. When I start to test the knee with the physios, they tell me to bend it to a certain level but I can't. I can't deal with the pain, either. As soon as I bend it to about 15/20 degrees, the burning, grinding pain is horrendous and my leg collapses. It just drops. It's as if a message has been sent straight back to switch off the muscles, which, I learn, is exactly what is happening.

It has now been more than five months since the Gloucester game and the message hits me loud and clear. There is no guarantee I am coming back to rugby as a player. None at all. I might never play again. Right now, I cannot even contemplate playing. But the doubts are way more extreme. It's not just a case of maybe I won't play again. It's am I going to run again? Can I even jog? What am I going to be able to do, physically, in later life?

The England physios, Pasky and Barney Kenny, come up to Newcastle, and they read the last rites on the season, and the Lions. That's hard enough to hear, but they want to strip my rehab right back. The kneecap isn't sitting properly in its groove, they say, so it's grinding, which is causing the unbearable pain on the raw, unprotected part of the back of the patella.

So I have a new course of action – retraining my quad muscles to fire in the right order. That means sitting on a chair at home, connected up with electrical pads to a machine that records the impulses on my inside and outside quad muscles. I have to contract the inside quad before the outside one. I sit on the chair, watching the success and failure of my muscle retraining on screen. And I have to do this for three whole weeks.

This is crucial. If I can't get this to work, I'm finished.

Shelley and I discuss where I am; or rather, I offload to Shelley about where I am. I feel things are slipping away from me. I'm missing an entire season. Everything I'm desperate to hang on to is retreating – it just seems it's not meant to be. I'm not even a rugby player any more. I don't know what I am — a face, a name maybe, but for many people, just a reminder of a crazy moment that occurred almost six years previously on the other side of the world. And that's the same moment I have been trying to leave behind ever since.

There is very little Shelley can say. She just listens and helps me accept reality. And she is great. She reminds me of the impermanence of all this. The fact that the world is ever changing is a major part of my spiritual training.

But I still wake up every morning to the realisation that I am another day further away, and face another day of not being involved. It feels unnatural, but I know I have to find a way to accept it, and try to see it in a positive light. I want to rediscover my inner strength and develop my spirituality.

Before 2006, I'd tackle every set-back by working hard, hammering the work ethic. It would be so simple for me to flick the switch to Tunnel Vision mode and slip back into those old habits. But if I am to succeed in a world that is always evolving, I know I have to keep adapting, too. And that has to be the new game plan.

● ● ●

It is good to know that, despite my knee injury, which is finally showing signs of coming good, there are decent people who are interested in working with me.

I get a call from Mike Catt, now a player-coach at London Irish.

What can I do for you, mate?

I know you might be out of contract, he says, and so you might be interested in looking elsewhere. I just wanted to put the case forward for my club.

I get a similar call from Richard Hill at Saracens. And that's really nice of both of them, two guys I would love to work with again, but the problem is that after all the years with Newcastle, I can't see myself playing against them. I don't want to come back here as a player for another team. I realise that I'm lucky to be in a position to be able to take that decision, but this is an instinct that, deep down, stops me from entertaining the idea of other English clubs. I think it's going to have to be abroad.

From the other furthest extreme, I get a great offer from Pat Lam, now coach at Auckland Blues. That really would be a great challenge, and I love watching Super 12 rugby. From the days of Carlos Spencer, Michael Jones and Jonah Lomu, I have kind of been an Auckland fan. But this one I can't really entertain, either. I still want to play for England.

And then I get a big surprise – an offer of a short-term summer contract with Wigan rugby league team. I would massively enjoy that. I'm a huge fan of Wigan, the club that produced my great old friend Jason Robinson as well as other legends including Andy Farrell and Kris Radlinski. This opportunity would be incredible.

But I have to let the chance go. Another time, maybe it could work, but right now I'm just coming back from a bad knee injury. I can't jeopardise my future by playing another sport that I'm not so familiar with.

Another factor is what type of club I want to join. At Newcastle, I've loved the underdog card. It would be great to have some silverware, that's always the goal, but I don't want to move to a club just because there's an obvious possibility of winning trophies and medals. I prefer the idea of fighting hard and building something new rather than slotting into something that is already the finished article.

It's the bonds forged at Newcastle that I value, created through digging deep, and to a degree, facing the pressure of relegation. That was real strength-building stuff, and those are great memories. It's the sheer fulfilment in that kind of journey that suits me. So when Tim, Bilks and I look towards France, that's the thought that governs me. There are conversations with Stade Français and Perpignan, who then don't consider me a viable option due to my injuries. After a few visits, it comes down to a choice of two, Bayonne and Toulon.

What I like about Toulon is the potential to build. They may be a team of superstars, but they've only recently been promoted to the Top 14 and are flirting with relegation. I'd love the challenge of trying to help a team like that work. I'd like to play a part in bringing the best out of all those great players – and learn a bit myself while I'm at it.

CHAPTER 23

TOULON, on first impressions, is awesome. The Stade Mayol is a couple of hundred yards from seafront bars and restaurants, mid-April is ridiculously hot and people on holiday wander up and down the front. I love the atmosphere.

Toulon are playing Perpignan and, ninety minutes before kick-off, I'm sitting at a table literally on the beach, in this beautiful setting, eating a stunning lunch with Shelley, Tim, Laurent, my French agent, and Mourad Boudjellal, the President of the Toulon. Laurent tells us that Mourad would really like me to see the game, but I'm not keen. I'm still contracted to Newcastle. I'm here to meet people at the club, not to be seen publicly looking as though I'm cheering on a team other than my own.

Laurent says that it may be good to go and sample the amazing atmosphere, get an idea of what it's really like. Now I love playing in great stadia and in front of big, appreciative crowds but it's not important to my final decision. My values are much more key to me; remaining loyal to Newcastle is the priority here.

Out of respect, we end up cutting a deal. We will go for five minutes, nothing more. Apparently we can park in an underground car park, get a lift up to the stadium and watch five minutes from a box. That way no one will know that I've been there.

Fifteen minutes before kick-off, we pull up outside the stadium in a couple of black Volkswagen 4 x 4s. Fans are milling around. The place is heaving. We don't park in an underground car park at all. In fact, we get dropped off among the hundreds of supporters, who immediately get out their phones and cameras and start filming me.

I don't like this at all. I feel compromised and totally out of control. We are ushered through a side entrance. I was trying to keep everyone close but now I can hardly see Shelley and Tim because of the crush of people. I'm starting to lose the plot a little when the familiar whiff of Deep Heat assails my nostrils and I know instinctively where we are. Sure enough, we are led into the dressing rooms.

At this stage before kick-off, the players are about to come back in from their pre-match warm-up. They are in an end-of-season relegation struggle, and they are going to wonder what on earth I am doing in here. I will be a disruption to their preparation, and there will be a guy playing number ten who's got to go and play this game knowing that there's another number ten literally on the scene.

You couldn't challenge my value system more intensely than this if you tried. I can't be in here, but there's no way I can I go back out into the crowd.

I ask can't you find another room for us? I don't care if it's a cupboard, just as long as it's big enough for Shelley and me. Tim can fend for himself.

So they shut us in the doctor's room. But this is no good – this is where players come to get last-minute strappings.

So we run along the corridor, trying not to be seen and trying to find somewhere to hide. We are put in the coaches' changing room where I pace around, thinking about the arrangements we made over lunch and trying not to explode. I sit down and force myself to read a team-sheet over and over, as a distraction. I hear the clatter of studs as the teams come back in, and then the coaches come into their room. Despite pre-game anxieties and nerves, we all exchange introductions politely. Hello, how are you doing? They are great with me but this is still a disaster.

I have no intention of watching anything now. I tell Tim as soon as the players have gone out on to the pitch, we'll leg it the other way and get the hell out of here.

When the coast is clear, we make a hasty exit, but just as we are in the tunnel, I hear the clatter of more studs. One last player is coming from the physio room – player-coach Tana Umaga, who has come out of retirement to help the team. The last thing I want to do is say hi when he's on his way out to play a really big game like this one.

So I quickly turn my back and say to Shelley stand there and pretend we're talking. It's an absolute shocker. Tana jogs past, presumably wondering who we are and what on earth a random girl and a guy in a beanie hat are doing in the players' area on match day. Laurent asks us if we still want to watch five minutes, but I tell him no.

● ● ●

Three months later, I clock in at the Toulon training ground for Day One with my new club.

I come with a familiar sense of apprehension. It reminds me of joining up with the Lions, or even the early days with England. I feel the same massive pressure to perform. I want to prove myself. I want to nail every training session. I want every pass and every kick to be right on the money. At least I feel fit and strong. I have spent an entire month on holiday in Majorca, but I trained every single day with the aim of killing myself purely in order to be prepared for this.

The early morning gym session, I discover, is split between the 7am group and the 8am group. I slip in in-between and start to get on with some stretches and warm-ups. The 7am-ers come over one by one.

Ça va? This is their greeting with a handshake.

I have just about got through all these and got back to work when the 8am-ers start arriving. Ça va? Handshake. Same thing. And this is the same every day. I want to get down to work but the first lesson on Day One is I can't until I have given everyone the morning greeting. But I like it.

Today is fitness testing and it is massively important to me to do well. I'm flying on the chin-ups and dips, thank you Blackie, but the rowing test, never a strong point with my short little levers, kills me. Sonny Bill Williams, rowing next to me, is absolutely awesome, but I go for broke and am left lying in pain on the concrete outside, knowing that the running test is yet to come.

This is the one that slightly concerns me. Five minutes running on a hard track will be a good test for my knee. The backs run together and I go all out from the start, Blackie style, and I keep on going until, at the end, there is some distance between me and everyone else. Professionally, I think I've done myself and Blackie proud.

Every day, I notice the differences here. Our first official training session of the pre-season is open to the public and 5,000 people turn up – that's almost as many as an average Newcastle home gate.

One of the traditions of Toulon's pre-season is to spend two days in the Alps. Sleeping under the stars around a campfire is a good way to get to know your teammates, even if it does mean staying up all night listening to Kris Chesney, the ex-Saracens lock, snoring. However, it isn't particularly good preparation for next day's long walk, another tradition, especially as the temperature is 27 degrees. I decide to set the pace again, flick the old Tunnel Vision switch, put my head down and set off at the front. A few of the younger players stay with me, but drop off one by one. It is like running with Liam Botham.

When we finally arrive at our destination, a small outbuilding in the middle of the mountains, the guys collapse, but we are pointed towards a stupidly steep uphill slope. That's where we are going next. Groans all round. I flick the switch again and hammer on harder than before, just to make a point.

Among my new teammates, I'm so grateful for the warmth of my welcome. I think it's fairly obvious that I'm here to give my all for the cause, but there is no sense of you're the new boy, you've got to fit in.

My first encounter with Tana Umaga was in the 1999 World Cup game where I hit him with a bit of a cheap-shot late tackle. I remember him also from the 2005 Lions, when he got me with one back. But there is no mention of that here, just a quickly formed mutual respect. His competitive personality and meticulous approach to preparation aren't far off my own, but it's fascinating to see him when he steps away from being a coach and joins in the drills. His decision-making, his spatial awareness – sometimes it seems the best back in the club isn't even playing.

I also have history with Joe Van Niekerk, the big South African back-row forward, in some old battles with the Springboks, but he seems a massively good professional and a really genuine bloke. My old Newcastle teammate, Tom May, is new here, too, which helps, and I quickly build an affinity for the two enormously talented Argentinians, Felipe Contepomi and Juan Martin Fernandez Lobbe. Felipe's decision-making and speed of hand are as good as I've seen, but he keeps asking how I am. It seems he really cares. It's like finding an Argentinian Mike Catt.

I really like it here.

● ● ●

Pre-season starts early. My first game for my new club is in 35 degree July heat, and I have come all this way to find my great friend Jamie Noon on the same pitch. He has joined Brive and they are our visitors. When a big fight breaks out near our line, Noonie runs up and grabs me from behind, holding me in a kind of head-lock, muttering in my ear all kinds of threats about how he is going to beat me up.

This is all quite amusing until the Toulon flanker, Thomas Sourice, decides he needs to jump to my rescue. He charges over and is on the brink of battering Noonie before I eventually produce my best French and explain that he is my mate and this is a joke. Thomas then finds this funny, too.

My competitive debut in the League is not such fun. When Toulon had their relegation issues last season, it was felt they needed more reliability with their goalkicking. That, clearly, is one of the reasons why I am here.

But here we are, going into this big, big game for me, a night match against Stade Français, with everyone, and me in particular, desperate to get off to a good start, yet on the pitch in the warm-up, something is definitely not quite right with my kicking. The ball is flying a bit funny, swinging from right to left, yet there's no real wind to speak of.

All the crisis management and panic lights are suddenly flashing in my head. I have to sort this out quickly because I can't tell if the ball is moving on its own or if it's my fault, and right now I don't know where the hell to aim. I'm trying everything, but nothing's working. I hate it that this has come about right now, right at this moment. It's exactly like the Samoa game in the 2003 World Cup. During the team talk, I'm only half there; the other half is still trying to work out what's going on.

My first penalty attempt is from wide left, a reasonable distance away. I need this; just get this right. And I do. It goes right where I want it to go.

In fact, I get all the kicks that are within a reasonable distance. Anything longer, though, and I'm miles away. I've not even had a chance to look up and the crowd are telling me all about it. So I'm playing a game with regrets already rifling through my head. It's really frustrating. I miss three kicks and I want them all back again. I want to prove myself here. I so don't want to be kicking like this in front of my new team.

The game is close. The scores go up in threes. I could just do with a few more of them. So finally, I take a 45 metre snap-shot at a drop goal, which I get. We are three points up with five minutes to go. I want it to end here, but they work a drop goal move of their own to level the scores, and suddenly the game is over. A camera is thrust in my face on the field and I'm being interviewed in French. I do my best to explain. It's great to be out here with the team, but I'm very disappointed about the three chances I should have got.

Deep down, I'm finding this difficult. There is no explaining just how challenging it is to perform normally when the confidence and surety have been stripped away.

When this happens, I would rather be anywhere other than on a rugby pitch in front of thousands of people. So in one sense, I am kind of proud of myself. I guess I could have feigned an injury to get off the field or turned down the goal kicks and gone for touch instead. On the other hand, I'm severely disappointed about the game, because I know I could and should have done so much better and a great chance went begging. Either way, I know for sure that I'll be out on the Stade Mayol pitch early in the morning, kicking my life back into shape again.

●　●　●

It's not just a case of getting out here and playing my best. There are other issues. I have to manage the move here with Shelley, I have to manage recovering my car, having had it towed away on my second night here because I didn't understand the parking regulations, and I have to manage my knee.

At times, the pain behind the back of the kneecap returns. It doesn't get quite as bad as it used to be. Some days we have two rugby sessions and in the afternoon I'm running with a very pronounced limp. And sometimes I can't kick at all off my right foot because I can't support myself on my left leg. So I'm having to adapt to the way my body has changed and compromise my old habits, especially in the way I train.

I warm to my new environment, though. Martin Johnson, now the manager of the England team, and Brian Smith, his backs coach, visit me, and I take them down to the Toulon waterfront. They're interested in me being a part of the autumn internationals.

A few weeks later, I'm down at the port again with my mum and dad. Toulon have just beaten Bourgoin and I have scored my first try for them. I managed to pick up my own grubber-kick and step the full-back to score. I don't make a habit of scoring, and so I'm happy with that. Now I can relax in the open air in a restaurant by the sea. It feels good to be here.

● ● ●

For the first time in over a year and a half, I am an England player again. I'm back at Pennyhill, and it doesn't take long to get used to the game plan that Johnno and Brian Smith have put in place. I like it. It gives width and options, and it allows me the chance to roam a bit.

And it feels great to be back at Twickenham. The atmosphere is terrific. We kick off the autumn season against Australia, who have pretty good team. The speed of their ball makes them difficult to defend, but I enjoy the game. I feel very comfortable at the level of international rugby, even with my new knee, and I enjoy being able to play what I see in front of me. I feel the instinctive side coming back into my game. I like that.

Our game plan is to attack certain areas of the field and, in order to ensure the ball gets there, I can't afford to be caught with it. So at times I have to play a little bit deeper than usual, flatter when I want to do the attacking. At other times, the framework requires something else.

None of this is remotely understood by the media, and after we have been beaten, 19–8, a great deal is suddenly made of playing flat or deep. That is the tone of the questions that are put to me afterwards. That's all I'm asked about – are you playing too deep?

'Playing deep' seem to be buzz words. I'm told the TV makes a thing of it, too. Even Bilks, on the phone later, says I see they are talking loads about you playing deep.

I can't explain to the media what I'm doing because I'm not going to give away anything tactical. All I can do in my defence is tell people they are misunderstanding and oversimplifying the situation.

Yet after twenty months away from the England scene, I feel I've got back into it. Lewis and I have done our jobs as leaders, and defensively, I really feel I've made an impact. Yet once again, the storyline seems to centre around me. Generally, people feel that I did well, but no one can just leave it at that. There has to be something and this time, randomly, it's depth.

We play Argentina next and our victory is hard-fought against good defending, but for the subsequent game against New Zealand, a decision is taken to change what we are doing. We want to hit them with something they aren't expecting, play more direct with more use of forwards around the breakdown and ten channel, a game plan favoured by Wasps and the Lions of the previous summer.

I'm not familiar with this. It's very structured. I feel I'm filling a role instead of roaming and making decisions. At the beginning, it has to be prescribed in order for us to understand it fully, but, afraid of getting it wrong or getting in the way, I find myself constantly asking Simon Shaw am I doing this right? What else should I be doing? And when you have played seventy-odd games for England, that seems a little bizarre.

We lose to New Zealand, but respectably. When I return to France, I feel I have developed as a player. I remain uncertain about this new game plan, but overall, I'm actually pleased. I'm also particularly excited to be back in an environment created by Johnno. Like 2003, the ethos is one of respect and supporting the players.

●　●　●

After the autumn internationals, it's great to be back in France again, where friendships and a sense of familiarity are forming. At the bottom of the hill from where we live, Shelley and I are warmly received in the boulangerie and the boucherie, where the chat invariably heads in certain directions – how the season is going, how much better the weather is on the Med compared to England, how the England team is doing and how long I'm going to be playing in Toulon.

Down in the village of Bandol, we have our regular spots. The Bistrot always looks after us. In La Seyne Sur Mer nearby, my favourite spot is a beautiful restaurant on the beach, Bard'ô, where the owner, Andrew, sets us up regularly the day after games, sometimes with tables for family and friends. We have already set a recrod with a table for twenty-two. It's a great escape.

I have done some sponsorship work for SFR, the French telecom company, who have made some radio ads playing off my accent. They ask for my English pronunciation of words such as 'Euro'. Of course, this leads to relentless piss-taking at training. Whenever a chance presents itself, one of my teammates will throw in one of these words with my English pronunciation. Very funny indeed. But I love the atmosphere here.

Away games are an interesting challenge. As always, I like to get in some practice before a game, and so someone at Toulon arranges with a local rugby club for me to use their ground. It's amazing how quickly word can get round. Usually, the minimum that is required is to pose for a photo with the local team, who will almost certainly have pitched up. Sometimes, I find I have an audience of around a hundred people. You don't want to tell them to back off, but with pre-match anxieties in full flow, you don't want to be signing hundreds of autographs before a game, either. It's a tough one.

I do not remotely mind signing afterwards, because I love the opportunity to connect with the supporters. After away games, I hardly ever make it to the post-match meal because I get caught in-between the changing rooms and the reception, and when I'm asked to sign then, I'll sign every one if I can. The other players often bring me food while I'm signing. They really look after me. But later, they'll be waiting on the bus and we have to leave.

Most likely, we have a plane to catch, and anyway, it's not fair for me to hold up the rest of the team. So I make my apologies and get on the bus, often to find that someone has brought more food for me. There is a great, respectful spirit among these players.

•   •   •

Since I'm a rugby league nut, I was a bit of a fan of Sonny Bill Williams before I got to Toulon. His talent is enormous. He is phenomenal. He has gifts that could make him unique in the world of rugby. But he is struggling to come back from injury and to show all his abilities in the game, so he is not as effective as he could be. He is also quite complex, sometimes solitary. He reminds me a little of myself.

We have been chatting on and off for a while and the similarities are becoming clearer. Back at Newcastle, I'd always seen it as my role to try to assist the younger guys, such as Toby Flood, to develop their game. I kicked with Toby a lot, trained with him. When he was still at school, I actually coached his team. I feel a similar responsibility with Sonny, but I'm also just inspired by what this player is capable of.

I ask him if he wants to do some one-to-one training with me, and if there's anything he particularly wants to work on. Little does he know that I'm keen to learn from him in return.

So now we sometimes train together, perfecting each other's passing skills and movement, and he asks me loads of questions, on positioning – where should I be if this happens? – and on decision-making – what's the best thing to do if this happens?

I tell him rather than working out where you fit in, you've got to find a way of actually making the team and the game fit in with you. Basically, you need to spend the entire game doing what you're great at. If you manage that, the team will win – end of story. And so will you. You're going to be the guy who's taking it to the next level.

And he is. The guy has got talent that I could only dream about.

● ● ●

We play away against Clermont, just into the new year, and afterwards I'm due to stay overnight at a Lyon airport hotel and then fly to London to join England for an analysis day.

But at 11.30pm, I start vomiting and at five o'clock I still haven't stopped. It's like the South Africa 2000 tour all over again. So I leave a message with Gavin Dovey, the England team manager, that I can't make it.

At the meeting I miss, they discuss the New Zealand game and the new game plan, and it gets well supported. The decision is let's carry on. So by the time we meet up again for the Six Nations, it's firmly set.

We go into the Wales game with the same game plan, same tactics, and it's a solid start, a good win. I fall ill in the following week and play Italy in hot weather feeling pretty rancid, stuffy, no energy, nothing.

Everyone always ignores the fact that playing Italy away is damned hard. I miss a couple of easy kicks that I shouldn't have missed, and the game is pretty close, but we win and we get in place some of the rugby we wanted. In the shape I'm in, I feel pleased just to have come through it. The media, however, don't agree. Their questions afterwards make that clear. I feel hounded. I'm being killed for not being on top form.

We are to play Ireland next, but by now it seems commonly accepted that England aren't playing well and that's down to me. We've just beaten a good team away from home. There were a couple of kicks I could have executed better, but the reaction is grossly sensational, egged on by, of all people, Matt Dawson.

Have you read what Matt Dawson wrote in the *Daily Mail*? That's the question put to me by the press a few days later.

No, I haven't. I don't read the papers.

So they tell me. Dawson says that I am not, and never have been, a comfortable play-maker or decision-maker. Apparently, I can only play to a team plan and I have always relied on others – and he puts his own name forward here – to make the decisions for me.

That's nice. That seems to set the agenda for the entire week.

● ● ●

Before the Ireland game, after a meeting with the team leaders, Johnno asks me to stay behind with a few of the coaches. Look, he says, you've been taking loads of stick, but we just want you to know we think you're doing a perfect job for us, and we're actually really happy. Don't let it get to you.

That's great to hear, because I really need a boost right now. I have been strict over my relationship with Johnno. Ever since he shifted from ex-teammate and fellow World Cup-winner to team manager, I have made a point of ensuring a safe distance between us. He is the guy picking the team and so I have felt I should treat him like management, not like an old friend. We do have our moments when the guard drops and we find ourselves reminiscing about what we once went through together as fellow players, but Johnno is more relaxed about that than I am. I only want what I genuinely deserve; I don't want history and past friendships to complicate anything.

So, from manager to player, it's great to have that reassurance from him. Nevertheless, I'm certainly feeling the pressure, but I want to be positive. I'm desperate to go out against Ireland and be myself.

I need things to go well. But our game plan, still relatively new to us, requires a few phases before we really exploit them and the moment of exploitation never seems to arrive. As a number ten, I feel predictable and a bit restricted in what I can do and where I can go on the field.

I start going after the game a bit and taking on the defence at every opportunity, but it doesn't help having the other guys standing off. I look to offload the ball, but I don't have people to pass it to. I sense moments of hesitation around me, as if some guys don't want to interfere, as if they don't know how to react to me as a person or as a player. But I'm crying out for support. I'm not seeing too many other options, so I try to create situations myself.

How I could do with a Mike Catt to help out and share the responsibility; or someone to play with the ball while I step back to take a look. I feel I'm constantly in the game but unable to affect it.

Yet the scores are tied and, with ten minutes to go, I hit a right-foot drop goal on the turn to give us the lead. If only this can be enough. But then I make a criminal defensive error. I don't make many and this serves as an indication that too much is going on in my mind. I over-read the play and am caught taking the man outside the one I should be taking. So Tommy Bowe runs through inside me and that is more or less that.

It shouldn't be, because we have a chance to win at it the close. We have numbers and could attack them out wide, but we aren't ready to exploit those areas of the field. No one says anything, no one talks to me, no one lets me know where the space is and, with my head still spinning from their try, I take us somewhere else. The chance of a reprieve is gone.

● ● ●

I've now had two fairly good games and was up and down against Ireland – and I'm being hammered by the media. I'm being hit harder now than ever before. You'd think I'd attacked their families. It's madness.

It doesn't help that every Wednesday without fail at Pennyhill, I'm sent out to talk to them. The same guys who are killing me in the newspapers after the games sit three or four yards away asking me how do you feel? What is your reaction to the media criticism? You must feel pretty down. It must really hurt.

It's like a guy punching you in the stomach and then saying oh look, you've got a bad stomach, that's terrible. Tell us about your bad stomach.

Now I am really struggling, desperately re-evaluating the rugby. I don't know how to make this work. My response always is to tackle the challenge and overcome it with hard work. That's how I always understood rugby. Now something's just not working and it upsets me.

I feel increasingly isolated from the squad. It's as if there is some obligatory respect for me because of where I might have been and what I might have achieved. It's like they don't want to interfere or get in my way. And now the whole media are pinning me down as the reason why it isn't going well, so I feel like an old expert hand who's letting all these young inexperienced guys down. The whole complexity of the situation created by the media and the past has made it really tough for me to connect with some of the guys. I'm sure that I'm largely to blame for this. I'm starting to feel ashamed and embarrassed around everyone, which is probably making them feel a little embarrassed for me. It's getting awkward.

On the point of tears, I phone Tana in Toulon. I just want his opinion. Against Ireland, he says, you looked like you were out on your own out there.

Brian Smith asks me to meet him for a chat in the bar at Pennyhill, and I go along to see him half expecting to be dropped. We need to give Floody a bit of a run-out off the bench this week, he says. He hasn't come off the bench yet at all, and he needs some experience. I agree with that completely, but I still feel the confidence in me is seeping away.

So during training, I crank up the pressure higher than ever. I'm so desperate to conquer this game plan and understand where I fit in. I treat every training session like a mini game. They become so important, just briefly they kind of become my life.

And as ever, I go about convincing myself that I am going to be great on the weekend. But actually, for the first time, reality is utterly different. I'm a genuinely broken man. The emotional stress and pressure has dragged me to rock bottom. I feel the media are set against me and the squad are losing confidence in me. I no longer have confidence in what I am supposed to be doing, either. I'm a shell of myself; I am completely lost.

I ask Brian for another chat. I tell him I don't feel it's working for me, and I'm struggling badly, mentally. I want to be in an environment where I can go out there and smash it, but I'm going out filled with uncertainty. I tell him I'm struggling to deal with this, I'm struggling to sleep and struggling to lift my head up in front of the other guys.

Brian is really understanding and says that he can see how painful I am finding it.

But the guy who then goes out to play against Scotland wearing the number ten shirt – that's hardly me. I do everything I possibly can, in as positive and enthusiastic a mood as I can summon – that will never change, that is still the non-negotiable part of the deal – but my focus is wrong. I do not play with the certainty of a team leader, the way I enjoyed so much in the autumn.

Internationally, my world is falling apart and so every time I touch the ball, I analyse my performance. It's like every second of this Scotland game is on replay. Everything good: that's OK. Everything bad: I've failed. What's the point? I failed. I'm stuck inside my head. I'm not stuck in the game.

Shortly after half-time, I am put out of my misery. In a tackle I get knocked clean out and that's it. I'm forced to come off. Normally, I'd fight coming off, but not this time. It's not like there's a sense of relief – just oh well, that didn't go as well as I'd hoped it would. And so I sit in the changing room, listening to the noises of the game outside. Jonny Bloomfield, one of our technical coaches, gives me updates on the score. An unsatisfactory draw. Unsatisfactory all round.

● ● ●

The following Monday, on the Pennyhill training pitch, Brian says he wants another word. I knew this was coming.

Look, he says, we are going to go with Floody this week against France. He needs a run out.

OK, that's great, mate. I don't mind that all, and actually I don't think it's necessarily a bad idea.

But I also ask Brian where do you see me in the plan?

We still see you as the number-one fly half, but it's been a difficult Six Nations and Floody needs a run out.

It might just be me but his answer seems a bit mumbled. It's not said outright, and from the umm-ing and aah-ing and the search for the right words, I'm not totally convinced that his answer isn't just an attempt to make me feel better and hide the fact that their confidence has shifted.

But when I tell Brian that the change is not a bad idea, I really mean it.

You're going to get a kick-start reaction from taking me out of the team, I tell him. In fact, strangely, I couldn't be more sure of it.

It happened in 2008. Things weren't going well and the team looked to me to try to sort it out, but the minute they took me out of the game, people stopped standing back and started wanting to get involved and do it themselves. Again, I've come into an England situation that's not exactly going well and I've tried to contribute towards finding the solution. And at times the team has been leaving me to do what they think is 'my thing'.

You'll get a good response from this, I tell Brian. The younger guys will come into their own.

Not that it exactly helps my cause. Immediately, I say well done to Floody. If there's anything I can do to help you in any way, I tell him, let me know. But I'm as low as I can go. I feel ashamed around the squad. I'm just a contradiction. I'm billed as the leader and a big player, and yet I have become the media's nominated scapegoat and now I've been dropped. A leader should have a kind of aura, he should be the go-to guy, so the worst thing is to feel undermined in this way by being seen to be responsible for everything that's not working. Everything feels awkward. Around the hotel, I don't really know how to conduct myself.

So I ask is there any way I can take a breather from this week's Wednesday press grilling? I know there are a few French TV stations who want to do an interview on the Friday to ask about me being back in France, so can I just do that and avoid the rest of it? It's agreed and I'm truly thankful.

Friday comes and, contrary to the plan, I walk straight into my own personal press conference. All the media are there in force, and having pushed the issue, they now have the questions to follow. What are my feelings on a difficult Six Nations? What are the qualities of Toby Flood? How does it feel to be dropped?

So they get their story. And, twenty-four hours before a match, I get my confidence freshly assailed.

● ● ●

Thanks to the fix-ups from the Ireland and especially the Scotland game, we take on France with an improved and expanded game plan, and the boys play with freedom and a let's-go-and-try-this attitude, for which I'd been longing for most of my career.

I watch from the bench of the Stade de France and the team look great. I come on at the end and hit arguably the best penalty goal of my career, with no warm-up, from the touchline 60 metres away. We don't win but we deserve to and what I see confirms my fears. This team looks as though it's better off without me. In every team I've played in, I've always felt I could make it work, but now I'm looking at a team that is working better without me in it.

● ● ●

Back at Toulon, I have to try to pick up the pieces. I go to the Stade Mayol to do some kicking practice and find a huge banner, in the form of a bed sheet, hanging over one of the exits, high up in one of the stands. In big letters, written in English, it says 'Welcome home Jonny'.

I love that banner. I can barely express how good those words make me feel. I hit the first few kicks with tears welling in my eyes.

Outside the ground, after kicking, a few fans approach me. They tell me they are proud of me. They say when you came on against France and you hit the big penalty, we thought oh no, now you're going to do your drop goal and you're going to beat us like you've done before. We knew you were going to do it.

It strikes me that no one here seems to be in the same frame of mind as people back in England. My fellow players are the same. I return to team training and it's as if the situation with England had never happened. They welcome me back warmly. They seem genuinely pleased, almost relieved, to see me. They make me feel as if I belong again.

With that kind of response, I feel I can exhale and lose some of that weight of negativity. It just feels so right here.

●　●　●

By the end of the season, Sonny Bill is really flying. He is an awesome sight. I've never seen a guy tackle as fiercely as he does, but also, I've never seen a guy keep the ball alive with such ease, even when he's targeted by three or more of the opposition. His offloads out of contact are incredible.

I return to a side that has won five games in succession, and we carry on and win the next six. There are games where Sonny Bill does things that are so good it's almost comical. He reminds me of the great days alongside Inga, when you want to remain professional on the field, but you also want to laugh at what he's doing. Spurred on by the energy in the squad, we all start joining in, even the great Tana Umaga comes back from retirement again.

Week after week, after the game, our special team victory song, 'I Gotta Feeling', resounds around in the dressing room. It becomes synonymous with happy moments. Joe Van Niekerk, our captain, tells us beforehand how great it is going to feel when we hear the Black Eyed Peas blasting out again, when we come in with another win.

The team may have flirted with relegation last year, but this time we finish joint top of the League, and the season culminates with two huge matches. In the end-of-season knockout competition for the teams that finish top of the League, we play Clermont in the play-off semi-finals. The venue is supposed to be neutral but somehow we are in St Etienne, which is barely an hour from Clermont and eight hours from Toulon. Yet the atmosphere is unlike anything I've experienced. The heaving crowd splits in half, red and black on one side, yellow and blue on the other. The noise is constant.

We have to fight back from 10 points down with time running out. But Sonny Bill scores a try, which I convert, and then, with under three minutes to run, I am standing over a 45 metre penalty to draw level.

At this stage Juan Lobbe, our magnificent number eight, slightly carried away, decides to have a word to explain to me what our tactics are going to be after the restart.

Juan, I say to him, can you please fuck off! I need to concentrate on this penalty.

Oh yes, sorry, he replies. Good luck.

I get the kick and so it's on to extra time, but we quickly go behind and give ourselves another 13 points to chase. We move the ball all over the field with crazy offloads coming from everywhere and quickly get seven back. The game ends with our flying Fijian wing, Gabi Lovobalvu, stretching out to score and being tackled into touch. So close. It's is a hell of a way to go out, and even if you hate defeat as much as I do, it's impossible not to feel proud.

Having lost that by six points, eight days later, we then lose the Amlin Cup final to Cardiff by seven. We start well and hold a good lead, but it's a game too far for me and for everyone. I pull a muscle in my back, which I don't help by then attempting a penalty from the touchline, so I miss the last half hour. But for us all, after all we've been through, it's a sad end to finish the season without a trophy.

But this season with Toulon has been out of this world and now it's time to celebrate. I used to drink once every few years. I'm now probably down to once a year, if I'm lucky – and this is it. I want to spend time with my teammates and I want be there to say a goodbye to Sonny Bill and Tana, who are leaving to return to New Zealand.

The night out goes the way almost all of them do for me. And the after-effects carry on, just at they did after the 2007 World Cup final. The next day, when Shelley and I are due at a team barbecue, I'm still being sick. When we arrive, I get out of the car to help direct Shelley into a parking spot, but she drives into a wall because I'm neglecting my duty, bending over vomiting.

CHAPTER 24

HAVING picked up the pieces in Toulon, I do not want to have them scattered once more with England. Last time it felt so difficult, so awkward, and impacted badly on my game. My concern is what effect another dose may have on me, should I go on the upcoming summer tour to Australia.

The other issue now is this back injury. I'd probably just about be fit for the Test matches, and with such uncertainty, there is a good argument for staying at home and recuperating.

Philippe Saint-André is pretty astute and so I go to him for advice. He says you've got a bad back, it's going to take a while to heal, you've got the opportunity to have the summer off and get back firing for next season. Why not have a bit of a breather and do what's best for yourself for once?

A week later, I'm on the plane to Perth. It was inevitable, I suppose. I went on the Tour from Hell in 1998. I toured South Africa in 2007. I have never shirked a challenge. It's part of my values system that is never going to change. The England situation is difficult, but that's no reason to avoid it. Just because it hasn't gone my way doesn't mean I should immediately turn my back on it and run. I won't give up. What I need to do is face up to my problems with England and get everything back to normal.

As far as I know, I am still the first choice number ten. I need to show that I am worthy of that position.

● ● ●

My own sense of awkwardness, my own paranoia, is not helped by the fact that I am literally on the fringes of training. For the first couple of days in Perth, while the squad train as usual, I do my own exercises with the physios and conditioners on the touchlines to try to get my back completely better.

After three or four days, with a week to go before the game, we have our first leaders' meeting where we talk game tactics. How are we going to play? I get the impression that everyone is turning their attention to Floody. The conversation is directed largely through him. What possible moves should we do? I wonder if something has been said in training that I don't know about. Something seems pretty set.

The first I see of the actual make-up of the team is in a squad meeting a few days later in the team room when it's put up on the board. And, no surprises, I am on the bench.

During training, in the lead-up to the game, except for only a few minutes, I'm one of those making up the opposition. This is completely understandable because Floody needs time to get comfortable and confident, but I don't get the idea that I'm to be brought on. No one says at a certain point in the game, we'll look to get you on. I'm just there on the bench if I'm needed.

My consolation is that we have been told that pretty much everyone will start a game on this tour. What they're probably doing is giving Floody a shot for the first Test with me earmarked for the second. That would explain everything.

For some reason the Australian media, though, don't believe a word of it. When I do the usual midweek session with them, they won't let it drop. They say to me isn't this some kind of a ploy? Aren't we all being set up here? Surely at the last minute, we'll find out you're starting?

But I'm not. The last time I was in the Subiaco Oval in Perth was seven years ago and I was in the team playing South Africa in the crucial 2003 World Cup group game. Now I sit on the bench while the game plays out in front of me, and two thoughts are spinning round my head – maybe this just isn't right for me any more, and I still feel this is what I was born to do. One totally contradicts the other.

With eight minutes left, I get on to the pitch and everything suddenly seems so simple. Not easy, but it makes sense, I feel comfortable and natural. I've spent all this time doubting whether I belong here any more, yet I can still do exactly what I want to.

I just wish I had time to do more. In the changing room afterwards, I'm barely out of breath. I'm certainly not satisfied but I am slightly encouraged. The second half was a massive success for us. There's a lot to look forward to and to work on for the second Test in Sydney. That could be a great chance for me.

● ● ●

The following Monday, we train at the Sydney Oval and I am handed a bib. The instruction is: reserves, line up on that cone on one side of the pitch. And over I go.

That's confirmation of where I stand, my one shred of hope gone. Now it's clear. Things have changed.

Thank God I'm room-sharing with Taity, my good mate, who is not going through a particularly good time either. We try to help each other along. We share our problems and try to motivate ourselves and each other. Every night we tell each other how good we are going to be the following day.

I tell myself my skills are going to be so good tomorrow, I visualise myself tearing up the starting-team defence with my attacking play. But then I wake up in the morning with my heart beating at a million miles an hour and those old panic attacks kicking in. It's the humiliation I feel. I don't fit in, my motivation is falling and I can't do this.

I don't know how much of this is my own paranoia, but I have no idea what my teammates think of me now. All those years I've been talked about in a certain way; all those years I felt that I was thrown back in the team as soon as I regained fitness to sort everything out. Everyone knows how proud I am, but now it almost feels like it's the end of the road for me, and they don't know how to respond.

My only form of mental escape is to overindulge in my individual skills, which means I get back late from training every day because I stay so long kicking. Trying to improve has always been my way of staying sane. What this means is that I have little time to get ready for the afternoon weight sessions, so I ask Calvin if I can stay at the hotel and do my exercises in the small gym there. It's a bit easier, anyway. I still get recognised by rugby fans over here, and I have to admit that I like the peace and quiet and the relief of being hidden away from everyone for a while. It's sad to say but perhaps the hardest part of all of it is watching the other players laughing and joking with each other, clearly thriving in a situation that I find so painful.

Then comes the Wednesday media session. I sit down with the journalists, a smile on my face, and try to pull off the façade of not minding too much when they ask how does it feel to have been dropped? Tell us about Toby Flood, they say.

These are the same people who spent the Six Nations asking me about how badly I was doing, now asking me where do you see your career going? And do you think you'll get your place back?

But I have to bluff it. They ask me so what has Johnno said to you about where you stand? And has he told you what he wants from you? What have the coaches said to you about this? The trouble is, I have to make those answers up.

I wonder if I should initiate a chat with Johnno and Brian, but I don't. Maybe that's not the smartest response, but I feel quite stubborn now. By this time, I'm interested to see when they are going to make the move.

Yet on the surface, maybe it's not such a crazy situation at all. I've been dropped to the bench. It happens, all the time in fact. What's to get het up about? It makes for a very convincing argument – just get over yourself and get on with it like everyone else. Perhaps that's the way I should be dealing with it. If only I was that strong right now.

On our day off, I go for a long walk on the beach. I try to work it out in my head and see everything in a better light; I want to get back to being myself. But, on this tour, I know that's asking a lot. This tour is hurting me and I'm letting it drag me further and further down. It seems the only way I'll find the right perspective is by seeing it through and then getting far away from it all.

● ● ●

Never has the world seemed so false as it does after the second Test. I am on for the last half hour. When I come on, we are two points down, and after about a minute and without so much as a touch of the ball, I am called upon to kick a penalty from 40 metres out. That gives us the lead, which we manage to defend to the end.

Afterwards, the journalists say isn't it ironic, this situation? You come back to this ground where you won the World Cup, and again you hit the kick to win the game for England against Australia – you couldn't have scripted it better.

What a load of shit!

But I'm just too exhausted to respond with any passion. I've simply had enough of all this. It's been a long tiring year and, right now, I just want to get away to a big holiday with Shelley; and I want to get back to Toulon, where rugby feels the way it should and where I feel wanted and valued.

● ● ●

The day before that second Test, Johnno had suggested that we have a chat. I told him I was keen but that I'd rather we wait until after the game.

So later, in the early hours after the Test, we grab a couple of chairs in the team meeting room.

I tell him I'm surprised at what has happened. The last thing I heard was that I was your first choice ten, and now I've spent five and a half weeks on tour and I haven't heard a peep from anyone apart from being told to pick up a bib in every training session and wear it as a reserve.

Johnno explains it from a different point of view. He says the coaching team didn't feel that you were someone who needed an arm around your shoulders. We just wanted to let you get on with your normal stuff.

There's that problem again. Outwardly, I might look like I'm coping and just soldiering on, but right now I need as big an arm around me as possible. I tried to make it clear during the Six Nations that I was struggling.

I tell Johnno all the stuff in the media has just got stupid. Whatever happens, it's my fault. And I just don't feel a part of the set-up now, I don't feel myself, I'm certainly not enjoying it.

Johnno tells me I want you to fight for your place back.

But the thing is, I tell him, I'm not 20 years old any more. You know what I'm capable of, you know what I'll give. The mark of me is that I will give it every single time without fail, and I will be there to stand up and be counted at the end when it gets tough, always, every time, and that's never going to change. So I'm not going to fight for my place back. I'm just going to keep trying to get better and better the way I always have done.

The question for me, I tell him, is not how hard I work for my place back. It's more do I continue playing or do I retire from England rugby?

When I was a kid, this isn't what I pictured playing for England would be like. It wasn't how I ever imagined myself behaving or letting things get to me. Away from the field, everything has spiralled out of control, and for me, now, it's not even about playing rugby. It has become about something else entirely and I don't understand it any more. I don't like it. I'm no longer able to be myself and I'm not happy.

I tell him the way I'm feeling, I may not come back at all.

CHAPTER 25

Four months have passed since that conversation with Johnno and I finally have an answer. In Australia, I told him I may not come back at all and I felt the same when he came to see me in Toulon. I was very close to closing the book on my international career.

But after some serious soul searching and some decent week-in week-out rugby, I have finally come to my conclusion: I am in it for one last chapter. I am just happier with myself when I'm striving, even when it's against the odds, in fact especially when it's against the odds. What I'm saying is I've got to stand up and be counted again.

However, no sooner have I told Johnno that I am in, than I am out of action again.

Before meeting up with England for the autumn internationals, Toulon play Stade Français in Paris. It is a massive game in front of a massive capacity crowd and though my long drop goal at the end bounces off the bar and goes over, we are still narrowly beaten. The real worry for me, though, is that I feel totally incapable of tackling.

They have Mathieu Bastareaud, a hugely powerful centre, running at us and for once I am focussed on just cutting him down, I am not being stupid and trying to smash him into next week. However, there are times when I literally feel like I may as well not be here. When I try to put big shots on other people, they run straight through me. At the end of the game I am in so much pain. I am very worried that the pain in my shoulder will mean seriously considering the way I play the game. I feel useless out there, like a turnstile in defence.

So, as soon as I arrive in the England camp, I go to Pasky and the England physios. I tell them I can't lift my arms above 90 degrees, especially my left one, and I can't tackle or take contact on it. They send me off to Manchester to see Len Funk, the guy who operated on both my shoulders and, after some scans, Len is very open and honest. He says that this is what you'd expect to see in a rugby player who has played a lot of rugby and who's had two shoulder operations. Both shoulders are arthritic, he says, there are little bits floating around and a lot of stuff not quite right.

What it means, he says, is I'm not going to return to being a 22/23-year-old player and that, to a degree, if quality of life is important to me after rugby then the rest of my career is going to be one of pretty strict management.

What it also means is that, after deciding to monitor it week by week, we decide that proper rest for a good month is what is required. And so, having tortured myself over the decision of whether I wanted to carry on playing for England, I can't play this autumn anyway.

On the one hand it is good to hear there was nothing really serious with my shoulders, on the other hand it is disheartening to feel that this is going to be me for the rest of my playing days. Bear in mind my training ethics, that diving whole-heartedly into contact sessions has been the only approach I have known – I now have to reassess completely. Now I am going to be that Matt Burke figure, the one sitting on the sidelines saying: Look this is a contact session, I can't do it. The sort of guy who, earlier in my career, I probably would have judged without any empathy for copping out, putting on the smoking jacket and letting the young guys do it.

But at least, when it comes to the games themselves, I will still be able to take off the slippers and smoking jacket. The reason I am at this stage, physically, is in part because of all those times when Clive and Rob and the coaches and the physios told me to take it a bit easy on the tackling and I chose to ignore them. But really it was just wanting to make the biggest hits, to be the best, the best at everything – which means being the best defender in the game.

I still get it now, I still get guys saying to me: Oh leave it to the back row or whatever. But what I love is the fact that I'm at this stage of my career and I'm still being me.

● ● ●

Back in Toulon, the good news is that we have been joined by Carl Hayman which is not only awesome for the team, but it means the band – of sorts – is back together.

It's a bit of a different scenario now. We don't quite have the same studio set up unfortunately so we have sessions in Carl's garage or in the small upstairs spare bedroom in Shelley's and my place. There are also some properly talented musicians around. Fotu Auelua, our immensely gifted number 8, plays a mean guitar. Our physio and all-round good guy, Mattieu Stoss, is a great jazz drummer.

On vocals, Carl's wife Natalie is quite handy, though unfortunately when she isn't around, it is actually left to me once in a while to try. One strict rule is that there is to be absolutely no looking me in the eye when I'm on the mic. I can't bear the eye contact.

'Yellow Ledbetter' by Pearl Jam is a band favourite. My goal is that, soon enough, I might have enough confidence to belt it out without having to look at the floor whilst I do so.

Meanwhile, my shoulders start slowly to improve. I finally get back to playing in December. The pain returns for my first game, against Montpellier, but then it just lifts the following week in a really good Heineken Cup game against London Irish.

We then qualify for the Heineken Cup quarter-finals with a win in a hell of an atmosphere against Munster. I am ever reminded of the sheer intensity and magnitude of rugby out here.

And I am also feeling fit for a return to England.

●　●　●

If I say I'm going to be there, then it is a given that I'm going to be there 100 per cent. That has to be the way.

There is no point in pretending I don't have slight trepidations, but I arrive back in the England camp for the Six Nations pretty much where I need to be mentally and physically.

Johnno is just Johnno, checking how I am and genuinely wanting to know the answer. But, to settle in here, I know that the onus is on me. It helps that, from the success at Toulon, I've got my confidence back. I am not like I was last summer; not like a shell of my former self.

At the same time, Floody has been playing well for Leicester and I don't expect any change in the selection policy. So I put a lot of pressure on myself in training but it's good pressure, it's saying this is just a great opportunity, go and show what I'm all about.

I can't help my natural self, though. I still wake up in the mornings in that slight state of panic, getting het up about how people see me and what my role is. Yet this is a good challenge, it's my time to learn from Mike Catt again. When he wasn't selected, he just kept faith in himself and his ability, he didn't allow himself to be blown about by the wind. He didn't allow himself to feel awesome because he was selected one week, and then unimportant the next when he was not – not the way I have let myself feel.

This is my time to deal with that. It's just what happens in life. But it's still going to be difficult for me.

And so, as the Six Nations start and I resume my position on the England bench, I start every morning scoring about a five or a six out of ten on the panic scale. But then we get past Wales and then Italy and I get to a point where I am waking up unaffected and almost immune to where my name is on the team sheet, and used to the fact that my press interviews seem to involve talking solely about how good Floody is and how well he is doing in the England number 10 jersey.

The trouble is, I discover, the nerves and the anxiety of being on the bench are worse than when you play. I can't believe in the past I have had the audacity to look at the guys on the bench and think to myself, ah, I wouldn't mind being one of them at the moment, they're not going through all this enormous pain.

But when you start, you go out there and just get stuck in. On the bench, your body is in this state of constant preparation and guessing, and second guessing. It doesn't have to be like this; there are other guys who deal with it so much better than me. Steve Thompson just sits there, talking like he's on his sofa at home watching it. When he is suddenly told to get stripped and go on, he just does it. And I look at him and keep thinking, can I see any nerves in this guy?

For me it is a challenging situation. I know why they want me there. I'm either coming on to try to rescue a game if we're behind, or finish the game if we're in front. You've got to do all the right things and you have only a very limited time to get them done. There is no time to build into it, find the pace, maybe make a few mistakes and learn from them. If you get it right, you kind of keep your head above water, people will say well done, and that's that. Whereas if it takes you a while to get into the game and you miss a couple of goal kicks, then you just get that immediate, ah well that's why you're on the bench, that's why you shouldn't be playing.

So I just have to make the most of every chance I have and I speak to Blackie about this before every game. Key words: contribute, contribute, contribute to the team, contribute in any way. Make sure every second you're contributing.

Against Wales, I come on and put us two scores up and just about out of reach. Against Italy, I manage to make a decent tackle in the corner to stop a try. Against France, I come on in the 51st minute and the first thing I have to do is take a shot at the posts from 47 metres out. This one goes over and gives me back the world record for points scoring. And against Scotland, I come on when the game is tight and getting a bit tense; we score a try and the corner conversion puts us further ahead.

But my biggest asset will always be my obsessive side, the fact that I cannot stop looking for more work to do out there. And in these games, I might be able to hit goal kicks, and I might be part of creating the odd opportunity, but I know that I am contributing because sometimes in

10 minutes of rugby, I am making six or seven tackles, plugging holes and taking on the responsibility to direct the team as much as I can.

Yet still I can't pretend that it isn't a struggle being on the bench, though my difficulty is hugely eased by the response I get from the Twickenham crowd. When I am running round warming up in the in-goal area, people shout and say really nice things, and the whole time I'm feeling, this is amazing. And, later, when I do go on to the field – to hear their cheers, that is an amazing experience too.

* * *

My preparation for Toulon's Heineken Cup quarter-final pretty much sums up the end of our season. We are playing Perpignan in Barcelona, in the Olympic stadium, and on the morning of the game, as is always my way, I go to do some kicking practice. I go with Tom Whitford, the team manager, and we are able to practise in the stadium which is great.

Bear in mind all the places I've kicked in the morning before games, the playgrounds, the car parks, the farmers' fields, the God knows what. Here I am on what is easily one of the most beautiful pitches I've ever stood upon in one of the most stunning stadia I have been in, and yet it's the only place, while I am kicking, that I've ever trodden in shit.

I guess it's a fox. And I guess the offending material gets sandwiched between my boot and the ball because I notice immediately afterwards that there's a pretty horrendous smell. And then I look to see Tom take the ball fully into his chest, look at his shirt, smell his hands, and then quickly palm the ball off to one of the ball boys.

In the game itself, we get ourselves in a great position and then throw it away in the second half. Similarly in the league, we're handily placed and then lose it all in our final and most crucial game of the season, away against Montpellier.

It is a massively disappointing end to the season and a sad way to say goodbye to some amazingly good friends and truly world-class players, Fotu, George Smith, Felipe Contepomi, Paul Sackey. All of them are going.

For me, I am going too. To my last World Cup.

CHAPTER 26

I roll into Pennyhill Park for what will be my last pre-season before my last World Cup. And I feel pretty good. I might have just had the opportunity to take a long break, to relax, I might have spent much of it in Majorca, but I have been working perhaps harder than ever before. This is an incredible opportunity, maybe my last, and it goes without saying that I want to make the most of it.

At Pennyhill, the England squad trains hard, Monday to Thursday, for six weeks. We have Friday to Sunday off and then start again. Except I don't take the Friday to Sunday off at all. For each Saturday, Calvin Morriss gives us each a session to do on our own while we are away, not huge sessions, just something to keep us ticking over. But I put myself on a different schedule. Up in Newcastle, I get together with Blackie and Sparks and train Thursday night, twice on Friday, twice on Saturday and a final session on the Sunday.

For me, though, it is clear that this camp will be a test mentally as well as physically. The pressure and responsibility is cranked up on the number nines and tens. Especially the tens.

We have sessions in the morning, one back line versus another back line, with the number tens making all the calls, in charge of running the plays. And in the afternoon, it starts all over again but this time it's the team session, one team versus another.

And then every morning, the tens have a meeting with Brian Smith in a small cottage by the team room just to look at the clips from the previous day's training and talk about it. What are you thinking here? Why did you do that? How could you improve this?

It is intense and very competitive, you feel there is something riding on everything, me v Floody v Charlie Hodgson. Charlie is a very, very good player and easily one of the best passers of the ball around. The three of us work together and against each other, we feel we are accountable for everything. There is no let up, it is very tough but the rugby relevance of it feels priceless.

But where I am really struggling is with the wrestling. The squad is doing a lot of wrestling as a technique to improve the way we manoeuvre our body weight and use power more effectively. But this is a bit of a tricky one for me because I am supposed to be managing my body, playing the professional.

However, the last thing I want in pre-season is to be on the sideline. On the one hand, I don't want to injure myself, not at this stage; on the other, I still don't have the mental toughness not to be a team man and not join in. And it doesn't help that the wrestling's becoming a big thing. Some of the guys love it, especially the coaches who watch all the sessions. We have bouts and every bout is recorded and your scores go up on the board in the team room with Manu Tuilagi and Matt Banahan generally topping the charts. And then they start showing these recordings on the TV in the dining-room during lunch.

The problem for me, because of my competitive side, is that it hooks onto me, begins playing on my mind, becoming very important, irrationally so, and I start to get anxious as I feel I am massively losing my standing within the group. My win-loss record is a dismal two bouts, two defeats. It feels as though everyone is beating me. We come out of one session with most of the guys laughing and joking and I walk away just feeling low about myself. When I don't compete well, it can really get to me, so much so that I feel I may as well just walk out altogether.

It seems to me we have to be careful here. Take someone like Mike Tindall for example – big, powerful, strong centre on the field and a senior man in the squad. But if he gets beaten in the wrestling too many times by Manu or by Matt Banahan or whoever, you start to mess with perceptions, you mess with the aura that he has built up. On the team room board, we don't post the weights that everyone is lifting, so why are we being reduced to wrestling facts and figures which aren't relevant on the field?

So I have a meeting with Brian and mention what I'm thinking. I think we need to be aware of what we may be doing here. I definitely get the impression that there are other players who feel the same. We've already had Ben Youngs injure his knee doing it. I am a proud person and if you are going to show these recordings during lunch, then I'm probably going to eat somewhere else.

But even so, all this is still killing me. Because this wrestling is right there in front of me. It is a challenge and one that I'm definitely coming up short in.

What I need is another focus, something to work on, see some results in and feel good about. I settle on the Team Fitness Test, just like in 2003. It is exactly what I need and first time out, I do it in 216 seconds, which just about lands me in the top five of the backs.

But now this is my goal. I work with Blackie and my brother on it every weekend, hammering out regular, good sessions. Big sessions, sometimes an hour or two without stopping. And the night before the next test, I am on the phone to Blackie, talking about my preparation, telling him how nervous I am about it, but also telling him how I am going to smash it. It just means that much.

The following day, I run it in 203 seconds, about seven or eight seconds faster than anyone else in the entire squad.

In the middle of the camp, we have a week off and I need to pop back to Toulon. So I go with Blackie and Sparks, we arrive in the evening and fit in a late night session in the dark. We then have to go to Germany to see the people at the adidas headquarters. We break off the meeting in the middle of the afternoon so we can do another training session. We carry on like this all week. At the weekend Shelley and I head down to Bristol for her sister's wedding, and then I am back at Pennyhill again, awaiting the final test.

And in that final test, I get my time down to 201 seconds, still six or seven seconds better than everyone else. Whether or not these final results are posted on the team room board, I don't know, it doesn't matter to me. I don't need other people to know about the good things, I just don't want them to know the stuff that is bad.

More importantly, I then get a phone call from Brian to say he's going to play me in the first Wales game. That is something I'm really excited about.

* * *

Sometimes you look at people like Sonny Bill Williams and you feel you see the future of the game. Against big teams, he runs hard and is able to throw offloads without any concern for his body, no matter how hard the tackle. He creates tries for fun. It takes the rest of us ten bloody phases and an hour of the game to make a try, but this guy can do it in one go.

These kind of guys are going to be where the game goes next and England have found one in Manu Tuilagi. I've played with guys like him before – Sonny Bill, Inga, Epi Taione – but Manu's very young and to be that good when you're that young is exceptional.

When I started as a professional, I tried to find a niche by being able to master all the skills in the game but to a higher level and from the first to the last minute. Now the elite game is also about size and strength and power. And Manu certainly has all that and the rest.

We play three warm-up games. Against Wales, at Twickenham, we win a tough game. We then lose to Wales in Cardiff and finish up against Ireland in Dublin where Manu is outstanding, big and strong and intimidating, a real weapon to have on your team.

As for me, I start in two of the three games, my first start for England for well over a year. But I am very hesitant to get too self-indulgent, to read anything into the team selections. I just have to see it as an opportunity, a fleeting moment where you think great, I've been picked to play. Whether I'm first or second choice or whatever, I am starting for England again.

And I think we go well, particularly against Ireland who beat us earlier in the year in the Six Nations, 24-8. We manage to put a few good things into practice that we've worked on, we defend well, we come away with a 20-9 win. Not a bad launch-pad for the World Cup.

● ● ●

Arriving in Auckland is like linking up with my past. I catch up with Tana Umaga who is now coaching over here; he looks physically very fit and is in great form. I love seeing Pat Lam, who is training for a marathon – rather him than me. And it is brilliant to see Inga again and his family. I love that.

Harley Crane comes round to the team hotel one day to take me out for a Thai meal. He is driving a low-riding Holden Ute and I jump and land straight on a half-drunk coffee on the passenger seat. Typical Harley. But it's great to catch up on old times and interesting too; he's got a family and a young son, and working and still playing and coaching rugby. He has the trappings of a grown-up life, but he is still hilarious, still hasn't changed.

Then when England move down to Dunedin, I catch up with some other old Newcastle teammates — John Leslie, Brent Wilson, Cory Harris — all fabulous people. I also get a chance to see my Argentinian friends. On England's one day off, we go down to the beach, and down there too are Argentina, our first opponents. It's a little bit awkward but it's really good to see Juan Lobbe, so we exchange a brief hello, and then agree to leave it until after the game.

But even people I don't know here know me. Awareness levels are through the roof in New Zealand and people here know their rugby so well. If I am out and about in Toulon, people might just say, in passing, hey, how are you? How's the team? But here, you put your head out of the hotel and they don't just want to say hello, they want to analyse the entire World Cup with you.

I feel a bit cramped by this. And it is quite clear that nothing we do here will go unnoticed.

● ● ●

The day before the game, as always, Floody and I have the window to do kicking practice with the match balls at the stadium and I find that some of my kicks are drawing left to right. The Otago Stadium is indoors, so it can't be the wind.

When you're kicking with wind, a ball will start straight before it catches the wind. That is fine, you can play wind like that, you get used to it. But these balls are drawing straight from impact, so you line up your kick and before you even have a chance to look up, it's somewhere else. That is a bit disturbing but I just tell myself that tomorrow I will be even sharper, even more precise.

The next morning, I do more kicking practice, but with practice balls, not the match balls, and I am absolutely nailing them. However, later at the stadium again, warming up before the game, I am kicking from a tight angle, I have Dave Alred behind me and I say to him: Mate just watch this, I've hit this match ball from here three times and it's missed near post three times.

I then say: Now watch this. I put down one of the other balls, a training ball, not a match ball, and it goes straight through the middle. Again and again, I'm hitting the same kick every time but it's non-match ball straight through the middle, match ball to the right, non-match ball straight through the middle, match ball to the right.

Going into the game, I still feel it'll be fine and for the first kick I've got, from the right hand touchline, I just pick the centre of the posts, smash it and it goes through the middle. I'm really happy with that.

The next one is fairly simple, from about 20 metres in from touch on the left, and I'm thinking I want to hit middle but look up and just watch as this ball keeps shifting further and further to the right, almost as if it's being pulled by a piece of string. It goes right across the posts. I want to shake my head and throw my arms up in the air but that won't help anyone. The real problem is now I don't know which balls are doing what or why. From then on, it's a joke.

The reason it's a joke is because there is no constant involved any more. When there is a constant, you can get feedback from what's going right and wrong, you can re-adjust, refine and correct yourself. The more you kick, you're ever more aware, ever more sensitive to feedback, so you know how to bring about the changes you require. The problem is that when you feel like you're smashing it and the feedback is telling you that everything is great, yet the ball is swinging both ways and missing one way and then the other, you're left with a very difficult situation.

With every kick that doesn't go over, you hear the crowd hushing even more, you are even more aware of them talking to each other, the collective murmuring round the ground, the impressively loud jeering from the large number of Argentinian supporters. Ah, another one, he missed that one as well. And to think that throughout the Six Nations, plus those games against Wales and Ireland before we came out here, I missed only a single kick.

In all, I hit eight kicks. One of them I'm definitely not happy with, one of them I didn't hit the exact line I was after, the other six I am really happy with. Only three went over.

Thank God, then, for Ben Youngs' try. We scrape through 13-9. I know I've got to get better, I've got to work harder. But also I know that I am kicking brilliantly and the balls are going everywhere.

●　　●　　●

The morning after the game I am out very early training with Dave; all that's on my mind is that I've possibly let the team down. But we're back to the training balls. We work on new stuff and different stuff with ever more attention to detail to help me smother the ball and hit an ever more assured line. It's going even better. I'm just kicking so well in practice; this is just the start of another great week's training.

We move up to Queenstown to train for the week and I am out again kicking early the next morning when I find out that there's been some incident regarding the boys going out for some beers.

Here in Queenstown, I do actually get away from the training pitch myself to enjoy some of the fabulous attractions; we go in a helicopter over some glacier lakes to a gold mine, and some of us go clay pigeon shooting (I'm not as bad as I thought I'd be, but Manu is a natural at this too). But I don't go out for the beers. It's been years since I've gone out after an England game; the last time was in 2007 and that was because it was the end of the World Cup. I'm not saying this is right; there's a balance to be struck and I'm probably the wrong side of one half of it.

When I was 20 or 21 years old, with England, I would go out after some games. I needed the mental clear-out before I could move on to the next one, I needed to liberate myself from all the pressure. I enjoyed it too. So I don't have a view on other people. It works for some, not for others.

What I cannot understand is the naivety of people going out to the extent that they did and it not crossing their minds it would find its way back to the media. We've already been warned several times about what it's like here, especially in the World Cup. You need to be a little reserved, careful, aware. With a camera on pretty much every phone these days, how could it not come back?

What is required is individual responsibility and not Johnno at his wit's end because the inevitable has happened and the night out has found its way into the newspapers. We've worked a huge amount on accountability on the field; the off-field thing just seems to be coming last and this is a conversation that needs to happen.

So we gather in the team room and people have their say and there are two sides to it. Some of the guys say you can't just stop doing everything because of the media, which is perfectly fair. On the other side of the argument is the big question that we need to ask ourselves: What are we here for and what have we worked so hard to be here for?

If there is any consensus, it's that we just need to be very careful from now on. But it is a conversation that I feel almost completely unable to contribute to. My own position is so far on the obsessive side of preparation and professionalism that I fear my point of view is not going to be shared by anyone.

● ● ●

Where I will not let my point of view go unheard is after the Georgia game. I watch the whole game from the bench and we win 41-10, but we don't adhere to the values that we had set at the start of this campaign about being ruthless, professional and together as a team. It looks like we lack urgency in what we're doing. There are also individuals playing for themselves, not showing respect for the opposition, throwing unnecessary fancy passes, not playing for one another.

The next day at the hotel, we have a team meeting with a harsh analysis of the game. At the end of it, Lewis speaks to the squad and when he is done, I ask if I can piggy-back on the back of his comments.

With his permission, I tell the squad that I cannot believe that it has come to this, where our defence coach, Mike Ford, who is as passionate as they come, has had to ask a group of players to buckle down and give it a bit more. I say that there are things we're doing in training that we're not doing in games and mistakes that we're making that we're not correcting, that there's sometimes a lack of hunger on the field, a lack of desire to get things right.

For me, the pure basics of rugby are not passing, catching, kicking; the basics are simply working yourself into the ground and doing whatever it takes for 80 minutes. The only reason that you don't change things, or that you don't work hard enough, is that it doesn't matter enough to you. And unfortunately, what that ultimately means is that the other 29 guys in this squad don't matter enough to you.

I don't often speak to the squad and hardly ever in this way, but I carry on. I say no one ever regretted giving it their best shot, but from now on we have to show how much it really matters to us. When we get things right, we're a great team and we can do whatever we want. But when we don't, we're just average. We've got one chance at this. If we don't take it, the regrets will last forever.

When I am done, my words are followed by silence. I hope it's the right kind of silence. Mark Cueto then comes up to me and says: Well done. He's a guy with great values and one of England's constant shining lights. He says to me: It just sounds right when you say these things.

I hugely appreciate his support. I tell him: Mate, it's all I think about, it's all I've got.

I might have just summed up my entire life in a two-minute speech.

● ● ●

After that first game, against Argentina, I'd learned my lesson with the balls and so for the Georgia game, which I didn't play, I went back to where I was in 2007, writing down on a piece of paper which of the match balls does what, and then memorising it for the game.

Going into the next one, against Romania, in which I am starting, we do our practice the day before as usual and there are only two balls that are messing around. Number two is leaking a bit left and number five is drawing so heavily that from in front of the posts 40 metres out, I need to aim a good two metres outside the left upright.

Before the match itself, though, my concentration is completely swung when I take a practice kick and it comes down and hits a woman in the crowd on the head. Way back in the Newcastle days, I once hit a touch kick and knocked out a bloke who was coming out of the food tent with packet of chips and a beer which finished up all down his shirt. On another occasion, I hit a winning kick against Bath and a man was so delighted to see it going through the posts that he neglected to move his head out of the way and he got knocked out too. I got a letter from his daughter after that saying how pleased her father was and could he have my autograph.

Here, I just want to apologise to the woman, but it's hardly the time and the place. Instead we get into the game, get off to a damn good start; we show the Romanians a proper respect and we are more ruthless. My first penalty is from 40 metres out. I look at the ball, it's a number four; I hit it well and it goes through the posts.

But after a try in the corner, I get the number five ball so I aim for the left post and before I've even looked up, it's outside the right upright. It's missed before it's even travelled 10 yards. We score again in the same corner and it's ball number two, the one which fades a little; I aim more or less middle, I don't hit it completely correct and it fades left and misses.

The next one I get, ball number one, is right under the posts, and goes dead straight. But then I have another kick from the left, 15 metres in, and it's the number five again and I'm thinking this is an absolute joke, it's just a lottery now because I don't know how far this ball is going to move. So I aim ever so slightly inside the left post just in case it doesn't draw at all, smash it as hard as I can and I watch it creeping closer and closer towards the right hand post. I'm thinking: Please stop, if this one misses, I'm not sure I can handle it.

The ball goes through but it's getting beyond a joke now. I only have one more kick, with ball number three, which is a dead straight flyer, and that's the end of it – or so I believe – because I am substituted at half-time to rest my shoulders which are still bothering me. We finish off the game well, Floody kicks well, a couple of great kicks from the corner, but then he hits one from the right hand side and it just goes nowhere near the target. He turns back at me on the bench and shows me a hand with five fingers outstretched. He doesn't like that ball either.

● ● ●

But that isn't the end of it. Not at all. It turns out that we are in trouble from the IRB because Dave Alred and Paul "Bobby" Stridgeon, our fitness coach, have attempted to switch the balls I was kicking during that first half.

I am asked for a meeting with Richard Smith QC, who is the England team lawyer. I tell him what I know. I tell him that I was desperately keen to avoid that ball number five, and that, one time, when Bobby had run on with my kicking tee, I had said to him: "Ball number five is drawing massively." It is not exactly surprising that I wouldn't want a ball that flies miles away from where it's supposed to.

Unfortunately, this then ends with a sanction for Dave and Bobby who are given a touchline ban from the next game, against Scotland. That's a really tough call, but whatever the circumstances we've done wrong and we're paying the price. What seems odd, though, is that we are not allowed to talk publicly about what is happening with the balls.

Dave is therefore bitter and angry, the same as me. But I just don't think this is that big a deal. They were all match balls. When people score and they do a celebration and punt the ball into the stand, it's exceptionally rare that the same ball ends up being the ball you kick the conversion with. Numerous times, after a try, I've said to the referee, there's no ball, and he's turned to the sideline and a ballboy has chucked a ball on – and it's a different one.

* * *

Though the ball-swapping issue dominates the media for much of the week, it doesn't really affect me. What affects me far more is the Scotland-Argentina game. I watch it in Floody's room, and we're having a bit of a chat and a laugh about other things and taking a few notes until Argentina score at the end of the game to steal the win and suddenly everything's changed.

We play Scotland next, and though it is still a pool match, the Argentina result means it has now become a knock-out game. If we lose by eight points, we'll be going home. I go back to my room slightly shell-shocked; I Skype Shelley and I'm hardly able to talk. The whole week is now different.

And yes, I do feel pressure about the goalkicking, but in training I am kicking brilliantly. The sheer effort I am putting into my training now is incredible, my focus on the strike of the ball is as intense as ever, and ironically, I am probably kicking as well as I've ever done in my life.

However, before the game, we warm up with ball number five and Floody says to me: This is all over the place, this one. That's all we need because the game is tough, as we knew it would be. Scotland are passionate, and the ball is wet and squirting around. They get penalties and start moving into our half; then they get kickable penalties, a drop goal and the lead.

We get down the other end; I have a couple of shots. The wind has been going left to right all day, but my first kick blows heavily left. It doesn't make any sense whatsoever. The second one is from a long way and I am bang online but surprisingly short, but the third is in a similar position to the first and I'm thinking: This is going to go right but the last one went left, so just aim dead centre. But the wind pushes it right. Here we go again.

I get the fourth and we go into half-time 9-3 down. This is tough. Yet I still have no kind of nervous hesitation in taking these kicks. I can't afford to have any. I'm just kicking too well in training, I'm still 100% confident that I'm doing the right thing.

If I was taking on these kicks just thinking, what the hell, I've got to have a go because everyone expects me to – that would be irresponsible. But every kick I take on, I still believe that this one's going to make the difference, my preparation has been so good I still believe I'm going to smash it over.

In the second half, I have two penalty attempts, both tough shots. I make one from the corner; the other is short and I should probably have kicked it into touch. We do not play particularly well, but we find a way to win and get ourselves through to the quarter-finals. But for me, as a perfectionist, there are big issues here to attend to. As a team, we went very quiet, we gave up all the initiative and let Scotland dictate. I don't know if it's the threat of an early exit, but I feel inside and outside me some teammates are looking at me for the solutions to a complex situation which I actually really need their help to find.

What doesn't help is that, for the second time, I have come away with a less than 50 per cent kicking success rate. I don't do less than 50 per cent. In big games where I have taken a reasonable number of kicks, I think the last time I did less than 50 per cent was four from eight against New Zealand in my first World Cup 12 years ago.

My feeling is that it's just horribly unprofessional and an extremely bitter pill to swallow that, at the biggest tournament in the sport, we're having to deal with this. Being unable to rely on my goalkicking makes performing physically and mentally draining. I'm getting hammered by the media again; nobody seems interested in the rest of my game. The rewards for my efforts are hard to find. The organisers can claim that all the balls are the same, but they're not. If they were, they wouldn't be doing this.

I'm sick to my stomach thinking about how hard I've practised my kicking over all those years and what little good it has done me at such an important time. It angers me. Deep down I know that I have never stood for poor results. I have never been able to accept average and yet this is what I'm staring at now. The worst thing is I don't know what I can do to make it better.

●   ●   ●

Against Scotland, it seemed as though there were a hell of a lot of Scots in that stadium. Or a lot of people wearing blue. I thought the same against Romania: there's suddenly a lot of Romanian fans around. And while the crowd is sometimes incredibly loud, it's been a long time since I've experienced that kind of noise whilst I'm kicking.

It's quite easy to go to every World Cup game we are in feeling like we're the villains, that we're not particularly well liked. The booing has been pretty full on, though I am told it is worse here for the Aussies. In a rugby sense, it doesn't affect me in any way, yet it's interesting and difficult to understand. I don't know how much of it is due to the bad publicity that has come from the Queenstown episode, but it's there nonetheless.

I don't know if we're not to blame as well, though. I don't believe that we are giving off the right impression here.

What I do know is that Johnno, Brian Smith, Mike Ford and the other coaches have been great to me out here. And as a playing squad, we're just not doing them justice.

● ● ●

We are to play France in the quarter-final and it is now not a case of Floody or me in the side, it is both of us. Me at 10 and Floody at 12.

Unlike most of the media, never at any point did I see the number ten issue as a case of me versus Toby. Yet I cannot deny the little part of me that is pleased to be able to have come back from some very hard times and reclaimed my place in the team.

Picking both of us is ideal as far as I'm concerned and I tell Floody that straight away: You're playing great, it's going to be awesome to have you on the same pitch, your positivity, your talking, your communication, every part of it is extremely important to me. And I mean it. It is great for me having another decision-maker out there to take the responsibility and the heat off, improve communication and move in and out of first and second receiver. It's like having Mike Catt out there again.

That is the good bit. On the pitch, the game itself spins quickly away from us. We lose a few set pieces, we give away a few penalties, we drop a few balls and we can't quite finish things off when it matters. Suddenly it is half-time and we are 16-0 down.

In the 65th minute, Matt Banahan arrives on the pitch next to me and I see that I am being substituted. I've picked up dead leg and have knackered myself out running on it. It's not a bad call. But the score is 16-7, still a long way back for us and my thoughts are simple: I hope to God we win. My individual feelings don't yet register.

We do continue the comeback, but not far enough. We finish 19-12 down and, just like that, our World Cup dream is snuffed out.

Afterwards, I take a look around the ground, I stand there absorbing it all, the stadium emptying and the French celebrating. This is Eden Park, New Zealand, the end of the World Cup, the last thing I see of a World Cup from on the field. I try to take it in. This trip has been at times terrible and definitely bizarre. And now, all too soon, it's over.

That's my last World Cup chapter, finished.

EPILOGUE

When I think back to that young lad playing mini rugby at Farnham, vomiting in the hedge through nerves, crying before games because he couldn't bear the thought of not getting it right, I wonder seriously how much has changed. I also truly wonder how the hell I ended up where I am now. Right through to the end of that last World Cup game, I still couldn't bear the thought of not being perfect. What if I didn't get it right? I still couldn't bear the thought of letting people down. The difference is that I finished off doing all this in front of thousands of people, millions of people.

On the eve of our France quarter-final, I received another fax from Blackie. This is what he wrote: 'I've learned that people will forget what you said, people will forget what you did, but people will never forget how you made them feel. Make us all feel wonderful. We'll never forget.'

No surprises – but once again he found something that made perfect sense to me.

For so much of my career, I've allowed myself to get massively caught up in the desire to try and control everything, especially the way people think of me. The longer it has gone on, the more I have seen how one day you're the hero, the next you're the villain, while I have been the same guy all along.

And all along, I feel as though my story has been carved from contradictions. I learned at mini rugby I wanted to be perfect, yet I have lived since then with both a desire for perfection and the knowledge that it's unattainable. When you're obsessive, like me, searching for something unattainable can become unhealthy.

Controlling my reputation and basing my fulfilment upon perfect outcomes – it's like falling through the air and grabbing at the clouds. What Blackie's fax says to me is that it's not the facts, figures and results that matter, it's how you make people feel.

Yet I know that I have spent many years trying to clutch onto things. Until 2003, I followed a path; it felt right, it *was* right, it always felt as if I was moving forwards. I sometimes think that ever since then, I've been trying to find my way back onto that path, trying to uncover my own quick-fix solution to get back to where I was back then.

Too often, England wanted the quick fix from me too. I was put back in to sort things out and it's probably my fault I let that happen. All those hours and hours of training, working on small skills, evasive ability, footwork, speed, handling skills, trying to develop as a player – what's really disappointed me is that so very rarely have I been able to use that. When things aren't right, it always has to come back to getting into the opposition half and keeping the scoreboard moving. I became more of a stereotype than I ever intended or wanted to be.

My fault again. I had a reputation and I wanted to be the person who lived up to it, who always came through when the pressure was on and the team needed it. After the World Cup win in 2003, I spent the next three years pretty much completely out of the game and so when I came back, I was desperate to be that person again. I never had nor gave myself the time to build again.

Ultimately I suppose I've been fighting a mental disposition, fighting who I am. Yet I know that my obsessiveness is what made me, what helped me towards whatever I have achieved.

I think of the two times I went out with Inga in Auckland – during the Lions tour in 2005 when I was mentally at a real low, and during the last World Cup when I was more mature and happier. Things have changed in between, yet it's almost the same battle taking place inside me. Many of the issues from 2005 are still there in 2011. It's just that I've become more mature, more grounded and adept at dealing with them. I can't change it, maybe I realise now that I can't afford to. I still strive to be perfect because it's what gives me my edge over others on the field. I just understand better that I'm not perfect and I know that's OK.

But if, as Blackie says, this is all about how I have made people *feel*, then I hope that I have made them feel good about rugby whilst I've been playing. The rugby supporters I have encountered around the world have been incredibly generous to me. I just hope that I have made them feel that there is an integrity in how I have behaved and what I have given to the sport, in the respect I have always had for my teammates and the honour I have felt in representing my country.

For me, this is massively important too: now my World Cups are done, I know I have given everything to this sport. Not just every match or even every training session, but every second, every moment, every opportunity. I could not have given more. I can't live with regrets and thank God that in this respect, I have none.

If I could review the footage of that 24-hour camera, then I could sign it off happily.

And of course, the camera doesn't stop after the World Cup. The day after France beat us, Harley Crane picked me up and we drove a couple of hours way out west, climbed up a huge sand dune and down the other side to get to a beautiful beach. And we played hacky sack together, just him and me for a long time before going for a swim in the sea. It was a trip back to the old times; so much fun.

But two days later, on the Tuesday, I arrived back in England. I was back in Toulon on the Wednesday and back on the field on the Saturday for the last half hour in a big win over Perpignan.

Being back just reinforced what is important. There have been times in my career when my team has won everything and there have been others when we've come up short. However, the results, the scoreboard, the outcomes are totally superseded by the journeys that took me to them. Winning and losing don't last. What do are friendships, the team, giving all you've got, memories, embracing the moment.

This is what's bigger: it's being in that changing-room after the 2007 World Cup quarter-final with Mike Catt and Martin Corry and sharing those special few minutes; it's the wow moments alone with Dave Alred, kicking balls with some of the best stadia in the world all to ourselves; it's hearing Inga fail to choke back the tears as he said goodbye to our Newcastle team, in a dressing-room awash with mutual respect; it's being with the Toulon boys listening to the Black Eyed Peas, being able to look them in the eye and knowing what we've been through together; it's sharing the daily path towards getting better with Blackie and Sparks and Mum and Dad too, living it, fighting for everything that mattered to us; it's sharing the battle with inspirational people like Jamie Noon, Sonny Bill, Hilly, Pat Lam, Felipe

Contepomi, and the knowledge that whether or not you see these guys ever again, it lasts forever. It's even the defeats, the 76-0 in Australia, the third Lions Test in Sydney three years later; whether it's the worst time in the world or the best, it's still about banking on each other, standing tall and helping each other to get through it. Emotionally, that's a special place to be.

I feel I made the most of being in those privileged places and that is why I'm proud of what I have done. I'm not necessarily proud of the World Cups and the Grand Slams won or lost, the amount of points I scored, this record or that. That doesn't come into it. What I am proud of is I have searched for the best of me and I have been a team man without fail. I made it all matter to me and I gave it my very best shot. Who in this world ever regretted doing that?

TESTIMONIALS

MATT BURKE

When we arrived in Newcastle, initially we only had the one car, so my first day, my wife Kate drove me to training. Eight in the morning and there he was, taking a shot at goal. We did training and he kicked some more. Everyone went for lunch, apart from Jonny, who maybe had a quick bite to eat but basically kicked all through lunch, too. We trained a bit more in the afternoon, and when I'd showered and Kate had come to pick me up in the afternoon, he was still in the same spot, kicking the goals. Kate said to me how come you can't be that dedicated?

I only worked it out when I was over in the UK, why he kept so much to himself in public. After one of the autumn internationals, we were in the BA lounge in Heathrow and he was tucked right out the back, and even there he was hassled by people. Everyone wanted a piece of him; it was like he was public property.

But one thing I felt was so hard for him was the media. No one gave him that freedom to be able to get over the injuries and get himself right. He was always judged on his performances in the past, and obviously in the 2003 World Cup. And when he wasn't playing for England, he was being judged against the incumbent ten. That was real tough.

MIKE CATT

I remember the slight young man Jonny was when he came into the England set-up, and I could really relate to it. In 1994, when I got my first international cap, nobody really knew me. Will Carling took me under his wing, and gave me that sense that I did fit in and could feel part of the team.

Back then, you had to win respect from some players. Until you'd got their respect on the rugby pitch, they wouldn't talk to you. When I turned up at my first club, Bath, I remember I threw a pass out to Jerry Guscott and he literally stopped in the middle of the training session and just threw the ball back at me. That's the way it worked back then.

So I knew how tough it was for Jonny, coming into an environment like that, especially at number ten. When you have to be the boss, it's so, so hard as a youngster or, as in my case, a foreigner, coming in and shouting the odds. You need people around you who can push you through – as Will Carling did with me.

I think the massive change for Jonny was on the social side of things. Back in the early days, he would have a few beers on a Saturday night. Phil Greening loved taking him under his wing. But he wasn't a hero then.

By 2003, he just couldn't relax off the field. He was so obsessed with what he had to do and how he had to do it that he didn't really want to go out. Hence Hilly and I insisted on taking him out on those Thursdays – just to get him out of the hotel. I don't think he got the balance right between rugby and the social side of things. He got too cooped up in his room. I still respected him enormously for it, because that's the way he wanted to do it.

And he achieved what he wanted. Totally. He was the best in the world. And he got there through that mental strength, the mental ability to do that hard graft. So everybody had a huge respect for him and we relied on him. There's no beating around the bush here, the team relied on him. In the same breath, he relied on us. He relied on the team to put him in those positions to win us games. But the respect for him was massive.

By 2007, I felt the expectation was huge, greater than ever. For the World Cup, there was massive emphasis on 'Jonny Wilkinson'. In 2003, it wasn't just about him; it was about that whole England side. In 2007, England needed him just to get to the knockout stages of the competition. That's how big the expectation was on his shoulders. After not having it for four years, it was right on his doorstep again. I think he found it quite daunting.

FELIPE CONTEPOMI

When Jonny arrived in Toulon, it was great. Look at how he trains. It's a real example to everyone. I know loads of people who train a lot, but he is unbelievable. He doesn't stop.

And he's a gentleman. It takes some time to get to know him, but he's loved by everyone here. I always say he's one of the few, maybe the only, English guy loved by all the French.

RICHARD HILL

I remember the Thursday outings with amusement. We never knew what time we'd actually be leaving because it all depended on how neurotic Jonny had got during the morning, and how many extra kicks had to be done.

But that was just the way he was. The only time I got a bit concerned was during the World Cup. I remember having a conversation with his dad in the build-up to the later stages, and there was a certain amount of worry.

The key was to try to get him to relax as much as he could, but sometimes that's easier said than done. In Sydney, we tried to grab him to go out for a coffee, but we failed. Maybe we shouldn't have worried. In hindsight, it's fairly clear that he had a pretty positive impact on our destination.

I don't think I'll ever forget that pre-World Cup summer camp. That was a complete eye-opener. I certainly remember being put in some fitness groups with him and it was just crazy. He was just smashing us.

It all fed his desire to be the ultimate player. He rewarded the forwards massively for our hard work. It got to the stage where, psychologically, we were playing with our opponents' minds. We didn't overelaborate and sometimes we maybe could have gone for tries, but the way he kept the scoreboard ticking over – it put opposition defenders on edge because they knew that every time they made a mistake, they were going to be punished.

I'll never forget the one he kicked in extra time in the final. What was it – 49 metres? I looked at their faces and just thought oh my lord, that's been a killer blow. They have not enjoyed that one.

PAT LAM

I remember when Jonny arrived as a 17-year-old at Newcastle, this young boy in a team of real established international players. The first time I saw him at training, I turned to Inga and I said: 'Mate, this is the closest thing I've seen to a New Zealand number 10.' His skill level, his tackling ability, but also his enthusiasm for the game and in particular the running game – I thought this kid's got something really special. If I was in any doubt, it was eradicated a little later in training when he hit me with a tackle and absolutely slaughtered me.

In those early days, I remember my wife and I had three of the young, single Newcastle boys round for dinner. My wife was particularly impressed by Jonny, his nature. She could see that he was a real quality person – and that was before he started teaching my 10-year-old, a young fly-half, how to kick. That's what Jonny was back then, a team man with a lot of values.

When Jonny was here in Auckland for the World Cup, he came round for dinner. We've now got five kids, teenagers, and Jonny was with them from six o'clock to 11.30 and they were talking about music and everything. I looked at Jonny and I thought how far he had come. Only the night before, England had lost to France, and here he was interacting with my family. After everything he had been through, he hadn't changed at all from that first time he came round to dinner. It was awesome to watch.

We went to say goodbye to him at the England hotel the next day before they left – and Jonny gave my boys the England team guitar. When they left, my boys said: 'What an inspiring guy to meet.' Teenagers don't often say things like that.

JAMIE NOON

I always looked up to Jonny. When I joined Newcastle, he was in the first team and had already played for England. It was strange because he's the same age as I am and yet he was so much more advanced. A group of youngsters around at that time wanted to be in that first team – and he was already doing it. Everyone looked up to him for what he'd achieved – but the way he was, the way he talked, the way he understood rugby, he was mature beyond his years.

At the same time, we all wanted to go out and have a good time. He came out with us at the start, but did so less and less. It was pretty obvious from an early point that he was getting a lot of attention. If he went out at night, or at any time, he'd be pestered. It was non-stop, brutal, and it was clear it was getting to him.

It was funny in those days, given the way some people have tended to categorise him as a player. I remember playing loads of games that were really tight and we'd say to him kick us down the pitch. And he'd say no, I don't want to kick, I think we should have a go. The way he played the game was important to him.

Yet overall, we saw that what he was doing was what he thought was necessary to be the best in the world. And obviously he achieved that.

So he became the benchmark for us. He always set the bar very high and we tried to work towards it. He instilled in us the desire to be the best. I still have that now.

As the 2007 World Cup rolled around, the big thing was the comparison with the last one. The closer we came to it, the more they showed the drop goal, and the more they talked about the victory in 2003, and 'Wilko is back'. I think that was a major stress for him, and extra pressure, extra expectation. I think he struggled with that expectation. His whole career culminated in one moment. After it, he was always compared with it, and I think, deep down, he wishes someone else had done it and not him.

MATTHEW TAIT

A lot of pressure fell on Jonny because of everyone else's expectations. He generated a feeling that everything will be all right, especially around the 2007 World Cup. I think he was aware of that. He kind of put people at ease, because of what he'd achieved, and how he was around the group. There was a feeling that if we were in a pickle, he would kick a drop goal or a penalty – and 99 times out of a 100 he did.

SONNY BILL WILLIAMS

I didn't expect him to be the person he was – so shy, so humble. I thought he's a world-wide figure who transcends rugby. I thought he'd have more of a swagger. But he's not like that. He's one of these guys who keeps his distance until you have earned his trust. I'm pleased to say that I was one of the lucky ones who got close to him. We clicked and became like brothers. He's quite a funny bloke but also a deep thinker.

Without Jonny, I wouldn't be where I am today. One day I asked him to help me out with some passing. Straightaway, he seemed to know what I needed. He knew my weaknesses. I really respect the way he educated me.

When you're in a team with Jonny, you don't want to tell him what to do. You don't want to jump into the number-ten position and push him out. That's his domain. But he gave me the confidence to get in there and mix it up, and I think that took a bit of pressure off him as well. I think, by the end, he must have got sick of my voice, always trying to run it.

Some days when I get to the gym, I can't wait to get through it. But every day Jonny is an animal in the gym and fearless on the field. And he's the best bloke I've ever met during my rugby playing days. Hands down.

OBE for services to rugby football 2004;
IRB Player of the Year 2003;
BBC Sports Personality of the Year 2003

A) JONNY IN TEST RUGBY

LIONS TEST APPEARANCES CAP BY CAP

CAP	DATE	OPPONENTS	VENUE	RESULT	PTS	T	C	P	D	Pos	Notes
1	30.6.01	Australia	Brisbane	W 29-13	9	0	3	1	0	FH	Four goals on Lions debut
2	7.7.01	Australia	Melbourne	L 14-35	9	0	0	3	0	FH	
3	14.7.01	Australia	Sydney	L 23-29	18	1	2	3	0	FH	Joint Lions record points in a Test
4	23.5.05	Argentina	Cardiff	D 25-25	20	0	1	6	0	FH	Lions record for points in a Test
5	25.6.05	New Zealand	Christchurch	L 3-21	3	0	0	1	0	IC	Only Lions Test start at centre
6	2.7.05	New Zealand	Wellington	L 18-48	8	0	1	2	0	FH	Last Lions Test appearance

LIONS SUMMARY

YEAR	SERIES	P	W	L	D	T	C	P	D	Pts	Notes
2001	v Australia	3	1	2	0	1	5	7	0	36	Record points Lions series v Aus
2005	v Argentina	1	0	0	1	0	1	6	0	20	Match accorded full Test status by IRB
2005	v New Zealand	2	0	2	0	0	1	3	0	11	
TOTALS		6	1	4	1	1	7	16	0	67	Alltime Lions Test points record

ENGLAND TEST APPEARANCES CAP BY CAP

CAP	DATE	OPPONENTS	VENUE	RESULT	PTS	T	C	P	D	Pos	Notes
1	4.4.98	Ireland	Twickenham	W 35-17	0	0	0	0	0	Rep	Youngest England cap since 1927
2	6.6.98	Australia	Brisbane	L 0-76	0	0	0	0	0	FH	First England start
3	20.6.98	New Zealand	Dunedin	L 22-64	0	0	0	0	0	FH	Injured and replaced after 43 mins
4	20.2.99	Scotland	Twickenham	W 24-21	9	0	3	1	0	IC	First points for England
5	6.3.99	Ireland	Lansdowne Road	W 27-15	14	0	1	4	0	IC	Gives try-scoring pass to Matt Perry
6	20.3.99	France	Twickenham	W 21-10	21	0	0	7	0	IC	Equals England penalty record for a match
7	11.4.99	Wales	Wembley	L 31-32	16	0	2	4	0	IC	Passes fifty points in Tests

CAP	DATE	OPPONENTS	VENUE	RESULT	PTS	T	C	P	D	Pos	Notes
8	26.6.99	Australia	Sydney	L 15-22	5	0	1	1	0	FH	Aussie Test Centenary match
9	21.8.99	United States	Twickenham	W 106-8	26	0	13	0	0	FH	World Cup warm-up game
10	28.8.99	Canada	Twickenham	W 36-11	11	0	4	1	0	FH	Passes 100 points in Tests
11	2.10.99	Italy*	Twickenham	W 67-7	32	1	6	5	0	FH	Sets individual England points record for a Test
12	9.10.99	New Zealand*	Twickenham	L 16-30	11	0	1	3	0	FH	
13	20.10.99	Fiji*	Twickenham	W 45-24	23	0	1	7	0	FH	Equals England penalty record for a match
14	24.10.99	South Africa*	Paris	L 21-44	3	0	0	1	0	Rep	England record 171 pts for calendar year
15	5.2.00	Ireland	Twickenham	W 50-18	20	0	4	4	0	FH	Combines effectively with Catt as his IC
16	19.2.00	France	Paris	W 15-9	15	0	0	5	0	FH	Youngest player to 200 Test points
17	4.3.00	Wales	Twickenham	W 46-12	21	0	3	5	0	FH	Equals the England pts record v Wales
18	18.3.00	Italy	Rome	W 59-12	14	0	4	2	0	FH	Replaced by Alex King 72 mins
19	2.4.00	Scotland	Murrayfield	L 13-19	8	0	1	2	0	FH	First Championship title
20	24.6.00	South Africa	Bloemfontein	W 27-22	27	0	0	8	1	FH	New England penalty goal match record
21	18.11.00	Australia	Twickenham	W 22-19	17	0	1	4	1	FH	
22	25.11.00	Argentina	Twickenham	W 19-0	14	0	1	3	1	FH	Third successive drop goal
23	2.12.00	South Africa	Twickenham	W 25-17	20	0	1	6	0	FH	
24	3.2.01	Wales	Cardiff	W 44-15	14	0	4	2	0	FH	Passes 50 conversions for England
25	17.2.01	Italy	Twickenham	W 80-23	35	1	9	4	0	FH	Pts record for a 6 Nations match
26	3.3.01	Scotland	Twickenham	W 43-3	13	0	5	1	0	FH	Reaches 200 points in 5/6 Nations
27	7.4.01	France	Twickenham	W 48-19	18	0	6	2	0	FH	Passes 400 Test pts to set England record
28	20.10.01	Ireland	Dublin	L 14-20	9	0	0	3	0	FH	
29	10.11.01	Australia	Twickenham	W 21-15	21	0	0	5	2	FH	Equals England drop goal match record
30	24.11.01	South Africa	Twickenham	W 29-9	21	0	0	7	0	FH	
31	2.2.02	Scotland	Murrayfield	W 29-3	7	0	2	1	0	FH	Passes 500 Test pts for Lions/England
32	16.2.02	Ireland	Twickenham	W 45-11	20	1	6	1	0	FH	Gives fly-half master class
33	2.3.02	France	Paris	L 15-20	5	0	1	1	0	FH	100th penalty goal for England
34	23.3.02	Wales	Twickenham	W 50-10	30	1	5	4	1	FH	First full house of scoring actions
35	7.4.02	Italy	Rome	W 45-9	13	0	5	1	0	FH	Passes 300 points in 5/6 Nations games

CAP	DATE	OPPONENTS	VENUE	RESULT	PTS	T	C	P	D	Pos	Notes
36	9.11.02	New Zealand	Twickenham	W 31-28	21	1	2	3	1	FH	England individual pts record v NZ
37	16.11.02	Australia	Twickenham	W 32-31	22	0	2	6	0	FH	England individual pts record v Australia
38	23.11.02	South Africa	Twickenham	W 53-3	8	0	1	2	0	FH	Labuschagne red carded for fouling Jonny in 23 min
39	15.2.03	France	Twickenham	W 25-17	20	0	1	5	1	FH	Match overshadowed by death 24 hours earlier of Nick Duncombe
40	22.2.03	Wales	Cardiff	W 26-9	16	0	2	2	2	FH	Equals England drop goal match record again
41	9.3.03	Italy	Twickenham	W 40-5	8	0	4	0	0	FH	Captains England for the first time
42	22.3.03	Scotland	Twickenham	W 40-9	18	0	3	4	0	FH	
43	30.3.03	Ireland	Dublin	W 42-6	15	0	3	1	2	FH	Jonny's only Grand Slam with England
44	14.6.03	New Zealand	Wellington	W 15-13	15	0	0	4	1	FH	All the points in first England win in NZ since 1973
45	21.6.03	Australia	Melbourne	W 25-14	10	0	2	2	0	FH	
46	6.9.03	France	Twickenham	W 45-14	18	0	3	4	0	FH	Passes 700 Test points for England
47	12.10.03	Georgia*	Perth	W 84-6	16	0	5	2	0	FH	Replaced by Paul Grayson 46 mins
48	18.10.03	South Africa*	Perth	W 25-6	20	0	1	4	2	FH	Equals England drop goal match record again
49	26.10.03	Samoa*	Melbourne	W 35-22	15	0	3	2	1	FH	
50	9.11.03	Wales*	Brisbane	W 28-17	23	0	1	6	1	FH	Fiftieth England cap
51	16.11.03	France*	Sydney	W 24-7	24	0	0	5	3	FH	New England drop goal match record
52	22.11.03	Australia*	Sydney	W 20-17	15	0	0	4	1	FH	Wins World Cup with late drop goal
53	3.2.07	Scotland	Twickenham	W 42-20	27	1	2	5	1	FH	World record third full house scoring actions
54	10.2.07	Italy	Twickenham	W 20-7	15	0	0	5	0	FH	Jonny's 21st successive win in England Tests
55	24.2.07	Ireland	Dublin	L 13-43	8	0	1	2	0	FH	Jonny's first England defeat for five years
56	26.5.07	South Africa	Bloemfontein	L 10-58	5	0	1	1	0	FH	
57	2.6.07	South Africa	Pretoria	L 22-55	17	0	1	5	0	FH	Captains England for second time
58	4.8.07	Wales	Twickenham	W 62-5	17	0	7	1	0	FH	Equals conversions record for match v Wales
59	11.8.07	France	Twickenham	L 15-21	0	0	0	0	0	Rep	Replaces Mike Catt 77 mins
60	18.8.07	France	Marseille	L 9-22	9	0	0	3	0	FH	
61	22.9.07	Samoa*	Nantes	W 44-22	24	0	3	4	2	FH	Passes 200 points in RWC matches
62	28.9.07	Tonga*	Paris	W 36-20	16	0	2	2	2	FH	

CAP	DATE	OPPONENTS	VENUE	RESULT	PTS	T	C	P	D	Pos	Notes
63	6.10.07	Australia*	Marseille	W 12-10	12	0	0	4	0	FH	Passes 200 penalties in Lions/England Tests
64	13.10.07	France*	Paris	W 14-9	9	0	0	2	1	FH	
65	20.10.07	South Africa*	Paris	L 6-15	6	0	0	2	0	FH	First player to score in successive RWC Finals
66	2.2.08	Wales	Twickenham	L 19-26	14	0	1	3	1	FH	Jonny's first Twickenham 5/6 Nations loss
67	10.2.08	Italy	Rome	W 23-19	13	0	2	3	0	FH	
68	23.2.08	France	Paris	W 24-13	14	0	1	3	1	FH	Equals Neil Jenkins's World Test points record
69	8.3.08	Scotland	Murrayfield	L 9-15	9	0	0	3	0	FH	Overtakes Neil Jenkins's World Test points record
70	15.3.08	Ireland	Twickenham	W 33-10	0	0	0	0	0	Rep	Replaces Toby Flood as centre 52 mins
71	7.11.09	Australia	Twickenham	L 9-18	9	0	0	2	1	FH	30th Test drop goal for England
72	14.11.09	Argentina	Twickenham	W 16-9	11	0	1	2	1	FH	Replaced by Andy Goode 74 mins
73	21.11.09	New Zealand	Twickenham	L 6-19	6	0	0	2	0	FH	
74	6.2.10	Wales	Twickenham	W 30-17	15	0	3	3	0	FH	
75	14.2.10	Italy	Rome	W 17-12	12	0	0	3	1	FH	Record tenth 5/6 Nations drop goal
76	27.2.10	Ireland	Twickenham	L 16-20	11	0	1	2	1	FH	
77	13.3.10	Scotland	Murrayfield	D 15-15	9	0	0	3	0	FH	Replaced by Toby Flood 44 mins
78	20.3.10	France	Paris	L 10-12	3	0	0	1	0	Rep	Replaces Riki Flutey 60 mins
79	12.6.10	Australia	Perth	L 17-27	0	0	0	0	0	Rep	Replaces Mike Tindall 72 mins
80	19.6.10	Australia	Sydney	W 21-20	3	0	0	1	0	Rep	Replaces Toby Flood 50 mins
81	4.2.11	Wales	Cardiff	W 26-19	3	0	0	1	0	Rep	Replaces Toby Flood 66 mins
82	12.2.11	Italy	Twickenham	W 59-13	6	0	3	0	0	Rep	Replaces Toby Flood 54 mins
83	26.3.11	France	Twickenham	W 17-9	3	0	0	1	0	Rep	Replaces Toby Flood 50 mins
84	13.3.11	Scotland	Twickenham	W 22-16	5	0	1	1	0	Rep	Replaces Toby Flood 65 mins
85	19.3.11	Ireland	Dublin	L 8-24	0	0	0	0	0	Rep	Replaces Toby Flood 50 mins
86	6.8.11	Wales	Twickenham	W 23-19	13	0	2	1	2	FH	Becomes England's most-capped back
87	27.8.11	Ireland	Dublin	W 20-9	10	0	2	2	0	FH	First Englishman past 100 pts v Ireland
88	10.9.11	Argentina*	Dunedin	W 13-9	8	0	1	2	0	FH	Third Englishman to play 4 RWCs
89	24.9.11	Romania*	Dunedin	W 67-3	9	0	3	1	0	FH	Replaced half-time by Toby Flood
90	1.10.11	Scotland*	Auckland	W 16-12	9	0	0	2	1	FH	Lands 400th place kick for England
91	8.10.11	France*	Auckland	L 12-19	2	0	1	0	0	FH	Replaced by Matt Banahan 64 mins

* indicates matches in Rugby World Cup tournaments

FIVE/SIX NATIONS SUMMARY

YEAR	P	W	L	D	T	C	P	D	Pts	Notes
1998 Triple Crown	1	1	0	0	0	0	0	0	0	
1999	4	3	1	0	0	6	16	0	60	
2000 Champions	5	4	1	0	0	12	18	0	78	New 6 Nations points record for a season
2001 Champions	5	4	1	0	1	24	12	0	89	Alltime 6 Nations points record in a season
2002 Triple Crown	5	4	1	0	2	19	8	1	75	
2003 Triple Crown, Champions, G Slam	5	5	0	0	0	13	12	5	77	England drop goal record for a season
2007	3	2	1	0	1	3	12	1	50	Passes Neil Jenkins's 5/6 Nations overall pts record
2008	5	3	2	0	0	4	12	2	50	Top 6 Nations scorer for the season
2010	5	2	2	1	0	4	12	2	50	
2011 Champions	5	4	1	0	0	4	3	0	17	
TOTALS	43	32	10	1	4	89	105	11	546	England 5/6 Nations points record

RUGBY WORLD CUP SUMMARY

YEAR	P	W	L	D	T	C	P	D	Pts	Notes
1999	4	2	2	0	1	8	16	0	69	Leading English scorer in tournament
2003	6	6	0	0	0	10	23	8	113	England record RWC points haul
2007	5	4	1	0	0	5	14	5	67	Leading English scorer in tournament
2011	4	3	1	0	0	5	5	1	28	Third Englishman to go to 4 RWCs
TOTALS	19	15	4	0	1	28	58	14	277	England RWC overall points record

ENGLAND TEST SUMMARY

YEAR	P	W	L	D	T	C	P	D	Pts	Notes
1998-2011	91	66	24	1	6	162	239	36	1179	Most pts, conversions, penalties and drop goals for England

OVERALL ENGLAND/LIONS TEST SUMMARY

YEAR	P	W	L	D	T	C	P	D	Pts	Notes
1998-2011	97	67	28	2	7	169	255	36	1246	Most prolific kicker of penalty goals and drop goals in Test history. Second most prolific points scorer in Test history (four behind Dan Carter of NZ)

RWC 1999 held in Britain, Ireland & France

England appearances at RWC 1999

Full-backs: M B Perry (It, NZ, Tg, Fj, SA)

Threequarters: A S Healey (It, NZ, Tg, SA[R]); N D Beal (It[R], Tg[R], Fj, SA); W J H Greenwood (It, Tg, Fj, SA); P R de Glanville (It, NZ, Fj[R], SA); J C Guscott (It[R], NZ, Tg); M J Catt (Tg[R], Fj, SA[R]); D D Luger (It, NZ, Tg, Fj, SA)

Half-backs: J P Wilkinson (It, NZ, Fj, SA[R]); P J Grayson (NZ[R], Tg, Fj[R], SA); M J S Dawson (It, NZ, Tg, Fj[R], SA); A S Healey (Fj)

Forwards: J Leonard (It, NZ, Fj, SA); G C Rowntree (It[R], Tg, Fj[R]); P J Vickery (It, NZ, Tg, SA); D J Garforth (It[R], NZ[R], Fj); P B T Greening (It[R], NZ[R], Tg, Fj, SA); R Cockerill (It, NZ, Tg[R], Fj[R]); M O Johnson (It, NZ, Tg, Fj, SA); D J Grewcock (It, NZ, Tg[R], SA); G S Archer (Tg, Fj); T A K Rodber (NZ[R], Fj[R]); M E Corry (It[R], NZ[R], SA[R]); R A Hill (It, NZ, Tg, Fj[R], SA); J P R Worsley (Tg, Fj); N A Back (It, NZ, Fj, SA); L B N Dallaglio (It, NZ, Tg, Fj, SA)

Head Coach C R Woodward **Captain** M O Johnson

RWC 2003 held in Australia

England appearances at RWC 2003

Back-three: J T Robinson (Gg, SA, Sam, U[R], W, F, A); O J Lewsey (Gg, SA, U, F, A); B C Cohen (Gg, SA, Sam, W, F, A); I R Balshaw (Sam, U, A[R]); D D Luger (Gg[R], SA[R], U, W)

Centres: W J H Greenwood (Gg, SA, U[R], W, F, A); M J Tindall (Gg, SA, Sam, W, F[R], A); M J Catt (Sam[R], U, W[R], F, A[R]); S R Abbott (Sam, U, W[R])

Half-backs: J P Wilkinson (Gg, SA, Sam, W, F, A); P J Grayson (Gg[R], U); M J S Dawson (Gg, Sam, W, F, A); K P P Bracken (SA, U[R], W[R], F[R]); A C T Gomarsall (Gg[R], U)

Forwards: J Leonard (Gg[R], SA[R], Sam, U, W, F[R], A[R]); T J Woodman (Gg, SA, W[R], F, A); J M White (U[R]); P J Vickery (Gg, SA, Sam[R], U, W, F, A); S G Thompson (Gg, SA, Sam[R], W, F, A); M P Regan (Gg[R], Sam); D E West (U, F[R]); M O Johnson (Gg, SA, Sam, U[R], W, F, A); D J Grewcock (U); B J Kay (Gg, SA, Sam, W, F, A); M E Corry (U); R A Hill (Gg, F, A); J P R Worsley (SA[temp], Sam, U); N A Back (Gg, SA, Sam, W, F, A); L W Moody (Gg[R], SA, Sam[R], U, W, F[R], A[R]); L B N Dallaglio (Gg, SA, Sam, U, W, F, A)

Head Coach C R Woodward **Captain** M O Johnson (Vickery was captain against Uruguay)

RWC 2007 held in France, Wales & Scotland

England appearances at RWC 2007

Back-three: J T Robinson (US, SA, A, F, SA); O J Lewsey (US, SA, Sam, Tg, A, F); M J Cueto (US, Sam, Tg, SA); P H Sackey (SA, Sam, Tg, A, F, SA)

Centres: M J Catt (US, A, F, SA); J D Noon (US, SA); M J M Tait (US[R], SA[R], Sam, Tg, A, F, SA); A D Farrell (US[R], SA, Tg[R]); O J Barkley (Sam, Tg); D J Hipkiss (Sam[R], Tg[R], F[R], SA[R]); T G A L Flood (A[R], F[R], SA[R])

Half-backs: J P Wilkinson (Sam, Tg, A, F, SA); O J Barkley (US); M J Catt (SA); S A Perry (US, SA); A C T Gomarsall (SA[R], Sam, Tg, A, F, SA); P C Richards (US[R], SA[R], Tg[R], A[temp], F[R], SA[R])

Forwards: A J Sheridan (US, SA, Sam, Tg, A, F, SA); P J Vickery (US, Tg[R], A, F, SA); M J S Stevens (US[R], SA, Sam, Tg, A[R], F[R], SA[R]); P Freshwater (SA[R], Sam[R]); M P Regan (US, SA, A, F, SA); G S Chuter (US[R], SA[R], Sam, Tg, A[R], F[R], SA[R]); L A Mears (Tg[R]); S D Shaw (US, SA, Sam, A, F, SA); B J Kay (US, SA, Sam, Tg, A, F, SA); S W Borthwick (SA[R], Sam[R], Tg); M E Corry (US[R], SA, Sam, Tg, A, F, SA); J P R Worsley (US, Sam, A[R], F[R], SA[R]); L W Moody (US[R], SA[R], Sam[R], Tg, A, F, SA); L B N Dallaglio (US, Tg[R], A[R], F[R], SA[R]); T Rees (US, SA); N J Easter (SA, Sam, Tg, A, F, SA)

Head Coach W B Ashton **Captain** P J Vickery (Corry was captain in the pool games against South Africa, Samoa and Tonga)

RWC 2011 held in New Zealand

England appearances at RWC 2011

Full-backs: B J Foden (Arg, Gg, Rom, S, F)

Threequarters: C J Ashton, (Arg, Gg, Rom, S, F); M J Cueto (Rom, F); D A Armitage (Arg, Gg, Rom[R], S); E M Tuilagi (Arg, Gg, Rom, S, F); M J Tindall (Arg, Rom, S); S E Hape (Gg); M A Banahan (Gg[R], S[R], F[R]); T G A L Flood (F)

Half-backs: J P Wilkinson (Arg, Rom, S, F); T G A L Flood (Gg, Rom[R], S[R]); R E P Wigglesworth (Arg, Rom[R], S[R], F[R]); B R Youngs (Arg[R], Gg, Rom, S, F); J P M Simpson (Gg[R])

Forwards: A J Sheridan (Arg); D R Cole (Arg, Gg, Rom, S F); M J H Stevens (Arg[R], Gg, S, F); A R Corbisiero (Gg[R], Rom, S[R], F[R]); D G Wilson (Rom[R]); S G Thompson (Arg, Gg[R], Rom, S, F); D M Hartley (Arg[R], Gg, S[R], F[R]); L A Mears (Rom[R]); L P Deacon (Arg, Rom, S, F); T P Palmer (Arg[R], Gg, Rom, S[R], F); C L Lawes (Arg, S, F[R]); S D Shaw (Gg, Rom[R], F[R]); T R Croft (Arg, Gg[R], Rom, S, F); J A W Haskell (Arg, Gg, Rom, S, F[R]); T A Wood (Gg, Rom[R]); L W Moody (Gg, Rom, S, F); N J Easter (Arg, S[R], F)

Head Coach M O Johnson **Captain** L W Moody (Tindall was captain in the pool game against Argentina)

B) JONNY IN CLUB RUGBY

EUROPEAN CLUB RECORD

CLUB	SEASONS	P	T	C	P	D	Pts	Notes
Newcastle	1997-2008	30	4	53	88	2	396	
Toulon	2009-2011	12	0	20	31	3	142	Amlin Cup Runners-Up 2010
TOTALS	**1997-2011**	**42**	**4**	**73**	**119**	**5**	**538**	Average 12.8 pts a match

LEAGUE CLUB RECORD

CLUB	SEASONS	P	T	C	P	D	Pts	Notes
Newcastle	1997-2008	138	25	196	302	22	1489	Champions 1998
Toulon	2009-2011	37	3	42	110	25	504	
TOTALS	**1997-2011**	**175**	**28**	**238**	**412**	**47**	**1993**	Average 11.4 pts a match

Jonny was also a member of the Newcastle team that won the RFU Cup in 2001.

C) JONNY IN INTERNATIONAL SCHOOLBOY RUGBY

THE 1997 ENGLAND SCHOOLS (18 Group) GRAND SLAM

22 March 1997, Twickenham   Won 20-10   v France

Scorers *Tries:* Brading, Best *Conversions:* Wilkinson (2) *Penalty Goals:* Wilkinson (2)

29 March 1997, Dublin   Won 16-9   v Ireland

Scorers *Tries:* Brading, Best *Penalty Goals:* Wilkinson (2)

8 April 1997, Preston   Won 55-18   v Scotland

Scorers *Tries:* Tindall (2), Roques (2), Wilkinson, Mears, Sheridan, Dawson *Conversions:* Wilkinson (6) *Penalty Goal:* Wilkinson

12 April 1997, Narberth   Won 18-17   v Wales

Scorers *Tries:* Tindall (2) *Conversion:* Wilkinson *Penalty Goal:* Wilkinson *Drop Goal:* Wilkinson

ENGLAND SCHOOLS (18 GROUP) PLAYERS 1997

Full-backs I R Balshaw (Stonyhurst College) *F, I, S;* L M Best (Durham School) *W*

Threequarters: L M Best (Durham School) *F, I, S;* P C Greenaway (Colston's Collegiate) *S(R),W;* T E Southall (Poynton HS) *F, S;* M J Tindall (QEGS Wakefield) *F(R), I, S, W;* S D Brading (Bedford School) *F, I, S, W;* T A May (Tonbridge School) *F, I, W;* S Amor (Hampton School) *W (R).*

Half-backs: J P Wilkinson (Lord Wandsworth) *F, I, S, W;* D J R Smaje (RGS High Wycombe) *F;* J Grindal (King Henry VIII, Coventry) *I, S, W*

Forwards: D L Flatman (Dulwich College) *F, I, S, W;* A Hubbleday (King Edward VI, Fiveways) *F, S(R);* L A Mears (Colston's Collegiate) *I, S, W;* J J Dawson (Dulwich College) *F, I, S, W;* R Siveter (Colston's Collegiate) *S(R);* A J Sheridan (Dulwich College) *F, I, S, W;* S W Borthwick (Hutton GS) *F, I, S, W;* A W S Roques (Sevenoaks School) *F, I, S;* M McCarrick (Sevenoaks School) *F, I, S, W;* A J Beattie (Hampton School) *F, I, S, W;* A Sanderson (Kirkham GS) *I(R);* R Holmes (Norwich School) *W;* S Williams (Colston's Collegiate) *W(R);* D A Giles (Kirkham GS) *S(R)*

Coach: G Wappett

Tony Roques led the team from blind-side in the first three games and Jonny Wilkinson did so from fly-half at Narberth, where his late drop goal against Wales secured the Grand Slam.

Balshaw, Tindall, May, Wilkinson, Flatman, Mears, Borthwick, Sanderson and Sheridan went on to win full senior England honours

ENGLAND SCHOOLS (18 GROUP) INVINCIBLE TOUR TO AUSTRALIA 1997

v Northern Territories under-20	W 115-3
v New South Wales Country	W 72-8
v Australian Capital Territory	W 41-3
v NSW Combined High Schools	W 64-5
v Victoria	W 111-0
v Queensland	W 54-8
v Queensland Select XV	W 48-15
v AUSTRALIA (27 August 1997)	W 38-20

England Schools Scorers *Tries:* Danielli (2), Tindall, Sanderson, Grindal *Conversions:* Wilkinson (2), Lofthouse (3) *Penalty Goal:* Wilkinson

Players who appeared in the Test against the Australia Schoolboys are in bold below. (Replacements used in italic bold)

ENGLAND SCHOOLS (18 GROUP) TOUR PARTY TO AUSTRALIA 1997

Full-backs **I R Balshaw** (Stonyhurst College); L M Best (Durham School)

Threequarters: P C Greenaway (Colston's Collegiate); **M J Tindall** (QEGS Wakefield); **J P Wilkinson** (Lord Wandsworth); **M Walker** (Dinnington CS); **S C J Danielli** (Cheltenham College); S D Brading (Bedford School); *S Amor* (Hampton School); P D Christophers (RGS Lancaster)

Half-backs: **J Lofthouse** (Sedbergh School) (*captain*); *D J R Smaje* (RGS High Wycombe); C D Hill (St Joseph's, Ipswich); **J Grindal** (King Henry VIII, Coventry)

Forwards: **D L Flatman** (Dulwich College); **A Hubbleday** (King Edward VI, Fiveways); L A Mears (Colston's Collegiate); J Collins (West Buckland School); D A Giles (Kirkham GS); **J J Dawson** (Dulwich College); *J G Hynes* (King Edward VI, Fiveways); R Siveter (Colston's Collegiate); **A J Sheridan** (Dulwich College); **S W Borthwick** (Hutton GS); **A W S Roques** (Sevenoaks School); *M McCarrick* (Sevenoaks School); **A J Beattie** (Hampton School); **A Sanderson** (Kirkham GS); *A L Balding* (Caludon Castle CS, Coventry); S Williams (Colston's Collegiate);

Coach: G Wappett **Captain:** J Lofthouse

Balshaw, Tindall, Christophers, Wilkinson, Flatman, Mears, Borthwick, Sanderson and Sheridan went on to win full senior England honours; Danielli did so for Scotland

Jonny was also a member of the England Schools (16 group) squad in 1995.

Statistical section compiled by John Griffiths.

INDEX